CULTURE, COMMUNITY AND CHANGE IN A SAPPORO NEIGHBORHOOD, 1925-1988

CULTURE, COMMUNITY AND CHANGE IN A SAPPORO NEIGHBORHOOD, 1925-1988
Hanayama

John Mock

Japanese Studies
Volume 8

The Edwin Mellen Press
Lewiston•Queenston•Lampeter

Library of Congress Cataloging-in-Publication Data

Mock, John Allan.
    Culture, community and change in a Sapporo neighborhood, 1925-1988
: Hanayama / John Mock.
       p. cm. -- (Japanese Studies ; v. 8)
    Includes bibliographical references and index.
    ISBN 0-7734-7974-0
    1. Sapporo-shi (Japan)--History.   I. Series: Japanese studies
(Lewiston, N.Y.) ; v. 8.
    DS897.S2M63   1999
    952' .4--dc21
                                         99-23114
                                          CIP

| This is volume 8 in the continuing series |
| Japanese Studies |
| Volume 8 ISBN 0-7734-7974-0 |
| JaS Series ISBN 0-88946-157-0 |

A CIP catalog record for this book is available from the British Library.

The Edwin Mellen Press
Box 450
Lewiston, New York
USA 14092-0450

The Edwin Mellen Press
Box 67
Queenston, Ontario
CANADA L0S 1L0

The Edwin Mellen Press, Ltd.
Lampeter, Ceredigion, Wales
UNITED KINGDOM SA48 8LT

Printed in the United States of America

To my parents,

Esther and Vern Mock

Table of Contents

Introduction

The decision to do field research in the neighborhood of Hanayama was made in a number of small steps, not all at once. The original proposal for the research focused on what is called linguistic register. It was for a sociolinguistic analysis of the use of language, particularly the production of sounds--what most people would call "accents"--in the maintenance of social stratification, of class barriers. Although this was never officially stated, I had been told that the proposed sociolinguistic study had an excellent chance of receiving grant support if it were planned for the more central parts of Japan, the areas around either Tokyo or Osaka. I had been advised, by more than one source, that anything proposed for Hokkaido would not be likely to receive grant support. I was told by one employee of a granting agency that no one really cared about Hokkaido and that I should concentrate on the "real" Japan. Whether there was a bias toward the major cities of the south or the quality of the grant proposal was just too low, the research for this study was not funded by any granting agency.

The decision to work in Sapporo--as opposed to some other area of Hokkaido--came from the ability of my wife and I to support ourselves, Maureen working in a private women's high school full time and my working part-time for a local women's college. The decision to live and work in the neighborhood of Hanayama was a result of employment geography. We wanted a nondescript neighborhood, with commercial and residential aspects, within walking distance of Maureen's school. We also had absolutely minimal resources so a very small apartment was an essential. The apartment building where a friend helped us find a place to live was in Hanayama. After making sure that the apartment was tolerable, a quick check of the neighborhood indicated that it would do very nicely as the site for the proposed sociolinguistic research, a conclusion that was to prove completely false. In the event, as I started looking at language use and sound production, it became quickly evident that the proposed sociolinguistic work would not be possible because there were an enormous number of regional dialects spoken in the neighborhood. Because literally everyone in the neighborhood was an immigrant, sorting out linguistic register from dialectal variation would have been a full time occupation in itself. As a secondary effect, it also convinced me that the idea of Japanese homogeneity was a myth that probably had other, perhaps equally interesting, manifestations.

Other factors were also involved in the eventual decision to do an ethnographic history of the neighborhood. I am quite tall in the United States which makes me extremely tall in Japan. My coloring, "mousy brown" in the United States, become "blonde" in Japan. Thus, the subject of the research had to be something that a very tall, blonde foreign male could reasonably accomplish. In the process of gathering the preliminary social stratification data needed for the soon-to-be-defunct sociolinguistic study, it became increasingly clear that one area where an oversized foreigner could excel was in the area of being a "stranger". I am so obviously an "outsider" in Japanese society, that I become, in a sense, a safe person to talk to, a classic example of Georg Simmel's stranger.

The rules of personal privacy seem to apply less to me than for other, more reasonably sized and colored foreigners. Once it became clear that I was extremely interested in virtually all facets of life in the neighborhood but particularly the history, the older residents of the neighborhood began to have a minor competition to tell me as much as they could about the neighborhood. After I had been in the neighborhood for almost a year, the younger residents, including the entertainers who were socially cut off from the rest of the neighborhood, apparently decided that I was able to keep my mouth shut and also began to talk to me, telling me their side of the story.

I developed my status as "stranger" as much as I could. Part of this approach involved not passing along gossip from one resident to another and other such obvious tactics. Other tactics that I needed to develop were unique to my situation. My height, in fact, became something of a standing joke and a point of local interest not only in "my" neighborhood but for a goodly distance around. In the central ward of Sapporo, I was "the foreigner" in general terms or, if specifics were needed (a rare event at a time of very few foreigners), the "giant foreigner". I became the "foreigner-of-the-neighborhood" (*kinjo no gaijin*) to the local children. Much to my wife's chagrin, she, in turn, became the "wife-of-the-neighborhood-foreigner" (*kinjo no gaijin no okusan*). As the "neighborhood foreigner", I eventually because widely recognized and achieved a place in the neighborhood, a social standing that let me ask questions pertinent to ethnographic research.

The primary purpose of this book is to provide an ethnographic account of a part of Japan not previously treated. *Ura nihon*, the back of Japan, has been under represented in the literature and this is a contribution toward the correction of that imbalance. Further, this is a part of Japan with a story that contributes significantly to the saga of the modern state. As the fifth largest city in Japan and as one of the fastest growing of the regional centers, Sapporo is an important city. As the cultural center for the northern half of the country, a discussion of Sapporo contributes to an understanding of the range and variety of cultural forms that make up modern Japan. The story of the northern territories themselves is, of course, also part of this story. Finally, as the focus of this book is on social change in one Sapporo neighborhood, the work contributes to our understanding of how social change can work in cities, in Japan, and in complex industrialized societies. The history of the neighborhood of Hanayama shows a pattern of evolution that has characteristics representative of other industrial urban centers in Japan and elsewhere. The neighborhood itself provides the focus, or the lens, through which other areas are examined.

Methodologically, this study has two general parts. The first part was two years of intensive participant observation research conducted in 1975 and 1976. The second part has been an ongoing interest in what has been happening in the neighborhood with a variety of return visits of various lengths but no further intensive period equivalent to the first two years. As a result, while there is some very detailed material up to 1976, the material from 1976 to 1988 is necessarily somewhat less complete.

LIST OF TABLES

LIST OF FIGURES

FOREWORD

Hanayama is an ordinary place, and as Robert E. Park, the founder of American urban sociology, once wrote, ordinary places are places of extraordinary interest. John Mock's detailed ethnography of Hanayama fulfills this promise of extraordinary interest by carefully situating the community itself in several important contexts, each of which is significant for our understanding of the community and each of which signals the original contributions this study makes to the understanding of contemporary Japanese urban life.

In the most direct terms, Mock's study of Hanayama, in the city of Sapporo, the capital of Hokkaido, extends the scope of Japanese ethnography simply by his choice of research sites. His work on Sapporo is, to the best of my knowledge, the first anthropological or sociological monograph about the city to appear in English, and thereby enables us to understand more fully the range of urban lifestyles and experiences of contemporary Japanese city dwellers. Urban life in Japan became a topic of great interest to foreign scholars with the publication of Ronald Dore's classic study, City Life in Japan (1958), but the majority of research on Japanese urbanization in subsequent decades has followed Dore's lead in concentrating on Tokyo. There are few studies of regional centers and smaller cities (of course, everything is smaller than Tokyo), so Mock's book is important in extending the comparative possibilities.

But it is more than that.

As Mock himself notes, the study of Japanese society and culture, by foreigners as well as by Japanese, has not focused much attention on the northernmost of the four major islands, Hokkaido. Hokkaido is culturally and socially outside the mainstreams of Japanese consciousness of their society's history, central cultural tendencies, and major social trends. Hokkaido has been--and to a certain extent remains--a periphery.

It is only a slight exaggeration to say that Hokkaido became Japanese only in the 19th century. It was a frontier society then, and so it remains at least in the imagery of mainstream Japan. If Hokkaido were located next to Wisconsin or Nebraska in the United States, it would be a perfectly venerable and well-established heartland, but the heartland of Japan lies far to the south around the ancient capitals of Nara and Kyoto, both of them dating from the 8th century, and around the megalopolis of Tokyo, which became the de facto capital at the beginning of the 17th century and has remained the center of national life ever since. In a society where the frontier experience shaped so <u>few</u> places, those that owe their origins to such settlement continue to stand out as distinct, even a century or more later.

So, in the popular imaginary of ordinary Japanese, as well as in the careful plottings of foreign social scientists planning to do research in Japan, Hokkaido has remained an outlying case. Little foreign research has been done in or about Hokkaido, and the most that many foreigners know about the place is that it was and is home to the indigenous Ainu.

John Mock's study of Hanayama therefore is a significant contribution to Western scholarship on Japan precisely because it puts Hokkaido and Sapporo on the map of contemporary Japan, so to speak. Mock does so with a blend of local history and contemporary ethnography that enables his study of a neighborhood to speak as well as about the particular social and cultural dynamics of frontier experience that have shaped Hokkaido's distinctive version of contemporary Japanese life. Put another way, every community is distinctive in some fashion and Hanayama is no exception; Mock's analysis enables us to understand how the historical development of Hokkaido, the patterns of migration that it stimulated, and the particular socio-economic circumstances that shaped the settlement of Sapporo are reflected in the specific details of contemporary Hanayama, thereby illuminating both the neighborhood itself and Hokkaido's place in contemporary Japan.

Few studies of urban communities, of cities in Japan or elsewhere, link contemporary ethnography to careful accounts of the local historical context, and fewer still are able successfully to link the local context to broader historical trends of social, political, and cultural life at the level of the state and the society as a whole. In Hanayama, Mock has done this by juxtaposing his own historical and ethnographic data with what Hanayama's residents themselves tell of the oral history of the neighborhood. Mock has made a distinctive methodological contribution by distinguishing among categories of residents not only by age, gender, and occupation (including, interestingly, the large segment of the local population who work in mizu shôbai, the entertainment world of bars and clubs), but also in terms of the demographic history of the neighborhood during the 20th century and the different streams of migrants who settled there at different times. The comparisons among and between residents of Hanayama reveal enormous amounts of variation, thus highlighting both the unique historical circumstances of Sapporo's settlement as well as the social and cultural complexity inherent in this ordinary but extraordinary slice of urban Japanese life.

Theodore C. Bestor
Professor of Anthropology and Asian Studies
Cornell University

ACKNOWLEDGMENTS

It is impossible to thank everyone who contributed to the production of this work in appropriate detail, particularly over the thirty or so years involved, so I will simply have to make do with this rather superficial form.

I cannot thank sufficiently the Japanese of Hanayama who literally made this study possible. Especially important to me was Kumiko Onoda who tutoried me in Japanese, helped me with the actual research as a field assistant, and has remained as a friend and comrade both in Japan and the United States. Drs. Asai and Okada of the University of Hokkaido were most helpful in shaping the research. Professor Wakizo Takata has helped me lwarn what little I know of Japanese society and has served as a staunch friend. Mr. and Mrs. Eichi Shinya and my landlady, Mrs. Sakuraba, introduced me to the rich detail of Japanese urban life while being incredible kind to a large, bumbling foreigner. I would also like to thank the Ouchi family, the Araya family, and Ogawa-sensei of Nemuro-Shibetsu for being good friends.

Intellectually, Scott Whiteford, Bernard Gallin, Dave Dwyer, Iwao Ishino, and Jack Donoghue were all crucial in my learning how to be an anthropologist and doing the research. Bill Ross set an example of a scholar and a gentleman that I would like to emulate. David Plath has, over the years, read various materials and consistently been instrumental in my understanding of my own culture, of Japan and of anthropology.

Special appreciation is due to Maureen Honey who encouraged in ways too numerous to mention, including sharing the field experience of living and working in Hanayama. Recognition is also due to Herb Whittier and Pat Whittier who have functioned somewhat like academic older siblings.

Finally, I would like to thank my family for putting up with me over the last many years and actively assisting in this project. My father helped me with the maps and other figures, my mother edited parts of many, many drafts, and my brothers provided useful comments on assorted aspects of the analysis.

CHAPTER I

"Despite the natural division of the country...unity and homogeneity characterize the Japanese"   (Reischauer 1988:8)

The predominant view of modern Japan is that of a homogeneous society dominated by the two major urban conglomerates in the central part of the country, the Tokyo and Osaka metropolitan areas. Looking at the vast majority of the work produced in English and Japanese about Japan, one would get the impression that a bucolic past of rural peasants has been replaced by a complete urban society located in either Tokyo or Osaka. The myth of Japanese homogeneity obscures the range of social variation found throughout Japan and the focus on the two great urban centers hides a wealth of diversity found in the other urban centers and more rural areas.

Modern Japan is clearly an urban society. However, it is not wholly represented by the large metropolitan centers of Osaka or Tokyo or a combination of the two. At a minimum, approximately two thirds of Japan's population lives away from these two areas. This would suggest that there is more to Japan. Between Cape Soya and Cape Sato and on to Okinawa, the range of cultural variation, degrees of urbanism, and patterns of social change is enormous and worthy, at the least, of study. The other areas of Japan have significant roles to play and, from an ethnographic perspective, important stories to tell. Modern Japan is simply too complex for a single voice, or the voices from one type of area, to tell the whole story.

Ura nihon, the "back of Japan", is used to describe either the Sea of Japan Coast or the whole of Japan away from the Kanto and Kansai (the areas around Tokyo and Osaka respectively). The fact that this term is used in the second meaning suggests that the Japanese see a duality between the great urban centers and the rest of Japan. There is a reasonable argument that understanding both sides of this dyadic relationship is essential for comprehending modern Japan. Historically, the population of Japan was much more evenly distributed than it is now. For the past century and even before, there has been a major exodus of population from the rural areas and smaller urban centers into the larger cities and great metropolises. As in Great Britain, the rural areas used to have a much denser population than it has now, and the great metropolitan areas were relatively and absolutely much smaller (cf Miur 1980). Part of this major rural urban migration has included the flow of people into a series of cities that might be considered regional, a second tier below Tokyo and Osaka. These centers include Fukuoka and Hiroshima to the south of Osaka and Sendai and Sapporo to the north of Tokyo. These cities have had extremely rapid growth rates even through they have also experienced an out-migration to Tokyo and Osaka.

These cities, and their hinterlands, provide Japan with a wealth of variation in linguistic, cultural, economic and ideological forms. They are not smaller versions of the metropolitan centers but rather display unique characteristics of their own which contribute to the heterogeneity that makes up much of the color and flavor of modern Japan. There is considerable national and local pride taken in knowing and recognizing what a given area is famous for, ranging from dialectal variations, local pickles, types of sake, notable landmarks, or perceived regional characteristics. For a foreigner living in Japan, it is an important sign of being accepted when one's Japanese acquaintances start talking about all of the regional variations and texture of the society rather than making flat pronouncements about "we Japanese...", the dreaded *wareware wa* statements that promote the myth of national homogeneity. It seems that Japanese embrace all this variation rather unconsciously but will also make broad statements about what Japanese do, ignoring regional and local variation. It is, therefore, among the anthropologist's tasks to bring out these differences.

In this light, Sapporo can be examined as a representative of the regional cities of *ura nihon* and as a city with its own unique structure, history and contribution to the overall fabric, to the woof and warp of Japanese society. As a regional city, Sapporo is the political and cultural center of Hokkaido. Hokkaido is by far the largest of Japan's prefectures and is, in a very real sense, the last remaining "frontier."

The northern territories were colonized only in the latter half of the nineteenth century and this short history, combined with a climate markedly colder than much of the south and the relative availability of land, makes Hokkaido's center a place notably different than other parallel cities.

Sapporo simply does not look like other Japanese cities. As only one of two major cities that were planned (Kyoto was planned and built in the ninth century), Sapporo has the grid pattern favored by nineteenth century urban planners, wide streets and a clearly coherent "downtown," both extremely unusual features for a Japanese city. While all cities are unique, Sapporo's uniqueness is immediately apparent to even the most casual observer. Stepping out of the train station, one is immediately confronted by broad street and avenues, looking more like a city in the middle of North America than East Asia.

The downtown construction is concentrated between the train station to the north and the entertainment district of Susukino to the south, a relatively small and concentrated area. With the construction of the Shinkansen, the "Bullet Train" station to the west, it is likely that this concentration will be diluted, as in other Japanese cities, but up to the 1990's, it has been maintained. Other Japanese cities tend to have multiple centers, like the nuclei of a cluster of amoebae (Asahara 1989; Cybriwsky 1991). In addition, the sense of business district concentration is highlighted by the sheer geographical size of Sapporo. The city is so spread out, so physically large, that the concentration of somewhat taller buildings in the downtown area differentiating it from the surrounding lower areas, appears very marked.

The early plan for the city was based on the assumption that flat land was plentiful and relatively inexpensive. Sapporo's growth is constrained only to the west by mountains and to the distant north by the Sea of Japan coast. Even in today's skyrocketing real estate markets, land in Sapporo is relatively inexpensive--although the downtown prices now are said to rival that of other cities in Japan. Another immediately apparent difference between Sapporo and most other cities is its rate of growth. New construction, even during economic downturns, continues at a high pace in Sapporo than elsewhere. Since the end of the Pacific War in 1945, Sapporo has consistently been one of the fastest growing cities in Japan.

Only Sapporo, like the other planned city in Japan, Kyoto, was designed to be a capital. Also only Sapporo and Kyoto are the major Japanese cities that are not natural ports although now an artificial harbor on the Ishikari Bay coast has been constructed.. When the Meiji Oligarchy decided to promote colonization of what were then considered to be the far northern territories--Hokkaido, the islands currently under dispute with Russia, the Kuriles and Sakhalin--Sapporo was a tiny village. It was strategically located on flat, well drained land between the largest known coal deposits and the nearest good port. So, Sapporo was designated to become the capital and the site of the primary military base for the entire north. As the capital of the Northern Territories, Sapporo was also settled in part by the *tondenhei*, the colonial militia, as well as controlled drafts of settlers from other parts of Japan, mainly the Tohoku region, the northern part of Honshu.

Visually, Sapporo was distinguished from other Japanese cities not only by its broad streets but also by its own particular wood construction. The forests of Hokkaido were readily available and wood was fairly cheap. The climate of the northern regions, moreover, was such that the traditional Japanese vernacular design was inadequate for the winters so houses were built more along the styles of Western housing, often with clapboard. As the unpainted wood aged, it turned a silvery, "weathered barn" grey. Even as recently as the 1970's, the dominant color of the residential areas of Sapporo, and most of the other areas of Hokkaido, was the grey of weathered wood. In addition, the thatch or tiles favored in the traditional architecture were both expensive and not terribly efficient in the cold climate, so painted metal roofing was used even quite early. As roofing techniques were improved, the metal sheets were enameled rather than painted, usually a darkish red or blue. Thus Sapporo, looked at from one of the many mountains to the west, was a city of barn grey housing with predominantly red and blue roofs. The concentration of larger buildings in the central core surrounded by an ever expanding sea of residential stretching to the north, east and south.

Thus, Sapporo is a city that looks, and in some important ways is, different from the other cities of Japan. As the regional capital of the recently settled far north, Sapporo represents an area of Japan with an unusual history. An examination of the social history of Sapporo, then gives us a view or perspective on Japan that contrasts with the view from the great cities of the south. As a regional center, Sapporo does represent urban Japan. However, the story of the northern territories--or at least a small part of it--can be read through the lens of one small neighborhood in the city and that neighborhood's adaptation to all of the changes that have occurred from 1925 to 1988. The main purpose of this work is to tell a story, to describe the ethnographic history of the people who lived in this one part of Japan; to add their voices to the chorus that makes up the song of the modern state.

The Neighborhood: Hanayama

The neighborhood of Hanayama was part of one of the original tondenhei or colonial militia settlements. The area that is the modern neighborhood was two and a half of the original farms. The original unit was five farms, a total of about seventy-five acres, which has since been divided into two neighborhoods. The colonial militia were originally divided into the old *go-nin-gumi*, "five-person/family groups", where each person--the head of the family--was responsible in some ways for the behavior of the other four and their families, a formidable means of social and political control. Lying between the main road running south from the train station to the major military base and what was designated as a shopping street in the original design, the neighborhood is about thirty-seven acres and had a population, in 1988, of about 1,600 people.

In 1925, Hanayama had a population of about 200 people and formed a tightly integrated social entity. This state was maintained while the neighborhood population trebled its 1925 size during the next forty years. Even in 1965, the neighborhood, with its population about 550, still represented a well integrated social whole. In 1975, the population had again doubled, to about 1,100, and the neighborhood was in the process of disintegration as a social entity. By 1988, the end of the Showa period, apartment buildings had almost completely replaced the original single family houses, the population had increased to about 1,600 and the social integration of the neighborhood was completely gone. Later, all of the single-family houses were replaced by other forms of housing. Hanayama is a neighborhood that is old enough to have a "time line" that can be traced.

The newer, purely residential neighborhood are, at most, only a few decades old. Other neighborhoods were rejected at potential research sites for other reasons. The primarily business neighborhoods were considered to be inappropriate for a study of changing social relationships because too few people lived in them. This left most of the older part of the city, composed of neighborhoods of mixed residential and small business.

As a neighborhood of the other, mixed type, Hanayama shares a number of important characteristics with other neighborhoods in its group. The history, demographic aspects, political representation in the larger urban arenas, economic activities and connections and social patterns are reasonably representative of all of the older, mixed neighborhoods in Sapporo and is probably not unrepresentative of this type of neighborhood throughout Japan.

When the research began, in 1975, Hanayama was a mix of small shops, small businesses, and, predominantly, residences including fourteen small apartment houses, four company owned duplexes and the rest in single-family houses. There were shopkeepers, landladies running the apartment houses, older white-collar families whose children had grown and younger white-collar couples who were either just starting out or who had school age children. In one corner of the neighborhood was a cluster of company housing where a group of eight blue-collar families lived. In the early days, but well within the memory of the older residents, there had been two farm families actively working the soil now covered with buildings. Finally, there were a lot of entertainers such as musicians, hostesses and bartenders who created a colorful and striking contrast to the more conservative residents of the neighborhood.

Physically, the neighborhood was bounded by three major streets. The narrow streets inside the neighborhood were public paths and social gathering places and, in good weather, noisy playgrounds for small children after school. The shopping street along one boundary was a constant bustle of customers and shopkeepers, particularly in the late afternoon. On the opposite boundary, the major road hummed with traffic filling all four lanes with parking on both sides. The ebb and flow of commuter traffic and the major bus routes gave a pulse and beat to the life of the neighborhood.

In the winter, when Sapporo has a wonderful combination of ice and snow on the ground and day after day of clear sunshine, the children still played in the streets while the adult socializing moved into the warmth of the shops. As the snow fell and was packed down on the streets, driving cars in the neighborhood became more and more difficult and eventually some of the interior roads became only used by foot traffic.

By 1988, there had been massive changes in the structure of the neighborhood. The grey wooden single-family houses had virtually all been replaced by apartment buildings, small to very large. Some of the roads had been enlarged and re-paved to allow easier automobile access.. Changes in the social fabric of the neighborhood reflected the changes in the physical structure. While the Neighborhood Association still existed, it had become almost completely ineffectual with only the shopkeepers and a few of the other residents even providing token membership. The bulk of the neighborhood residents were almost completely uninvolved in anything resembling "neighborhood affairs". In effect, during the Showa Period, the neighborhood moved from being a social entity with substantial ties and functions, to being only administrative unit.

CHAPTER II

Physical and Historical Context:
Japan and Hokkaido until 1925

The social organization of the neighborhood of Hanayama is rooted in the ecological and historical context of the prefecture of Hokkaido and the city of Sapporo. Hokkaido and Sapporo share much of the ecological and historical base common to the rest of the archipelago of Japan. Yet more than any area of older parts of Japan, Hokkaido and its premier city, Sapporo, have historical and ecological roots differentiating them sharply from the common Japanese experience. This is indicated by the use of the term -*do* instead of -*ken*. In this context, *do* means "prefecture" but it also means "way, path, road". Thus, Hokkaido can be translated as "North Sea Prefecture", "North Sea Road" or even "The Way to the Northern Seas". The colonial history of the prefecture and the city and the development of Sapporo as a center of tertiary industries--commerce, government, transportation and communication--are closely connected to the climate, topography, and location of natural resources. For example, the neighborhood of Hanayama exists because of its location on fertile land halfway between the Yubari coalfields and the port of Otaru. Hanayama's historical cycle, from an agricultural village to a densely populated portion of a large urban center directly reflects Hokkaido's development and the concomitant growth of Sapporo.

Hokkaido--Physical:

The primary distinctive feature of the island of Hokkaido is its geographical location. Hokkaido lies at the extreme northern end of the Japanese Archipelago (45° 42" to 41° 23" north longitude, 139° 45" to 145° 50" latitude). It is a large (70,508 square kilometers, or 31,200 square miles, about 22% of the area of Japan), roughly diamond shaped island about 450 by 400 kilometers across the points of the diamond (see Figure 1). Hokkaido lies about 300 kilometers from the coast of the mainland of Soviet Siberia (at the closest point), about 45 kilometers south of the island of

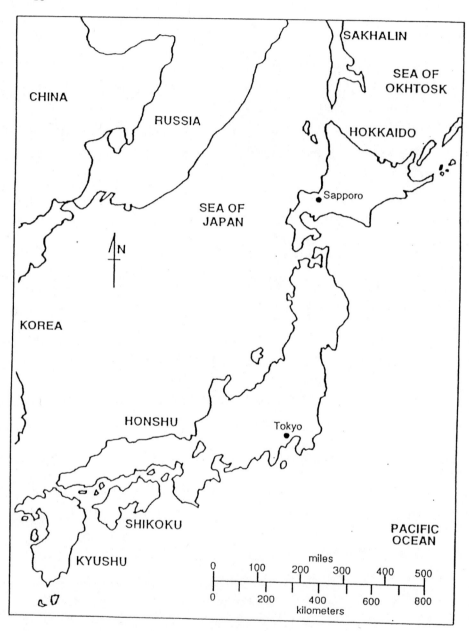

Figure 1.   Northern Japan and Adjacent Areas

Sakhalin, and less than 30 kilometers to the west of the first of the main Kurile Islands, both Sakhalin and Kuriles being currently controlled by the USSR. Hokkaido can therefore be described as an intrusion of Japanese territory thrust into a horseshoe of Soviet controlled, and heavily militarized, territory.

Hokkaido is the most geographically isolated of the major Japanese Islands. The Tsugaru Straits separating Hokkaido from Honshu, the next island to the south, are about 17 kilometers wide at the narrowest point and are noted for difficult currents and weather patterns. In 1985, right at the end of the Showa Period, the *Seikan* (Aomori-Hakodate) Tunnel was completed connecting northern Honshu and southern Hokkaido. The Seikan Tunnel is only for rail traffic so ferries still operate from Aomori City and other points.

Like the rest of Japan, Hokkaido, consists primarily of old volcanic formations, many still active, creating a series of mountainous ridges separated by relatively flat valleys. There are three rather large plains in Hokkaido of which the Ishikari and the Tokachi are the most usable because of the climates. The plains on the eastern end of the island and to the north are limited in their agricultural potential because of the long, severe winters. The Ishikari and the Tokachi plains, along with the smaller plains and valleys of the Oshima Peninsula, are fertile and support most of Hokkaido's population. The mountainous backbone of the island is not high with the southern peaks reaching 1500 to 2500 meters above sea level. However, they are rugged which, when combined with climatic factors such as snow, serves as a barrier among the various parts of the island. The pattern found in the rest of Japan of isolated valleys and plains separated by mountain walls is also found in Hokkaido. However, because of Hokkaido's relatively recent occupation by Japanese, the internal isolation has not had the same social significance, primarily because of better modern communication systems. Had Hokkaido been settled by Japanese in large numbers before the development of railroads and telegraphs, the isolating effects of the climate and the terrain would have been far more drastic than in the south. The late nineteenth century colonization emphasized the plains and the sea coasts both because that was where the natural resources and fertile land were and in an attempt to construct a prefecture that could have adequate modern communications. Even today, all of Hokkaido's large cities are on agricultural plains. During the winter, with its severe weather patterns, they are often isolated from one another and from the south.

The climate of Hokkaido is moderate to severe, with cool summers and cold winters, much like central Sweden, New England or the Canadian Maritime Provinces. Because of the action of the ocean currents and the movement of air masses from continental Asia, the southwest part of the prefecture is markedly warmer than the northeast. In fact, in some ways the east-west axis is more important in terms of temperature and precipitation than is the north-south axis. The precipitation levels are fairly high for all of Hokkaido with higher precipitation in the west than in the east, as is true of Japan as a whole, but in no region could Hokkaido be called arid. As shown on Table 1 and Figure 2, Hokkaido is considerably cooler than other parts of Japan but even the coldest lowlands have a growing season of sufficient length for agriculture. Further, there is adequate rainfall for all of Hokkaido. The combination of precipitation, sufficiently mild temperatures, and stretches of flat land allow parts of Hokkaido to be among the richer agricultural areas of Japan in spite of the more severe climate. Hokkaido produces most or all of Japan's oats, potatoes, azuki beans, string beans, beets, peppermint, and asparagus. In addition a large proportion of Japan soybeans (10%), feed corn (39%) and about 22% of the country's total dairy cattle come from Hokkaido. Hokkaido ranks as the third largest of Japan's rice-producing prefectures with about 4.5% of the national total, behind Niigata's approximately 7% and Akita's approximately 5%.

Aside from the agricultural resources of the plains, Hokkaido's major natural resources are timber, minerals, and seafood. Hokkaido's densely timbered mountains also provide hydroelectric sites. Hokkaido timber is mostly extracted for pulp with most of Japan's construction wood coming from North America, primarily from

Table 1.   **Comparative Climatic Data**

Temperature (F°)

Station	Mean of warmest month (Aug)	Mean of coldest month (Jan)	Days of growing season	Precipitation Cm.	Inches
Southwest Japan					
Kagoshima	80	44	253	221.4	87.17
Kumamoto	80	40	211	180.1	70.91
Fukuoka	80	41	203	161.2	63.46
Hiroshima	80	39	221	151.3	59.57
Osaka	80	40	219	133.0	52.39
Kochi	79	41	241	260.7	102.64
Central Japan					
Nagoya	80	37	207	161.7	63.66
Hamamatsu	79	41	281	118.4	46.61
Tokyo	78	38	215	161.0	63.39
Nagano	76	29	166	99.1	39.02
Fukui	79	36	205	233.9	92.09
Tohoku					
Sendai	75	31	181	112.9	44.45
Yamagata	75	29	168	123.6	48.66
Morioka	73	26	148	102.1	40.20
Akita	75	29	175	179.5	70.67
Hokkaido					
Sapporo	70	21	129	108.0	42.52
Asahigawa	69	14	127	109.3	43.03
Obihiro	67	13	121	95.7	37.68
Kushiro	64	20	141	109.8	43.22

Source: *The Climatographic Atlas of Japan.* Tokyo, 1948

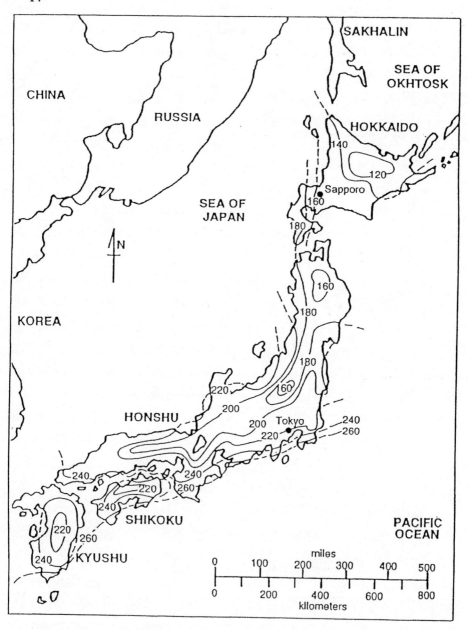

Figure 2.   Days Frost Free

Alaska and the Pacific Northwest.. The mineral deposits are mainly low grade coal with some gold, silver, copper, iron, and petroleum. The major natural resource of Hokkaido is in the surrounding sea containing the richest fishing beds in Japan's territorial waters. Since the twelfth century, three primary marine products--herring, salmon, and commercial seaweed--have been taken from these waters, and these fishing grounds remain among the richest currently being exploited by the Japanese.

The specific sections of Hokkaido are worth looking at in some detail because each region contributes economically to the development of Sapporo. Also, the subsections of Hokkaido have geographical features, such as drift ice (see Figure 3), not found in Old Japan that play a role in the historical development of the prefecture and its capital. Hokkaido can be divided into six major sections (see Figure 4): the Ishikari-Yufutsu lowland, the Kitami-Abashiri plains, the Konsen plain, the Tokachi Plain, the Central Fault Depression and its five basins, and the hill and mountain lands (including the Oshima Peninsula) that separate the assorted plains and lowlands.

The 4,289 square kilometers of the Ishikari-Yufutsu lowland is the heart of Hokkaido comprising the most extensive alluvial lowland. It has become the center of agriculture and its related industries and settlements. The northern part of the lowland, facing the Japan Sea, is primarily poorly drained peat soils of indifferent fertility. As Trewartha describes it,

> ...the drainage handicaps of the Ishikari Lowland present the most serious obstacle to its more complete occupance, for in the spring, with the melting of the heavy snow cover, the plain is a quagmire. (1965:346)

Along the Sea of Japan is a line of barrier beaches with dunes and a smooth contour without natural harbors. In recent years, a large artificial harbor has been constructed in northern Sapporo along the Sea of Japan using enormous amounts of concrete and late twentieth century technology. Around the northern and eastern edges of the Ishikari are a series of interconnected diluvial terraces, slightly higher than the lowland and having better drainage, comprised largely of volcanic ash.

The southern portion of the lowland is mainly composed of a low volcanic ash

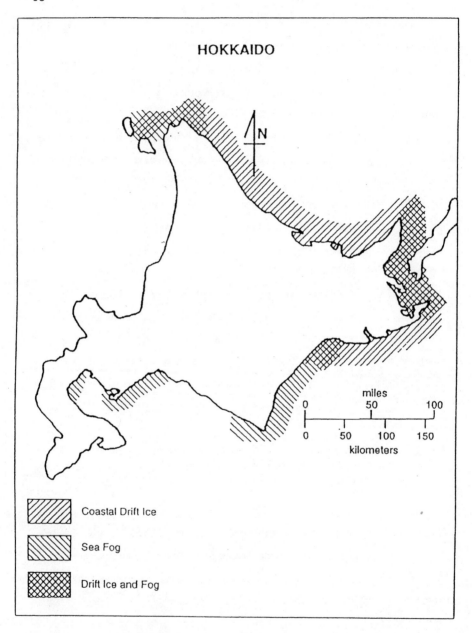

HOKKAIDO

Figure 3.   Coastal Drift Ice and Sea Fog

upland called Chitose. This area drains south into the Pacific Ocean rather than north into the Sea of Japan, even though the upland averages only about twenty-five meters in height. The inferior soil, built up from fresh volcanic materials and having poor ground water has made agriculture difficult, supporting a population density much less than the Ishikari alluvial lowland.

The Yufutsu Lowland, bordering the Pacific Ocean, combines a desolate assortment of features, including poor drainage, cool summers, sea fog (see Figure 3), and lower fertility, in an area which supports a very low population. On the seaward side, most of the area is beach ridges and on the inland side are considerable areas of marsh. What agriculture there is tends toward animal husbandry since much of the non-marsh makes adequate, if sparse, pasturage. Unlike the Japan Sea coast, however, there is a small natural harbor site at Tomakomai, which has been improved into a good functional port that serves Japan's largest pulp and paper mill situated there.

The lowlands as a whole support about equal amounts of paddy rice and non-irrigated crops. Enough rice is grown to make it one of the more important rice-growing areas of the entire country. Of the non-irrigated crops, oats, soybeans, potatoes, buckwheat, peas, and wheat are those more important. Orchards and dairying are also important, particularly operations near Sapporo.

In the mountains to the east, immediately adjacent to the lowlands, are the Ishikari coalfields, Sorachi in the north and Yubari in the south. These fields, extending about one hundred kilometers north and south and about twenty kilometers wide and now almost completely played out, were the largest in Japan. The coal was in complicated geological formations, the seams often thin and steeply inclined, and generally of a mediocre quality. There is a complete absence of high grade coking coal in Japan.

The five basins of the central depression are all small. Tombetsu Basin (124 square kilometers), the northernmost, has no flat flood plain of any size. The agricultural population is sparse with most workers employed in logging and lumbering. Nayoro Basin (379 square kilometers), about seventy-five kilometers long, has a distinct floor, of which much is poorly drained but some portions are suitable for paddy rice. Forestry is important. A like pattern is found in Shibetsu Basis (109 square kilometers), the smallest of the five basins.

Next to the south is the largest and most important of the five, Asahigawa Basin (also called Kamikawa Basin, 555 square kilometers). With well-drained soil and flattish land, this is one of the most prominent growing areas in Hokkaido. Because of the agricultural base and the historical importance of early communications by railway (completed in 1898), the Kamikawa Basin supports the second largest city in Hokkaido, Asahigawa. Furano Basin, the southernmost of the five basins (185 square kilometers) is small but the next most densely populated of the five after Asahigawa. Furano has about an equal distribution of rice in the lowlands and non-irrigated crops on the fringing uplands.

The climate in all of these basins is severe with warm summers but very cold winters and short growing seasons. Further, because of the surrounding mountains, Asahigawa has the dubious reputation of having less sunlight--more cloud cover--than anywhere else in Hokkaido. For all of these disadvantages, these basins, particularly the two southernmost ones, are important agricultural and forestry centers. The surrounding mountains also provide considerable hydroelectric resources.

The Tokachi Plain (3,827 square kilometers) is made up of three upland diluvial levels, the highest reaching elevations of 500-600 meters, and a lowland flood plain of newer alluvium. The Ando ash soil, of low quality and a very fine texture, is subject to wind erosion. Along the coast the summer months are cool and foggy, preventing any agriculture for about five kilometers inland. The interior is warmer in summer than the coast but with more severe winters. In fact, the Tokachi Plain as a whole competes with the Central Depression for having the most severe climate in Hokkaido (see Table of Comparative Climatic Data, Table 1, note Obihiro). Most of the agriculture on the Tokachi Plain is of a mixed type, combining dairying, oats, maize, potatoes, hay, soybeans, kidney beans, flax, sugar beets, and some horse ranching. Only about two percent of the total cultivated areas is paddy rice. The smooth coastal contours provide no natural harbors and the sea fog is such that even fishing is relatively undeveloped.

The Konsen Plain, about the same size as the Tokachi Plain, is similar to the Tokachi in that both are primarily upland plains with littoral lowlands. The coast of the Konsen Plain is washed by the cool Oyashio Current from the Bering Sea. As a result, the summers are both cool and extremely foggy (See Figure 3). Both Kushiro and Nemuro average 86 days a year of fog, with about half the days in June, July and August being affected (Trewartha 1965: 360). The soil is low-grade Ando ash which, like that of the Tokachi Plain, is subject to wind erosion and resists improvement. The major emphasis of agriculture is on dairying with an average farm size, about seventy acres, being larger than that of any other part of Japan. Feed crops dominate here and include hay, legumes, oats, barley, and potatoes, as well as grassland. Rice is entirely absent.

A large fishing fleet takes port in the natural harbors along the coast of the Konsen Plain. However, since World War II, this fleet and the port towns have declined markedly because Soviet occupation of the Kuriles has greatly inhibited Japanese exploitation of the rich fishing waters to the north and east. As a result of the cool, foggy climate of the coastal areas, agricultural alternatives are difficult to implement. The whole of the Konsen Plain supports a sparser population than any of the other lowlands on the island.

The Kitami-Abashiri Plains are divided into three parts: the Shari ash upland in the east, the wet alluvial lowlands of the Abashiri River close to the coast, and the inland Kitami Basin. The Shari volcanic upland has only recently been settled but already has a population density almost twice that of the Konsen Plain. While some rice is grown in the Abashiri flood plain, most of the land is dry field crops. It is surprising that rice is grown at all; Abashiri has a July average temperature of 62°F and an August average of only 66°. Not unexpectedly, however, the major economic emphasis here is marine and forest products. The Kitami Basin (474 square kilometers) is the agricultural base of the Abashiri district. Considerable rice is grown in the poorly drained, coarse alluvium of the basin floor but the diluvial uplands are more extensively utilized than is the wet flood plain.

A plurality of the island's sugar beets and white potatoes are grown in the district, with emphases on dairying, with its associated feed crops, and legumes. Farms average twelve to seventeen acres, smaller than those of either Tokachi or Konsen. The entire Sea of Okhotsk coast is sparsely populated, as might be expected given the climate. The summers are cool and short with long, severe winters. To add to these conditions are the summer feature of sea fog and the late winter and early spring feature of drift ice as shown in Figure 3. The sea fog and drift ice are important because they inhibit agriculture and reduce maritime activities such as fishing and transportation. Those areas having either or both of these features are more isolated from the rest of the country and have sparser populations than other, similar areas. The feature of drift ice is unique to the Hokkaido coast and was another geographical feature of the severe climate with which the Japanese had to learn to cope.

The hill and mountain lands comprise the majority of the area of Hokkaido. These areas are less densely populated than the equivalent areas of Old Japan, with exceptions found here and there in small pockets of lowland. These rugged areas are the principal source of lumber, wood products, and hydroelectric power as well as the mineral resources of the island. Further, the national parks located in the volcanic lands (see Terrain Subdivisions of Hokkaido map, Figure 4) have drawn many summer tourists from Old Japan.

The most important highland area is the Oshima Peninsula, the southwest extremity of Hokkaido. In the interior are most of the non-coal, mineral resources being exploited, including small deposits of copper, gold, silver, tin, iron, and sulfur. Three of the natural harbors on the coastal margins have become important ports. Hakodate, to the south, is the oldest Japanese-occupied area of the island, the most important fishing port, the terminus for the Honshu-Hokkaido Ferry until 1985 and

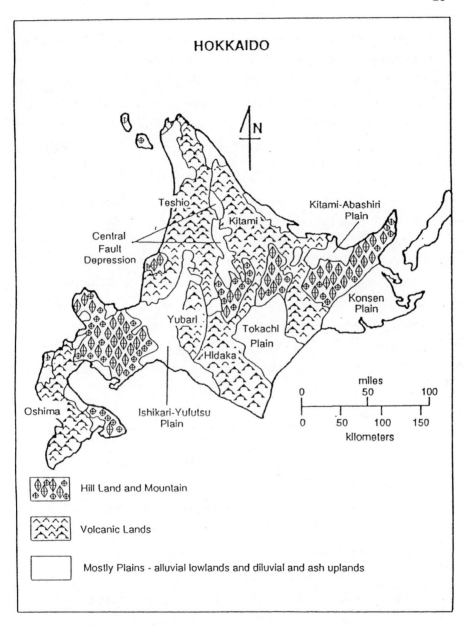

Figure 4.   Terrain Subdivisions of Hokkaido

the connecting port for the *Seikan* Tunnel from that date, and the southern terminus of the Hokkaido railroad system.. Otaru, on the easternmost corner of the Oshima coast on the Japan sea, is primarily the port for the northern Ishikari, including Sapporo. Muroran, near the eastern end of the Pacific Coast of the Oshima Peninsula, is the largest steel-producing area north of Tokyo, manufacturing about 9% of the nation's pig iron and about 6% of its steel (Trewartha 1965:366). Although the local coal and iron ore resources are exploited, much of the ore and all of the high grade coking coal must be imported.

The composite picture of Hokkaido is one of an underpopulated area (66 people per square kilometer, the national average being 277) The economy is based not on manufacturing and construction industries but rather on extractive industries such as agriculture, fishing, and forestry, and tertiary industries such as commerce and services. Hokkaido is uniquely geographically and perceptually isolated from the rest of Japan by physical topography and its severe climate. A third factor which enters into the perceptual separation of Hokkaido from the rest of Japan is Hokkaido's unique history, or rather, from the Japanese point of view, Hokkaido's lack of historical depth. All of the other major areas of Japan can claim historical roots--as being Japanese--for at least two thousand years. Hokkaido's Japanese occupation can be traced only back to the sixteenth century in even a minor way, and only back to the nineteenth century in terms of any real historical significance.

Hokkaido--History:

Prior to the Meiji Restoration in 1868, Japanese occupation of Hokkaido was confined to the Oshima Peninsula with the primary settlement at Hakodate (see Figure 5). Along with a number of fortified trading posts along the southern coast of the peninsula, Hakodate had been settled as early as 1514. This area was the seat of one of the major feudal clans, the Matsumae. The political control of this area see-sawed between the Matsumae (1514 to 1798, 1821 to 1854) and direct control by the Tokugawa government (1799 to 1821, 1854 to 1868). The settlements began as small trading outposts, then became exploitative colonies, and finally residential

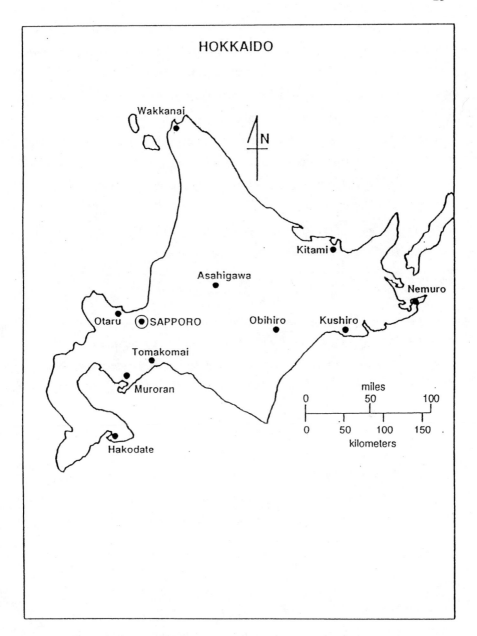

Figure 5.   Cities of Hokkaido

colonies. This pattern, first exhibited on the southern tip of the Oshima Peninsula, was generally followed in the colonization of Hokkaido by the Japanese, with new colonies moving generally north along both the east and west coasts.

The indigenous Ainu population had originally occupied all of Hokkaido, the Kuriles, Sakhalin, and the Tohoku region of Honshu. At one time the Ainu may have inhabited all of Japan as well as Kamchatka and South eastern Siberia and were slowly pushed back. Japanese actions *vis a vis* the Ainu were overtly exploitative and, in some cases, directly genocidal, much like the policies of the European settlers in North America but apparently not as brutal as the British in Australia (Bodley 1987 and Hughes 1987). The native populations were considered not quite human and treated accordingly. The Ainu were never a serious consideration in terms of national policy planning, including those plans made and executed for the colonization.

During the Tokugawa period, Hokkaido was distinguished as the ultimate northern frontier. During the Restoration, the Matsumae-fortified town of Hakodate was the final stronghold of the Loyalist forces. After this resistance was crushed, control of Hokkaido was given to the *Kaitakushi*, the Colonial Bureau, a division of the national government set up in 1869 specifically to colonize and develop the Northern Territories of Hokkaido, the Kuriles, and Sakhalin (or Karufuto as the lower half of the island is called in Japanese). In 1881 the Kaitakushi was dissolved, and Hokkaido, to be governed directly by Tokyo, was divided into three departments: Hakodate in the west, Sapporo in the center, and Nemuro in the east (see Figure 5). In 1886 the departments were abolished and Hokkaido was made an administrative entity of ten districts with a capital at Sapporo, at that time a small town of about 12,000.

The Tokugawa isolationist policies had frozen potential Japanese movement into the north, maintaining contact at its earliest exploitative stage. The Tokugawa saw Hokkaido and the other northern islands as being outside of Japan, subject to light resource exploitation, such as fishing and fur trading, primarily focused in or near the Oshima Peninsula. Permanent settlements were strictly limited and expansion was extremely slow or non-existent. With the Restoration, a number of considerations contributed to a sharp shift in policy concerning the Northern Territories. The Meiji, fearful of the Imperial Russian expansion that had begun by 1868 into Siberia and the northern islands, sought control of the Northern territories both as a defense against the Russians and as an area suitable for the intensive colonization and exploitation. The basic concept was to survey the area to be colonized--to a large extent with hired American advisors--develop transportation and communication links, and exploit any discovered resources.

The oligarchical Meiji's colonial policy was indecisive. The major national focus was the industrialization of Old Japan, not the colonization of the north. Until 1881 the Kaitakushi was in direct control of colonial efforts and policies in the Northern Territories. These policies included the formation of the *Tondenhei*, the Colonial Militia, conceived of as a peasant militia spread widely throughout the Northern Territories. Many of these Tondenhei were former samurai and provided both a never-tested military bulwark against Russian expansion and a series of nuclei for civilian settlements. These militia were given plots of land, some tools, and seed. The land grants were relatively generous. The standard plot size for Hokkaido, adopted in 1889, was 5 *cho*, about 5 hectares or 12.25 acres. This was far larger than the usual farm size in the rest of Japan. Further, there was an attempt to provide low cost loans for further expansion of their holdings. There were some problems, such as absentee speculation and fraud, with well-connected people buying up land--or getting the Kaitakushi to give it to them--but, given the levels of overall confusion during this period, the program went much as planned. "In the quarter century ending in 1900, when military colonization was abandoned, nearly 40,000 soldier-colonists and 557,000 civilian immigrants had entered Hokkaido" (Trewartha 1965:321). The major drawback was that the planning itself was on too small a scale. In 1900, after thirty years of active colonization, Hokkaido had a total population of about a million. Although Hokkaido was some twenty-two percent of the total land area of Japan, this is a low figure, a population density of only 13 people per square kilometer. In the eyes of the national government, the colonization of the Northern Territories had a low priority and few of the scarce national resources were committed to it.

Further, the Kaitakushi appears to have had little idea of the conditions in the north or even of its own ultimate goals in colonizing. The geographical conditions were mapped out by a number of the Kaitakushi-sponsored working groups, but the effect of the Hokkaido winter, particularly in the Southeast and Northeast coasts (see Figure 6) and cold coastal plains, was not fully appreciated until long after the initial colonization period and almost no allowance was made for these difficulties.

An excellent example of this lax government attitude is found in the development of cold-weather strains of rice. Soon after its formation, the Kaitakushi was advised that rice growing would be difficult in Hokkaido's climate. Its response was a half-hearted attempt to promote the growing of other crops more suitable for the climate, notably wheat, millet, and potatoes. Since the migrants were primarily familiar with rice cultivation, an educational program was needed for the rapid development of cold-resistant strains of rice. The educational program, endorsed by the American advisors the Kaitakushi had imported at great expense, was deemed too costly. The underfunded program launched to develop cold-resistant rice strains resulted in a very slow spread of rice horticulture and hardship for the colonists. As the map of the rice frontier shows (Figure 6), it took more than half a century for the Japanese to develop strains of rice sufficiently hardy for all of Hokkaido's lowlands. Much of the adaptation that occurred had to be on an individual level, each colonist or group of colonists had to devise methods and approaches to cold climate farming with minimal assistance from the government. The whole of cold weather agriculture did not have to be newly invented, of course, as many of the colonists were from the Tohoku region of northern Honshu where the climate is similar to that of Hokkaido although not as extreme. Although the Kaitakushi were not effective in the niceties of colonization, there was one aspect of the move into Hokkaido that was clearly understood and toward which most of their effort was directed: the exploitation of

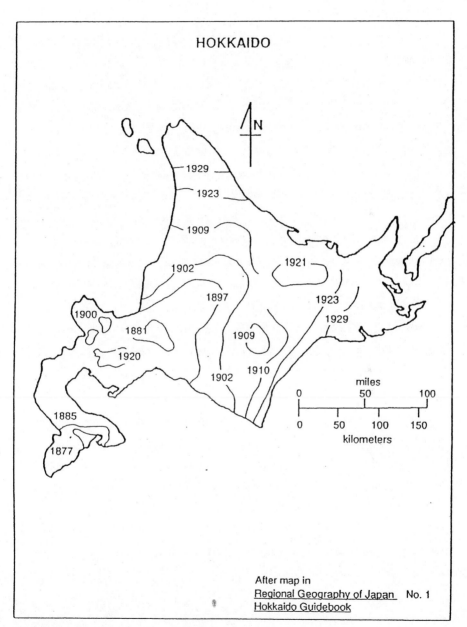

After map in
Regional Geography of Japan   No. 1
Hokkaido Guidebook

Figure 6.   The March of the Rice Frontier

the mineral resources of the island.

One of the first things that the Kaitakushi found from their explorers was that there were, in addition to the large coal deposits in the Hokkaido mountains, silver, gold, zinc, iron, and some petroleum. The development of transportation links during the nineteenth century, predominantly railroads and ports, follows a pattern of construction closely following the opening for exploitation of these mineral resources. For example, the first railroad, built in 1881, linked Sapporo and the Yubari coalfields with the port of Otaru. The largest port on the island, Hakodate, was by-passed because it was too far from the coalfields. Given the primitive state of the internal combustion engine and the rugged nature of the topography, the railways and ports rather than roads were important for transportation. This reliance on rail and sea communications influenced the patterns of Hokkaido settlement. Railroad development in Hokkaido radiated out from the Sapporo-Otaru-Yubari Coalfields nexus slowly expanding to cover the entire island. The pattern of settlement followed the coasts and the development of the railroads as shown by the map of railroad development, Figure 7. As shown, the immediate concern was the connection of the Yubari Coalfields to the port of Otaru. After the completion of the first links, the main thrust was to penetrate the interior going into the Kamakura Basin, then south to the Tokachi Plain and east to the Konsen Plain as well as north into the smaller northern basins. The railroads were obviously developed to complement the sea routes by penetrating the interior. Where the railroad did run along the coast, it was either a case of no inland route being available due to unsuitable topography or because the coast was not accessible to ships because of a lack of ports.

The main thrust of immigration into Hokkaido came from the Tohoku region of northern Honshu. Most of the civilian migrants settled either in the growing port towns or in the militia settlements along the major rivers (see map, Figure 8), largely concentrated on the northern part of the Ishikari Plain. With the military colonization policy at the end of the nineteenth century, the civilian migration continued as demonstrated by the continued increase in population as shown in Figure 9. The defeat of China in the Sino-Japanese War of 1895 and Czarist Russia in 1905 firmly established Japanese supremacy in the Northern Territories, at least until 1945. Between 1900 and 1925, the development of Hokkaido continued but with decreasing national emphasis. The frontier in Hokkaido was, to some extent, supplanted by other territories thought to be more commercially valuable, more strategically located, or less secure, such as Taiwan, Korea, and the Pacific Islands mandated to Japan by the League of Nations after World War I. As a result of these unique features, Hokkaido had certain aspects in marked contrast with Old Japan, even with the Tohoku region which it most closely resembles geographically.

A few items comparing Hokkaido and Old Japan might aid in understanding the socioeconomic patterns found in Sapporo. Although the population density of Hokkaido is lower than that found in Old Japan, the degree of urbanization is similar if one uses the "Densely Inhabited District" (DID) criteria. Using DID figures for 1960, Hokkaido had 42.1% of its population living in DIDs, while the national average was 43.7%, with only seven of the Old Japan prefectures having higher percentages of the populations living in DIDs. All of these denser populations are located in the three great metropolitan-industrial areas, plus industrial Fukuoka in northern Kyushu (Trewartha 1965). At the same period, the ratio of sexes in Hokkaido showed a preponderance of males (102), while the national average showed a deficiency of males (96.5) and the Tohoku region had proportionately even fewer males.

Another oddity is that Hokkaido's farms are the largest and among the richest in Japan, with a history of independent ownership derived from its "land grant" past. As Table 2, the Regional Subdivision of Japan table shows, Hokkaido's modern agricultural income per farm is almost 75% higher than that of the next highest region. Hokkaido also had the third highest per capita income (in 1957) of any region in Japan. In the earliest periods, this was not the case but the strong resource base of the island did allow for a great deal of individual economic independence. The land

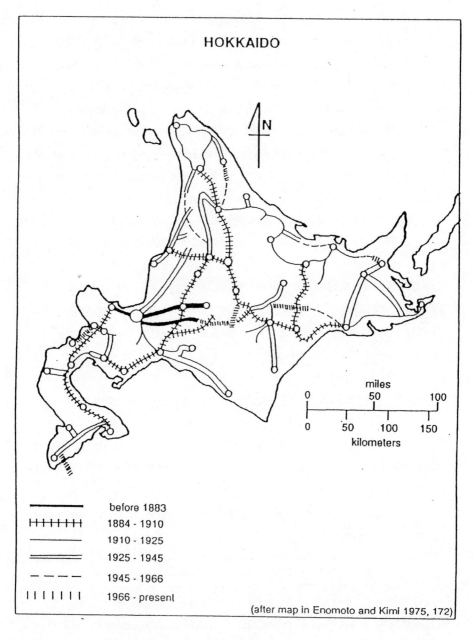

Figure 7.   Railroad Development in Hokkaido

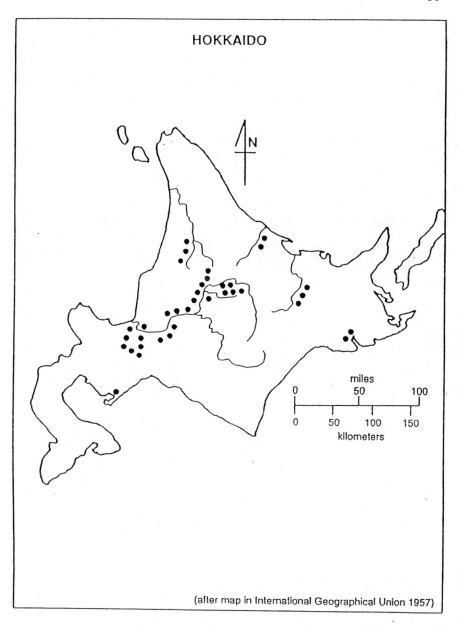

HOKKAIDO

(after map in International Geographical Union 1957)

Figure 8.   *Tondenhei,* Colonial Militia Settlements in Hokkaido: 1876-1899

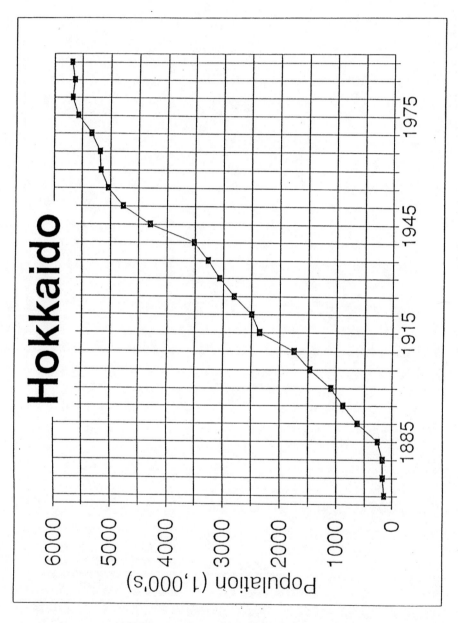

Figure 9.   Hokkaido Population: 1875-1995

Table 2.   Regional Subdivisions of Japan

REGION	Per capita income in 1957 (1000 yen)	Index (Japan = 100)	Percentage of population supported Primary industry	Secondary industry	Agricultural income per farm	Industrial production income per capita (Japn=100)	Population change during 1955-1960
S. Kyushu	67.1	72	58	18	72	31	-2.5%
Tohoku	72.0	78	53	20	127	35	-0.3
Sanin	73.8	80	52	17	76	32	-3.6
N. Kanto	74.0	80	53	17	114	49	-1.7
Tosan	76.9	83	53	16	83	43	-2.3
Shikoku	79.3	85	48	20	84	56	-2.5
Sanyo	82.2	89	42	21	83	99	+0.1
Hokuriku	87.1	94	41	21	107	81	+0.7
N. Kyushu	89.5	96	33	31	82	90	+1.9
Tokai	90.3	97	33	21	88	144	+6.3
Hokkaido	93.5	101	40	27	172	53	+6.5
Kinki	113.4	122	23	31	84	179	+10.4
S. Kanto	123.1	133	18	29	111	157	+15.8

grant structure of colonization caused a very high level of individual ownership of land. This economic environment strongly contrasts with Old Japan's small, relatively poor farms and long, sometimes bitter, history of tenantry and all that tenantry entails (Cf., Bix 1986).

Thus, there is an unusual set of circumstances--at least for Japan--where there was a relatively strong resource base and, because of the sheer physical and psychological distance from the central government, a sense of political and social independence. At the same time, the recent colonization of the area allowed for the use of more modern transportation modes, notably steamships and railroads, which, in turn, mitigated some of the isolating effects of the rugged terrain. The clumping of settlements along rail or shipping routes allowed the concentration of communications in one place, the city of Sapporo.

Sapporo: Physical

Sapporo, the Capital of Hokkaido, was designed and built to be an excellent example of the "central place" described in Central Place Theory. All roads lead to Sapporo. The major industries in Hokkaido have their central offices in Sapporo, and a large portion of the total population of the prefecture, about 35%, lives in Sapporo. The focus of political power, including the prefectural offices, is in Sapporo, and the social and intellectual orientation of the population of the environs of Hokkaido is oriented toward Sapporo as much if not more than toward Tokyo, a rare situation in a country so focused on its primary metropolis and capital.

Sapporo, an Ainu word meaning "extensive dry land," lies at the northern end of the Ishikari Plain. The plain on which Sapporo was built is primarily volcanic in nature, being the result of aggradation by the Ishikari river and its tributaries. "Ishikari," the name of the river from which the plain gets its name, is also an Ainu word meaning "to wander" or "to meander." The Ishikari Plain is mainly poorly drained with numerous peat bogs, hence the significance of the name of the city, it was apparently one of the few dry, flat areas to be found. Sapporo is extremely large, physically, for a Japanese city because of two factors: it is unrestricted by natural features on three sides, the north, east, and south; and the second, more important, element is that it was planned by an American along American ideas of urban development. The result is a checkerboard of wide avenues intersected by wide streets and a diffusion of the population far greater than that found in any other Japanese city.

Unlike most of the great Japanese cities, Sapporo was not a port although an artificial port has recently been constructed in the adjacent City of Ishikari, on the bay just north of Sapporo, which functions as a port for the City of Sapporo. In a land divided into small plains by rugged mountains, the historical development of most cities was largely abetted by easy access to the sea, the easiest mode of transportation. Hokkaido is as rugged as Old Japan but the later development of the island allowed

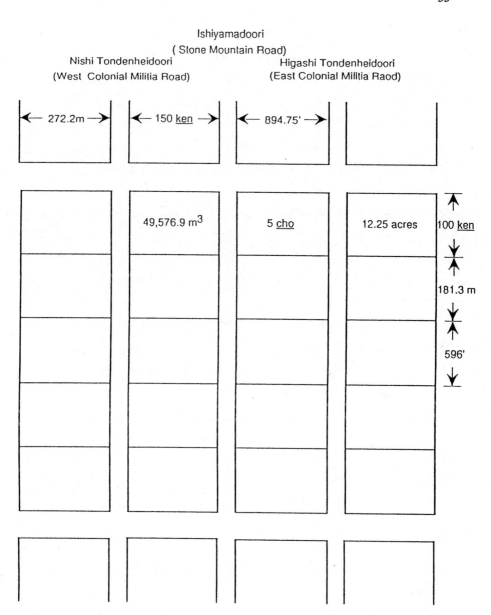

Figure 10.   Pattern of Sapporo Tondenhei, Colonial Militia, Land Grants

for different kinds of planning. The original exploitation plans, developed in the early Meiji period (1870-1890), looked primarily to the exploitable raw materials available in Hokkaido and ways of moving them to the south. The Ishikari Plain, where most of the raw materials on the island are concentrated as well as a large portion of its arable and more fertile land, has coasts on both the Sea of Japan and the Pacific Ocean. The Pacific coastal area, as discussed previously, is swampy, relatively infertile, and a considerable distance from the coalfields that were the primary interest of the early Meiji planners. The town of Tomakomai is the only port on this coast of any significance and its natural harbor is poor. The Sea of Japan coast has a smooth contour with no natural harbor at all. However, adjacent to this northern end of the Ishikari Plain, in the northeastern corner of the Oshima Peninsula, is a good natural harbor at Otaru. Thus, Sapporo occupies a strategic position near the island's best extensive farm land and between the coalfields and the best available port. Why Otaru was not chosen to become the future capital of the Northern Territories is not clear. Its distance from the Ishikari coalfields, its physically constricted location--being hemmed in by mountains--and its distance from a suitable wide open space for a military encampment might have been factors.

Sapporo--History:

The pre-Restoration town of Sapporo was not a very imposing place. It was a tiny hamlet on the banks of the Ishikari River, of mixed Ainu and Japanese habitation, subsiding on agriculture and river fishing. In 1872, four years after the Restoration, the population of the town was only 624 people occupying about 5.5 square kilometers along the banks of the river. This population appears to have been stable for the previous century. Sapporo was only one of many small villages scattered throughout the Northern Territories primarily concentrated on the more fertile plains and along the coasts.

To support the planned nexus of the rail line from the Ishikari Coalfields to Otaru, the Kaitakushi emphasized military colonization on the northern Ishikari Plain. By 1880, the date of the completion of the railroad, the major military base in the

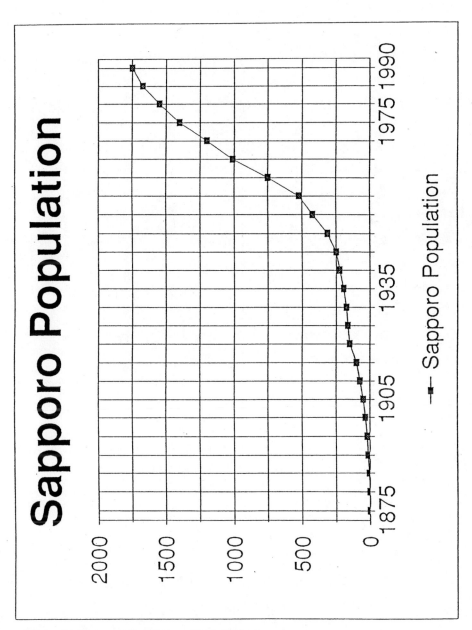

Figure 11. Sapporo Population: 1875-1995

38

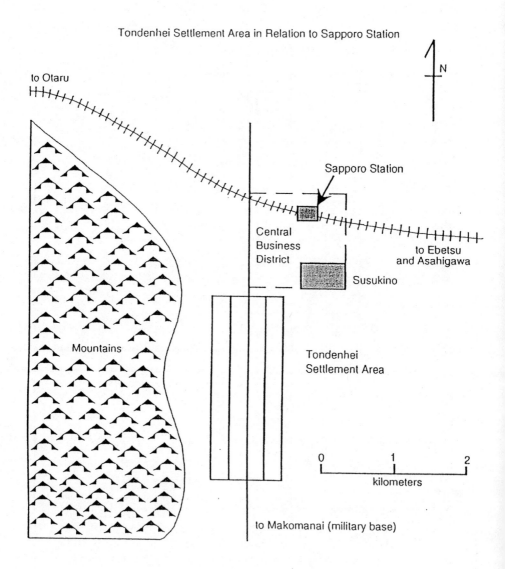

Tondenhei Settlement Area in Relation to Sapporo Station

N

to Otaru

Sapporo Station

Central
Business
District

to Ebetsu
and Asahigawa

Susukino

Mountains

Tondenhei
Settlement Area

0   1   2

kilometers

to Makomanai (military base)

Figure 12.   Sapporo Growth Pattern

Northern Territories had been established at Makomanai, a few kilometers south of the railroad station at Sapporo; the area between the station and the military base had been heavily colonized by Tondenhei. It was on this axis, railroad station to military base, that the city was planned and constructed. The element of planning in the construction of Sapporo probably cannot be stressed too much. The only other major city in Japan to be planned is Kyoto which was built in the eighth century. Aside from its unique historical aspect, much of the later development of the city reflects this original planning. In fact, it has only been in the last couple of decades that the city has finally "outgrown" the original plans made in the early 1880's.

The Tondenhei settlement south of Sapporo followed the line pattern common to most of the Hokkaido military colonies. Each colonizing household was given 5 *cho* (12.25 acres) of land in a surveyed grid, the area judged necessary for its support. In the case of the settlement south of Sapporo, the major road running from Sapporo station south to the military base at Makomanai and on to, among other things, a stone quarry that provided much of the building material used in the construction of the city, was surveyed as a dividing line between two double rows of Tondenhei homesteads. Dividing each of the double rows of homesteads was a narrower road (see map, Figure 10). Each of the colonists was given not only the land but also some tools and seed. It should be remembered that this particular areas has some of the more fertile land on the island and the least isolated; thus the planners could be selective about the recipients of these grants. As a result, the settlers moving into this area were among the most stable and skilled of all the migrants into the Northern Territories.

The post-Kaitakushi period (1881-1900) marked the fastest rate of population growth in Sapporo's history, an indicator of the increase of administrative and commercial functions of the period. Aside from the vast increase in railroad mileage focused on Sapporo (see Railroad Development Map, Figure 7), the commercial functions were mainly related to agriculture with only a small emphasis on secondary industry. This focus on primary industry and mining was a reflection of Sapporo's status as the capital of what was, in fact, a colony. The explosive development of secondary industry was concentrated almost exclusively in the core area of Old Japan. This period was the time of greatest tension concerning Czarist expansion into Siberia and the northern islands. The speed of Sapporo's growth reflects the degree of tension. By 1900, the population of Sapporo had increased to 40,578 for the official city or *shi* itself. The figures for the metropolitan area or DID, including the army base, would have been much larger.

The period from 1900 to the accession of Hirohito to the throne in 1925, the beginning of the Showa era, was characterized by steady growth of the city and the prefecture. With the successful conclusion of the Russo-Japanese War in 1905, Japan was ceded the southern half of Sakhalin (Karufuto) and the Kuriles. This cleared the way for a less tentative colonization of those areas surrounded by rich fishing waters. Karufuto and the Kuriles, part of the old district the Tokugawa called *Yezo* or *Ezo*, were brought under the administration centered on Sapporo. Thus Sapporo became the capital for an area comprising more than a quarter of the total land area of Japan. This area stretched so far east and north that it was almost as far from the outer edges of the hinterland to Sapporo as it was from Sapporo to the national capital at Tokyo. The total area stretched about one thousand kilometers east-west and almost six hundred kilometers north-south.

Aside from the physical growth of the territory, the commercial and transportation networks of the Northern Territories were greatly expanded. As the transportation links to Old Japan grew, particularly the railroads (see Railroad Development Map, Figure 7), the development of the primary industries of fishing, forestry, farming, and mining were increasingly made more commercially viable. The decrease in primary industries in Sapporo itself and the increase in secondary and more importantly tertiary industries, reflects the growth of the economy and population of Sapporo's hinterland. Sapporo's population continued to grow during this period at a rapid rate reaching about 73,000 in 1910 and more than 150,000 people by 1925.

The national government's previous efforts at the colonization of Hokkaido and Sapporo in the last quarter of the nineteenth century were distinctly less noticeable. With the conclusion of the Sino-Japanese War of 1894-5, Japan had gained the territories of Taiwan and Korea. The Russo-Japanese War had removed the threat of Czarist Russia in the north and had confirmed Japan's sphere of influence over Korea. The end of World War I saw the League of Nations mandate a number of previously German-controlled Pacific islands to the Japanese. Thus, the imperialist interests and efforts of the national government were directly more toward these new possessions than toward the region for which Sapporo was the capital. It should also be noted that given the communication technology of the period, the new imperial possessions, or parts of them, had greater ease of communication with the national capital than did the interior of Hokkaido or Karufuto or the more easterly Kurile islands.

By 1925, Sapporo had become a medium-sized city with a number of unusual features. First, its rate of growth (see Figure 11) was comparable to the growth experienced by the largest industrial cities of the south, but it was not undergoing the industrialization on a scale similar to that experienced by cities such as Tokyo, Osaka, Kobe, and Nagoya. Second, although Hokkaido and its associated smaller islands was considered part of the "homeland"--unlike Taiwan, Korea, and the mandated Pacific islands--Sapporo was more geographically isolated that any other equivalent-sized or larger city, either in the home islands or in any of the new imperial possessions. Third, and most important, Sapporo's hinterland--both in the sense of administrative control and commercial dominance--was more vast than any area in Old Japan, rivaling the new imperial possessions. Further, in terms of raw materials, minerals, timber, and sea resources, the Northern Territories, administered from Sapporo, were wealthier than any equivalent physical or administrative area in Old Japan. The importance of the Northern Territories frontier to the rising industrial strength of Japan is analogous, although on a smaller scale, to the relationship between Siberia and the rest of the Soviet Union or Alaska and the United States.

Unfortunately, there are not cities in either Siberia or Alaska comparable to the position of Sapporo to complete the analogy.

The Neighborhood:

The modern city of Sapporo is built around a central core incorporating the railroad station in the north, the entertainment district of Susukino to the south, and a business district in-between. From this core area, major avenues and railroad and subway lines radiate in all directions except west, the direction where there are mountains. The major direction of growth for the metropolitan area has been east and south (see map, Figure 12), along the railroad to the east and a major artery to the south.

The downtown business district is comprised almost exclusively of tertiary industries. Lining the major arteries radiating outward there is a scattering of secondary industrial concerns mixed with smaller tertiary establishments. Outside the city to the northeast and southwest are agricultural belts, primarily truck gardens. Due east and south are areas of secondary industries.

The neighborhoods of the metropolitan area can be classified into three types: non-residential neighborhoods made up of tertiary and secondary industries, purely residential neighborhoods existing on the extreme outskirts of the city and extending into the surrounding suburbs, and a mixture of residential and commercial areas making up most of the neighborhoods of the city. Without zoning restrictions, the growth patterns have been more or less organic, mixing small tertiary concerns, light secondary industry, and residential clusters.

The neighborhood which is the focus of this book lies between the railroad station and the military base in the south at Makomanai. It is about two kilometers south of the railroad station and about one kilometer south of the entertainment district that defines the southern boundary of the downtown area. This district lies south along the major north-south artery and, before its incorporation into the *shi* of Sapporo, was known as *Hanayama-mura*, Nose Mountain Village, the name used in this book for the neighborhood itself.

Hanayama is bounded on one side by *Ishiyamadoori*, Stone Mountain Road, the major north-south avenue; on the other side is one of the two *Tondenheidoori*, Colonial Militia Road, which bracket Stone Mountain Road, one to the east and one to the west. The neighborhood is of the more common type in the city in that it is a mixture of some tertiary and light secondary concerns but mainly residences. On the Stone Mountain Road side, it is lined with retail and light manufacturing enterprises. The Colonial Militia Road side is a solid strip of small retail establishments. In between are solid clusters of single and multiple family housing units, separated by narrow streets, rather dense by American standards (although well within the range found in the interior of large American cities) but not crowded by Japanese big-city standards.

Again, the lack of zoning ordinances makes for a mixture of housing that would be unusual in an American city. Hanayama housing ranges from the house of a bank officer, very large by any standard with spacious grounds, to very small (one room) apartments with no yards, with considerable variation between. There are also tiny, exquisite gardens interspersed with dilapidated houses with junk and trash piled along the street. In all, the neighborhood gives a jumbled effect alien to an American city.

Historically, Hanayama is as old as the city. During the Kaitakushi period, 1872 to 1881, land was allocated south of the then-existing town of Sapporo for Tondenhei, Colonial Militia, colonization. Over the next decade, 240 families moved into the area forming a roughly rectangular district of twelve-and-a-half-acre farms (see map, Figure 10). As mentioned earlier, each family received an allotment of land, tools, and seed. Unlike other parts of Hokkaido, even in the Ishikari Plain nearby, the better land was not withheld for later colonization but was allocated immediately because the planners wanted a Colonial Militia core of migrants strategically located between the military base and the railroad station. The land allocated was moderately fertile and the farms prosperous.

The original Hanayama residents, comprising two-and-a-half households of the original homesteads, came from Aomori Prefecture in the northern Tohoku region of Honshu. In the original Tondenhei records, preserved in the University of Hokkaido Archives, are carefully recorded data about each family such as the prefecture of origin, demographic material, tools and seeds granted, and ranks and military service records of each of the heads of the immigrant households. Although the northern Ishikari Plain was unusual in that very early (i.e., 1881) there were rice strains that would grow there, these new immigrants experienced some difficulties at first. It is unclear whether the trends in farming were the result of the rice-growing difficulties or the availability of a ready, near-by market, but in either case, it appears that very early there was an agricultural emphasis towards potatoes, wheat and vegetable crops. If, in the earliest days of the settlement, rice was the primary crop, it was quickly replaced by others more suitable to the climate.

By 1900 the city of Sapporo had grown considerably. Hanayama was not officially part of the city but functioned rather as a closely outlying farming area, being just about three hundred meters from the edge of the neighborhood to the boundary of Sapporo proper. A large daily market was established just south of the neighborhood retailing directly to local households and wholesaling to the retail establishments of the growing city. Although the Meiji land sales records are unclear, it appears that the original farms were maintained at least until 1900 without being alienated from the original colonists.

By 1910, the population of the city had almost doubled again. Hanayama was still not officially part of the city, but the urbanized area was steadily growing around it. The farms continued to function as before, and the nearby farm market had become a major wholesale center for the city. In 1911 the district was officially incorporated into the city of Sapporo. During this period the retail stores, a few of which had appeared very early along Tondenheidoori, proliferated to form an almost solid strip along the entire length of the street. Interestingly, it appears that at least during the Meiji period, the farm owners maintained ownership of the land but not the building housing the retail establishments. The retailers, all small-scale merchants, leased the land upon which they built their stores.

The population growth of the neighborhood reflected the expansion of the city itself. About 1880, fourteen people from three families make up the original land-grant settlement that was to become the neighborhood. By 1900, there were about ten families with about fifty-five people. By 1910 there were twenty-two families with about one hundred people. The people living in Hanayama in 1910 can be divided into three categories. There were still three active farm families, exclusively truck farming. About thirteen families of small-scale merchants lived in, over, or behind their shops, and about eight families of white- or blue-collar employees lived in single-family detached housing.

With the steady expansion of the city of Sapporo, including the incorporation of the nearby areas into the official city, Hanayama became progressively less rural as the city moved toward it. Even at the earliest stages, the movement of shopkeepers and white- and blue-collar employees reflected the beginnings of a shift from a rural farming district into a "suburban" area and, finally, into a fully urban area. The official incorporation into Sapporo-*shi* preceded Hanayama's transition into a fully urban, or even suburban, neighborhood, at least as far as population density is concerned. The population density of Hanayama was about 800 people per square kilometer, a moderately high number. It should be remembered, however, that 80% of its population was concentrated along three borders, on only about 10% of the land, with the other 90% of the land being working farms.

Even at this stage, the neighborhood was being drawn into the city. The first trolley ran along the major artery on one side of Hanayama as early as 1911. The retail shops were proliferating to serve an increasingly dense population in the surrounding area. Most importantly, blue- and white-collar employees were moving out into the district, particularly to Hanayama and nearby neighborhoods, because of their proximity to the downtown (one to two kilometers) and because of the relatively inexpensive land available. These trends were to continue through the focal study period ending in 1985.

46

Summary:

The severe climate and difficult topography of Hokkaido functioned to isolate the early colonial settlements from each other and from Old Japan. However, the technology available to the Japanese colonists in the latter part of the nineteenth century, particularly railroads, enabled the colonists to lessen the isolating impact more than if the colonization had occurred earlier. The pattern of colonization developed to maximize the exploitation of mineral and agricultural resources of the island. The choice of Sapporo as the capital of the Northern Territories directed the political, social, and economic focus of the region on to the city, led to a concentration of railroad communications, and set the stage for the development of tertiary industries in Sapporo. The neighborhood of Hanayama went through parallel stages of development reflecting the growth of the city. In the earliest stage, it was part of a farming community. As Sapporo grew, Hanayama became more closely connected with the city until its formal incorporation in 1911. The farm families were first joined by retail shopkeepers, then by blue- and white-collar employees of the city's growing industries. By 1925, the neighborhood had a mixed population of shopkeepers, farmers, blue- and white-collar employees with farming on the wane.

CHAPTER III

Phase I: 1925 - 1945

When we moved here (in 1925), there were just fields all around. In fact, the neighborhood stayed pretty open that way until after the war...There weren't any streets within the neighborhood, just paths. There wasn't even a horse trolley on Stone Mountain Road then, that didn't come until about 1930. If you wanted to go into town, you could always get a ride with a (farm) wagon...I worked at the main post office and walked to work everyday up until I retired (in 1958). It took me only about forty minutes to walk. It was a very nice walk. Now I wouldn't want to do it, but then it was all open and smelled good. There were just a few cars around until recently. Of course, the roads weren't paved like they all are now, either.

Mr. N, age 77

During the first fifty years of existence, from 1877 to 1925, the neighborhood of Hanayama developed a definite pattern: retail establishments grew along the major streets to the east and west and a progressively more dense scattering of private houses were constructed as people drawn to employment at the various expanding Sapporo concerns migrated into the neighborhood. This pattern of development continued throughout the 1925-1945 phase as a continuous stream of migrants, mainly white - and blue-collar employees, moved into the neighborhood.

In 1925 Hanayama was primarily agricultural with strips of mixed single-family housing and retail establishments along the east and west boundary roads. The farms were of the truck-garden variety, producing crops such as potatoes, squash, onions, radishes, and salad vegetables for immediate sale to the city markets of Sapporo, one of which was just south of the neighborhood. The farms had originally been solid blocks of land, but by 1925 the process of fracturing--breaking them apart for building sites--was well underway. The first two farm families were still the major landowners in the neighborhood and, aside from their farms, they retained title to most of the single-family housing plots and all of the retail establishment sites along Colonial Militia Road.

The retail establishments lining the east and west borders of Hanayama were very small scale. The most common design for these shops was to have a small salesroom--sometimes as little as four square meters--facing the street with sliding glass doors, as shown in Figures 13 and 14. The retail shops had their wares displayed in the sales room. As the salesrooms were rather small, by American standards (100 to 200 square feet), these rooms were very crowded as the shopkeepers tried to display the maximum amount of goods in the minimum amount of space. In fine weather, the sliding glass doors of the shop could be opened wide and the sales area would spill out onto the side of the street in stalls or trays protected from the weather by light awnings made of wood or cloth. The living quarters of the merchant family usually were attached directly behind or over the salesroom, these quarters comprising sometimes only a single six-mat room for a family or four or up to as many as four or five rooms, the living space of a normal, single-family detached house. Even the larger dwellings were crowded as the amount of space available for both domestic and commercial use was severely limited. Looking again at the representative shop floor plans (Figures 13 and 14), it is clear that the amount of space in these structures is very limited. In both shops represented, the first floor eight-mat rooms were used for cooking, eating, and as general purpose "living" areas. In the small shop (Figure 14), the six-mat upstairs room was unheated. This feature combined with the partly exposed stairway limited the usefulness of upstairs sleeping area. For example, during periods of extreme winter cold, the bedding would be brought downstairs to the warmer eight-mat room. The upstairs rooms in the larger shop (Figure 13) were more accessible than those of the smaller shop because of the interior stair. The larger shop upstairs rooms were used for storage, sleeping, and other "living" functions. The amount of space available in housing like the two shops presented here was further limited by the Hokkaido climate. Since all heat was from kerosene stoves that had to be turned off at night and because the level of insulation was very low, most family life tended to concentrate, at least during the winter, to the room or rooms that were heated directly. From their shops, which unlike the land they owned, the merchants sold almost everything that anyone would be likely to buy in an urban neighborhood: vegetables, meat, fish, fruit, noodles of various kinds, fresh *tofu*, housewares, medicine, inexpensive furniture, *tatami*, tools, and even calligraphy supplies.

Throughout this phase, the majority of the population lived in single-family houses scattered behind the retail establishments wherever land could be leased. Most of the houses of the neighborhood were large with spacious yards, by Japanese standards, and varied from the original Tondenhei farm houses to more modern houses as exemplified by the floor plan in Figure 15. Most of these houses had three to five rooms, including dirt-floored kitchens. The large six-room house represented in Figure 15 was owned by a relatively wealthy senior white-collar employee. Most of the everyday "living" activity was done in the central eight-mat room and the adjoining six-mat room. The largest room, the ten-mat, was usually reserved for entertaining and important guests. During the day, especially in the summer, the sliding doors would be opened between the various rooms creating a very large living area that was very light and airy blending with the garden directly outside. The Hanayama houses, like other Hokkaido houses, differed from those found in Old Japan in several important features. All of the Hanayama houses had metal roofs rather than thatch or tile. The Hanayama houses were relatively large due to the availability of inexpensive building materials of wood and stone and the relative cheapness of the land. Nearly all houses in Hokkaido had large vented kerosene stoves, called Russian stoves because the basic design had first been developed for use in Siberia, the traditional *kotatsu* or central hearth having proved inadequate for the severe Hokkaido winter. Finally, another adaptation to the Hokkaido climate, all of the exterior doors and windows were glass, often double glassed, rather than paper, usually with the traditional wooden shutters as well. The housing became denser as the population of the neighborhood increased.

But the population grew slowly--an average of about 1.1% per year, an approximate 25% net increase in two decades, a rise from about two hundred in 1925 to about two hundred fifty in 1945 (see Table 3). The slowness of the population

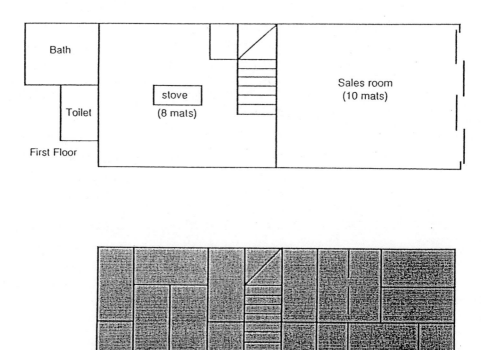

Figure 13.   Large Shop Floor plan

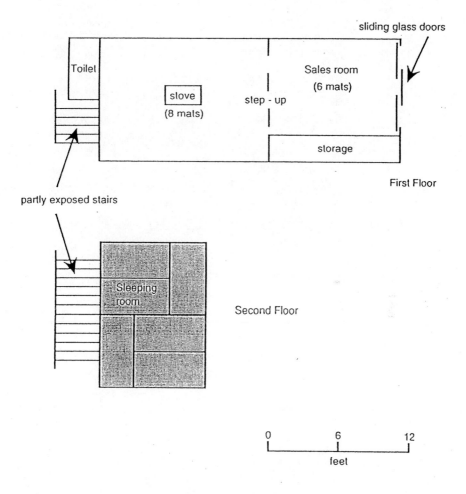

sliding glass doors

Toilet

stove

(8 mats)

step - up

Sales room

(6 mats)

storage

First Floor

partly exposed stairs

Sleeping room

Second Floor

0　　　　　6　　　　12

feet

Figure 14.　　Small Shop Floor plan

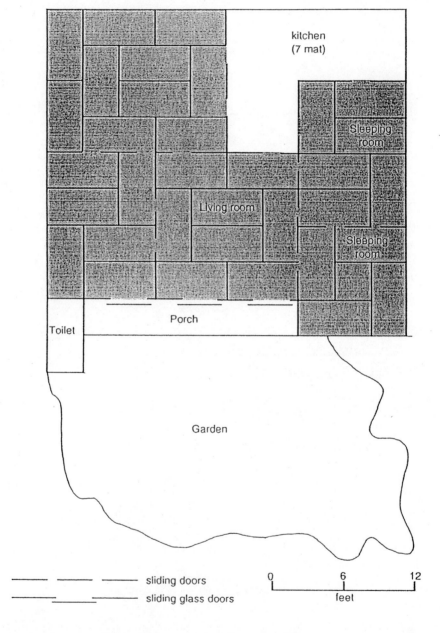

kitchen
(7 mat)

Sleeping room

Living room

Sleeping room

Toilet

Porch

Garden

—— — —— — —— sliding doors

——— ——— ——— sliding glass doors

0   6   12
feet

Figure 15.   Wealthy Hanayama House Built about 1920

Table 3. Population of Hanayama

	Households	Adults	(Approx) Population
1877	3	7	14
1900	10	---	45
1910	22	---	100
1925	43	121	200
1940	62	154	250
1950	88	217	350
1965	175	346	536
1975	394	704	1,052
1988	516	988	1,412

expansion is important here as will be seen later in the comparison of this phase with later phases in the development of the neighborhood.

The major feature distinguishing the 1925-1945 phase from the earlier period was the completion of the transition from semi-rural to urban. The earlier period had seen the transition from pioneer conditions with wild deer and bear--the early Tondenhei houses were constructed to be "bear proof"--to densely settled rural agriculture. Although the neighborhood was officially incorporated into the city of Sapporo in 1911, the agricultural aspect of the neighborhood was not terminated until the last truck farm ceased operating in 1943 when the heir took a job as a white-collar employee with the National Railway. Hanayama was fully incorporated into the city of Sapporo, socially and economically, in the period from 1925 to 1945. Both within the Hanayama neighborhood with its retail stores and outside the neighborhood where the population of white-collar residents increased, the economic base had shifted from primary agriculture to tertiary industry. This transition is reflected in the composition of the households of the neighborhood (see Table 4). The 1945 figures would be similar to those for 1940 except that there were no farm households later.

The numerical increase in the white-collar population and the eventual transition of the agriculturalists into white-collar workers corresponds to both the shift in the social hierarchy and the economic base of the neighborhood from semi-rural to urban. Although in 1925 the individuals with the highest social prestige in the neighborhood were older white-collar males (cf. Ramsey and Smith 1960), they did not totally dominate the neighborhood the way they would by the end of this first phase. At the beginning of the phase, the older white-collar group was socially equal to the farmers, who were the largest landowners but had the lowest occupational prestige, and the shopkeepers, a numerical plurality with a high capital investment in

Table 4. Composition of Hanayama in Phase I

| | 1925 | | | | 1940 | | | |
| | Households | | Adult Pop. | | Households | | Adult Pop. | |
	no.	%	no.	%	no.	%	no.	%
Shopkeeper	16	37.2	43	5.5	18	31.6	48	31.2
Old White-Collar	7	16.3	19	15.7	10	17.5	26	16.0
Young White-Collar	13	30.2	383	1.4	21	36.9	55	35.7
Blue-Collar	5	11.6	14	11.6	7	12.2	20	12.9
Farmer	2	4.7	7	5.8	1	1.8	5	3.2
	43	100.0	121	100.0	57	100.0	154	99.9

the neighborhood. By the end of the phase, the older white-collar group dominated the social order of Hanayama. Changes in the personnel of the former political structure of the neighborhood, the Neighborhood Association (*chonaikai*), reflected this shift in relative dominance.

The Neighborhood Association was only a recent, urban version of a historical series of government-sponsored or -approved organizations descended from the Tokugawa sumptuary laws. These laws had forced residential clustering by occupation and institutionalized the concept of collective responsibility for groups that lived and worked together. The original organization in Hanayama had been the Colonial Militia (Tondenhei) Association, whose membership had been the entire two hundred and forty original colonial families of the area divided into twenty-four groups of ten families each. The Tondenhei Association had been organized along para-military lines with a non-commissioned officer as the leader of each sub-group of ten families and a hierarchical structure designed to convey orders quickly and efficiently in case of the need for mobilization of the colonial militia. Membership had been restricted to Tondenhei and their families. Representation at Tondenhei Association meetings had been by households, that is, each household in the association having one representative, usually the head of the household. Thus, the official members of the Tondenhei Association were kin-based residence groups, not individuals.

As more non-Tondenhei migrated into the area, the Tondenhei Association came to represent a dwindling proportion of the populations. When in about 1911 the area was officially incorporated into the city of Sapporo, the Tondenhei Association had become ineffective through dilution, since no non-Tondenhei could join. Further, the explicitly military purpose of the Tondenhei had been rendered superfluous by the crushing Japanese victory in the Russo-Japanese War of 1904-05. It was about the time of the incorporation of Hanayama into the City of Sapporo that the Tondenhei Association was replaced by the Neighborhood Association. The Neighborhood Association, in turn, sent representatives to a ward association.

In 1925, the head of both the Hanayama Neighborhood Association (*chonaikaicho*) and the local district association were older white-collar males, but many of the secondary figures of the association were farmers, blue-collar, or shopkeeper males. The secretary of the Hanayama Neighborhood Association, a position of considerable power, was a farmer's son who had a blue-collar job outside the neighborhood. By 1945 the older white-collar males completely dominated the Neighborhood Association occupying all of the offices, with only a few shopkeepers listed as heads of the *tonari gumi*, the block associations, thirteen of which comprised the Neighborhood Association.

This shift in dominance occurred because the groups who had rivaled the older white-collar males, the farmers, and the shopkeepers had either disappeared or declined in relative strength. The farmers were gone. The economic position of the shopkeepers, no longer a numerical plurality, had been severely undermined by shortages related to the war. The older white-collar group, combined with the younger white-collar group, had gained a numerical plurality and, given the economic difficulties of the war period, had been able to invest in neighborhood land and buildings more rapidly than the shopkeeper group. A few of the older white-collar group had even bough out some of the shopkeeper's stores for use as rental property. Another factor was also important: one man was elected head of the Neighborhood Association annually from 1941 to 1945 and again from 1947 to 1950. He was an older white-collar male who was said to have a wide circle of acquaintances that he could mobilize to assist in neighborhood business, and an amiable personality, perceived as appropriate for such difficult times. As one of the then-younger white-collar males put it:

> For years after I moved here, the Neighborhood Association head was always the same man, Mr. A. During the war, you know, times were a little difficult and then after the war, well, we didn't know what to expect and things were even worse...Mr. A. always seemed to know everyone. Also everyone in the neighborhood liked him. We all knew each other fairly well back then, there weren't very many people. When I moved here (1938) there were only six houses (right around here)...Now that I am older, I am very impressed with Mr. A. He really knew many people. After the war, he even seemed to know all the Americans. He was a very good Neighborhood Association Head. He knew how to get along with people.
>
> Mr. S, aged 64

Thus, the rise of the white-collar group as the most powerful in the neighborhood combined with utilization of skills held by a white-collar male (white-collar males in general knew more people than members of other groups), exaggerated by the solidarity of the white-collar males who tended to vote together on issues previously discussed informally, resulting in the dominance of the white-collar group.

Underlying this migration into Hanayama by white-collar employees and their subsequent rise to social dominance was the basic pattern of urban growth in Sapporo as a whole. Sapporo's growth between 1925 and 1945 was somewhat erratic, population growth rates varying from 8.7% in 1941 to a negative 2.2% in 1945, but was one of the most rapid in Japan (See Figure 16   Sapporo--Percentage Population Increase: 1925-1975 after Wilkinson 1965:148). Furthermore, the dominant type of employment seems to have remained constant. Wilkinson's analysis by male employment composition lists Sapporo as having the same composition in 1920 and 1930. He gives no list for 1940 due to the difficulties in record keeping at that time. The 1950 categories are similar to the earlier ones with the addition of a commercial emphasis   to   the   already   existing   Administrative-Services   and Transportation-Communication emphasis (Wilkinson 1964:179). Thus, the relatively modest growth of the period was channeled primarily into tertiary enterprises. This is important not only because it means that white-collar employees were being drawn into the city, but also it meant that the economic situation of the white-collar employees in the city was relatively stable; there were no great fluctuations caused by shifts in the types of industries found in the city.

Despite the changes caused by the growth of Sapporo into a major commercial center, this urbanization appears to have been only minimally important to the majority of the population of the neighborhood in terms of their daily activities and social relations. Part of this was due to the employment of only about a quarter of the adult population (both males and females) outside the neighborhood (see Table 5), primarily in white-collar jobs in growing tertiary sector, e.g., government, the post office, or the transportation system. The other three-quarters of the adult population was either unemployed or worked within the neighborhood itself as housewives, craftsmen or shopkeepers. Although most of the income of the neighborhood came from city industries, a relatively small portion of the population was earning the income.

The second major type of economic contact between the people of the neighborhood and the larger city was the specialized area of wholesale marketing. Whatever their particular product line, all of the shopkeepers were supplied through carefully developed and maintained networks of personally known wholesalers. Considering the small scale of the stores, a given shopkeeper might buy all his goods from only one or two suppliers. It is likely that this business relationship was durable, lasting over a period of many years, and had developed non-business aspects. One shopkeeper described it as follows:

> I moved into the neighborhood in 1942 after I got back from China. My uncle owned this (drug) store and I started working for him. At that time, things were very difficult because of the war...Well, the shop was much smaller then, I've been able to enlarge it...At that time, my uncle used to buy from Mr. Yamada over nearer downtown, or 8th street, I think. He got almost everything from him and had for year. They had been in school together. Oh! a very long time ago, maybe Taisho (before 1925). Oh yes, Mr. Yamada is still alive. I send him a new year's card every year. No, I don't buy from him, he's retired but I did buy from his son for quite a while but not any longer (the son died).

Mr. T, aged 57

An item to observe in this quote is the maintenance of a social obligation--indicated in the sending of a New Year's card--even many years after the termination of the business relationship. The neighborhood stores, then, where the Hanayama population did nearly all its shopping, bought their goods from outside the

Table 5. Location of Employment (males and females)

	1925		1940		1950		1965		1975	
	#	%	#	%	#	%	#	%	#	%
Inside Hanayama	49	40.1	53	34.4	54	24.9	57	16.5	98	13.9
Outside Hanayama	26	21.5	40	25.9	80	36.9	167	48.3	384	54.5
Neither	46	38.0	61	39.6	83	38.2	122	35.3	222	31.5

neighborhood, but for the vast majority of the population this outside contact was only indirect. The major conduits are through the retail shops, from employment outside the neighborhood, and, to a much smaller degree, from the contacts of the farmers with suppliers and markets. Even with all three possibilities, less than half the adult population of Hanayama had direct economic contacts outside the neighborhood.

Even though the neighborhood was dependent economically on the larger industrial base of the city by means of wage labor and as a source of supply, only a minority of the adult population made the outside contacts. The neighborhood was closely connected to the larger urban environment through relatively small conduits, which meant that the social and political impact of the economic contacts between the neighborhood and the city were minimized, the people of Hanayama thus being able to maintain a strong sense of social autonomy.

Because the people of Hanayama were largely self-sufficient socially and economically, they saw themselves as distinct from other nearby settled areas. Their perception was aided by the slow rate of migration into the neighborhood and the rapid absorption of the immigrants who entered the neighborhood's social milieu. The few new families who did immigrate at any given time settled in scattered locations throughout the neighborhood rather than clustering together. The social mechanisms from the absorption of these newcomers were important in preserving the neighborhood's sense of itself. Before looking at how the absorptive mechanisms worked, an overview of the identity of the migrants into Hanayama seems in order.

Migration:

The migrants to the neighborhood between 1925 and 1945 were of the social groups already present, mainly white-collar employees. Only two new shopkeeper households and four new blue-collar households came into Hanayama, while a total of seventeen (six older and eleven younger) white-collar households moved in during the same period. Two blue-collar, three older white-collar, and three younger white-collar households moved out during the same period, leaving a net gain of two blue-collar, two shopkeeper, three older white-collar, and eight younger white-collar households. These fifteen households were composed of thirty-five adults.

Of the fifteen adults in the seven households for which reliable data are available, one was from a city larger than Sapporo (Sendai), two were from rural areas in Hokkaido, one was from Sapporo, two were from the Tohoku region of northern Honshu (both from small town, one in Akita and one in Aomori), and nine were from other urban areas in Hokkaido. This fits fairly well with the findings of White (1978) in his study of prewar migration to Tokyo. White argues that the significance of this pattern of migrant origins is that urban-urban or semi-urban migrants would not have felt as great a sense of dislocation and novelty as would the archetypical rural migrant. As Tauber puts it, such migration "would lessen the social adjustments and the psychological shock almost inevitable in direct transition from *buraku* to metropolis" (1958:127). In addition to the younger white-collar adults who came into Hanayama, there were reputedly also a few older white-collar households who came into Hanayama from other neighborhoods in Sapporo, that is, were just moving across town. These older white-collar adults, then, would have suffered the least shock or stress in relocation.

The seven younger white-collar households all knew someone in the neighborhood of Hanayama before they moved. In fact, all said that one of the reasons they moved to Hanayama was because they knew one or more people there.

> We moved here (in 1938) for three reasons. First, I had a job teaching at the elementary school over here and this is nearby. Second, several of the other teachers from the school lived in this neighborhood. Third, Mr. Ayama and Mr. Mori lived here and helped us find the house (that we moved into). [Mr. A had also been instrumental in getting Mr. S the teaching job.]

These existing contacts in Hanayama probably also helped cushion the shock of relocation.

The group of younger white-collar households in the Sapporo neighborhood for who reliable data are available were well educated (see Table 6). It is not clear just how representative this group is for the whole of Sapporo or even Hanayama; although all the informants tended to assert their "just average" nature, their high degree of formal education tends to support White's thesis (1978:82) that the prewar migrants tended to be among the better educated, as the Education and Occupation figure shows. Of the seven males, two had university degrees, two graduated from higher school, two from middle school, and only one had terminated his formal

Table 6.Education and Occupation of Phase I Migrants (Younger White-Collar)

Table 6.Education and Occupation of Phase I Migrants (Younger White-Collar)

	Lower Elementary	Higher Elementary	Middle	Higher	Higher School for women	University
Women (total)	1	2	2	1	2	
Men (total)		1	2	2		2
Post Office		x				
Elementary Teacher				x		
Prefectural Office						x
Railway		x				
City Office						x
Private Firms (More than 100 employees)			x	x		

education with the legal minimum of primary school. Further, the two university graduates were from important institutions: one was from Meiji University in Tokyo, which was and is one of the most noted of the private universities; the other graduated from the University of Hokkaido which, as one of the eight Imperial Universities, was one of the most prestigious institutions in the country.

The level of formal education for women in this group was not as high as that of the men, an imbalance found in the population as a whole due to institutionalized and universal sex discrimination. The one female who finished only the lower primary school was the mother of one of the males and had acquired her formal education a generation earlier, at the turn of the century, when three years was the minimum legal requirement and all that was available in the remote part of Hokkaido where she was born and raised. The higher schools for women were basically finishing schools where young women were prepared for marriage.

The proportion of males employed by the public sector is reflective of Sapporo's growth pattern. Five out of seven working for some form of the government bureaucracy was a very high percentage. Although there are no reliable figures, informants believed that this was fairly representative of the neighborhood as a whole at the time, five out of seven being perhaps more than usual; most said that about two thirds would probable be more accurate. One interesting point is that both the university graduates were public employees, one for the prefectural government and the other for the city of Sapporo, which indicates the prestige associated with employment in the public bureaucracy.

Thus a sketch of the migrants into Hanayama during the 1925-45 period indicates a basically urban background, relatively high educational levels for males, and an orientation toward tertiary institutions. As these migrants entered the neighborhood, they were readily absorbed into the social milieu by mechanisms explicitly and self-consciously applied for just that function.

On the individual level, new neighbors were introduced formally around their immediate section either by someone they already knew--the most prevalent reason for moving into the neighborhood--or by their immediate neighbors to whom they had introduced themselves. This process of conscious self-assimilation is exemplified by the custom of *O-hirome*, self-introduction. In the O-hirome, the newcomers say who they are and, in effect, ask to be accepted into the ongoing social life of the neighborhood. This custom involves one of a new couple, usually the wife, taking small gifts to at least the three houses immediately across the street and the immediate neighbors on each side or even to every house along the street. She then introduces herself--and, indirectly and *in abstentia*, her family--"gets to know" her neighbors and, more importantly, becomes "known" to her neighbors. Usually this is done with more than just the immediate vicinity. Aside from the direct introduction and exchange of socially crucial information, invariably with the ubiquitous tea, the newcomers become indirectly "known" to a wide circle of people throughout Hanayama as the volunteered information circulates throughout the neighborhood. this exchange of information can be seen as essential to the maintenance of neighborhood solidarity. As Roberts argues it, in a different cultural but still urban context:

> "Apart from shared and evident interest, it is the quality of information that they possess about each other that enables...groups to combine effectively and extend their organization..."(1973:11)

The information exchanged in the sort of face-to-face, intimate interaction exemplified by the O-hirome is of an extremely high quality, in Robert's terms, dealing not only with the major social criteria of relative status, such as occupation, age, and education, but also with more informal criteria that might well be the building blocks of long-term, close friendships, such as number, ages, and personalities of children; hobbies; possible compatible personality characteristics; and other trivia of life style. The arrival of a new household was something of an event and certainly of great social importance--with the concomitant focus on the event that such perceived importance entails.

Once the O-hirome had been accomplished and all important social information had been exchanged, one was officially and socially a part of the neighborhood, albeit still a newcomer. One then had to learn the *kinjo no tsukiai* (customs or relations of the neighborhood), a process involving pervasive interaction with one's new neighbors which further increased the depth of social relationships. One then also participated in the cycle of reciprocal exchange relationships (*tsukiai*) which are especially marked at New Years, weddings, childbirth, funerals, and other life cycle events.

For example, gifts were given at all these life-cycle events, sometimes directly to those involved but sometimes in the form of collections--often taken by the head of the tonari gumi--and careful records were kept of who gave. Careful track was also always kept of the value of gifts given and received. To give too much implied showing off. Giving too little might indicate that one was either poorer than one's neighbors or was stingy and had an uncaring attitude about other people. Worst of all was giving exactly the same value in return, suggesting a termination of the relationship with whomever the gift was given. As Mrs. Y, a young wife during the war, remembers:

> It may seem strange, but I think that it was a little easier then. Yes, one had to keep track of who gave what and so forth but that wasn't too hard. Also, nobody had any money then, so we all gave just little presents. Now when some gets married it is very expensive. During the war, when S-san got married, my husband managed to get a little sake from somewhere and that was all we gave. But it was all right.

I had to admit that at the time I was very silly and scared about being rude, so I carefully wrote down things so I could remember...Like who was getting married and so forth. My mother-in-law really scolded me one time when I gave too little for someone's funeral--said that I was making her son look stingy...Does that sound difficult? Well, you know, there weren't very many people then, so it wasn't hard to keep track. Only eight families on this street (1941)...But along...I guess it took me about a year to feel comfortable here. It might have been longer for other people, but I was so glad to have my own house (away from the in-laws).

There were also socially important visits. The most important of these visits was at New Year's when one would visit one's neighbors, thank them for their help during the previous year, and ask them for their indulgence during the coming year.

The gift giving, visiting, and mutual assistance during life crises reinforced the social bonds existing within the neighborhood. However, as Mrs. Y (quoted above) stressed, the degree to which any given individual or family actually participates in these events was, to an extent, governed by their own personalities. Certain events, such as O-hirome and New Year's visits, were, in their more formal aspects, "required" unless one wished to suffer the social consequences such as ostracism by one's neighbors, but beyond that the extent and enthusiasm to which one participated was a matter of personal choice.

At a minimum, however, these "formal" interactions among individuals served the important functions of introducing newcomers into the social milieu, exchanging the social data crucial to any social interaction, and providing a continuing framework for future interactions. All of these functions were essential to the social order because there was a pervasive cultural ethos in Japanese society that placed an extremely high value on interpersonal interactions as being, at least in their minimal form, essential for "getting on" (cf Benedict 1946; Dore 1958; Nakane 1970). Further, these interpersonal relationships form the basic building blocks of the social groupings which, to a large extent, defined and still define Japanese life.

Social Relationships:

The above discussion in the mechanisms of absorption in the neighborhood indicates the intense interest in social relationships which the people in Hanayama had during the prewar and war period. Mr. N, my oldest informant, put it as follows: "We had to get along. We had very little choice. Those were hard times." A somewhat less pessimistic view was expressed by another resident who saw this early phase as having some very positive aspects:

> It was better then. Children could run around without danger. We never had to lock our doors (because the neighbors would watch the house for us). Everyone had frontier spirit. Everyone knew everyone else and tried to help them when they could. There was a very good feeling in this neighborhood.

The social relationships which existed in Hanayama reflected this intense interest.

In any discussion of social relationships, there are three important features of Hanayama during this first phase to keep in mind. The first is that the total adult population of the neighborhood was small. The second feature was that the social and economic milieu of the neighborhood, in spite of the war, was relatively stable. People migrated into the neighborhood in small numbers, an average of less than two new households per year. Most of the people in Hanayama had been there for some time. The economic growth and rural-urban transition that distinguishes this phase was not rapid. The focus here, then, is on a small population in a stable environment. Third, for members of all social groups in the neighborhood there was a strong cultural value on having a broad network of trustworthy social relationships. Further, there were some very pragmatic reasons to invest resources in the development and maintenance of such relationships. The cultural value was derived directly from the rural Japanese experience where traditionally cooperation among an extensive network of people had meant the difference between success and failure. (For the classic discussions of cooperation of rural agriculturalists in Japan, see any village study, e.g, Embree 1939; Norbeck 1954; or Smith 1956; or, on a more abstract level, Benedict 1946; Harris 1977, specifically Chapter 13 or Nakane 1970).

The environment of the neighborhood reinforced this cultural value. Throughout the war period, for example, rationing was carried out on a neighborhood basis by the Neighborhood Association. Outside of the formal rationing system, itself requiring face-to-face relationships, there were also informal systems of food distribution. Almost everyone in the neighborhood had some sort of garden plot. By planning ahead and cooperating, duplication of effort was avoided both in actual work and in what was produced. Small scale exchange networks were commonplace. The other informal food distribution system involved "gray market" contacts with rural agriculturalists through which people in Hanayama were able to purchase goods otherwise unavailable. By what was in effect pooling their social resources, the residents of Hanayama were able to maximize their access to food because of their contacts with farmers outside the city. The government appears to have been aware of this sort of personal contact food acquisition network and, in fact, appears to have counted on it for certain kinds of food distribution. At least, it is clear that this sort of "gray market" was widespread and that the official rationing and distribution system was inadequate for the survival of the population (Havens 1978:114-132). In sum, the value of the maintenance of broad social networks was reinforced for the population of Hanayama as a whole by as basic a feature as the need to acquire food. Thus, a broad network was very adaptive for everyone.

There were also additional reinforcing features operative for only particular groups. For example, the broader a shopkeeper's network, the more business might be expected. Younger white-collar males who had a series of contacts, particularly with older white-collar males, might get a promotion or a business contact that otherwise might be missed. Older white-collar males seeking influence either in the Neighborhood Association or elsewhere could get it by mobilizing their networks.

The important point in that there was a cultural value toward the building and maintenance of extensive networks of social relationships, based, among other things, on residential proximity. The environment of the neighborhood was such that there were distinct advantages strongly reinforcing the value of network building; that is, the behavior of building and maintaining social networks was highly adaptive.

The resultant social networks from this combination of a strong value neighborhood knew every other adult although, as mentioned, it took awhile for new adults to become fully assimilated. In Mitchell's (1969) terms, within the neighborhood there were one hundred percent density and one hundred percent reachability--the extent to which personally important people can be contacted through the networks--everyone who had lived in the neighborhood for any length of time.

This complete density is evidence of a tight web of social relationships. An examination of three other characteristics of the social networks in Hanayama gives further evidence of the tightness of the web. The three characteristics--what Mitchell (1969) calls interactional characteristics--are durability of social relationships; the intensity of social relationships, the degree to which individuals are prepared to honor requests or respond to needs; and the frequency of contact.

The durability of the network links was directly proportional to the duration of residence in Hanayama. The groups who had greatest tenure in the neighborhood had the most durable relationships (see Table 7). From the chart, it is clear that the farmers, the older white-collar employees, and the shopkeepers averaged a long-term residence in the neighborhood. All three of these groups also had durable average relationships, especially with other members of the three groups. In all cases, the stability of the neighborhood residence pattern allowed the development of long-term relationships.

The intensity of the social relationships--the degree to which individuals are prepared to honor requests and respond to needs--is more complex. There are two major stumbling blocks in assessing this intensity: the first is that one is dependent upon the impressions of informants some thirty years after the fact; the second is caused by the emphasis on indirection or purposeful ambiguity in Japanese culture. Usually an onerous request would be made indirectly through a go-between so that the request could be rejected without having been formally acknowledged, and the rejection be formally ignored. On the other hand, the intensity of a social relationship might well be considered its most important characteristic.

relationship might well be considered its most important characteristic.

Table 7. Tenure in Hanayama (average years in neighborhood)

	1940	1950	1965	1975
Older white collar		22	22	21 24
Shopkeepers	23	23	20	18
Younger white collar		6	3	8 5
Blue collar	12	8	7	9
Farmers	30	--	--	--
Entertainers	--	--	0	1
Landladies	--	--	0	5

Further, those who lived in Hanayama were unanimous in their perceptions of the degree of intensity of the social relations of that period.

On the whole, the intensity of social relationships was very high. As the optimist quoted earlier, Mr. S, put it:

> What is "frontier spirit"? Well, it is helping each other. If somebody down the street, for example, got sick, we always took them food and someone watched their children. During the last part of the war, when things were pretty bad, I don't think that we would have gotten much food, even here in Sapporo, without help. Some people left but not from around here because we knew we could depend on other people (in the neighborhood). If somebody needed something--really needed it, like food or medicine for the children--they usually didn't have to ask.

There was, not surprisingly, a correlation perceived between very durable relationships and those with high intensity. A sense of duty also seemed to have been an important part of the intensity of the social bonds. Younger people felt that they were obliged to fulfill the request of older people, and older people, particularly the high prestige, older white-collar males, had a sense of *noblesse oblige*.

> As a young wife, when Mrs. Tanaka (a neighbor married to a high company official) asked me to do anything, I thought I had to do it

right away. I don't mean she was...(nasty)...but I had been living with my in-laws and back then a young wife did what she was asked--or told--to do. Of course, it worked both ways; Mr. Tanaka helped my husband (an employee of the city of Sapporo) and (my husband) got a promotion (because of Mr. Tanaka's help).

Mrs. Y talking about the conditions in 1940,
before the serious stresses of the Pacific war.

Finally, most of the social relationships were reinforced by frequent contact. Those least involved in the daily life of the neighborhood, the salary men and blue-collar workers employed outside the neighborhood, still had daily contact with most if not all the adults on their lane. Everyone walked out of the neighborhood in the morning and back into it in the evening. Their wives had even more frequent contacts.

Mr. Ayama used to go off every morning and not come home until evening, but I was here all the time. I think that I saw almost everyone...yes, every day. Sometimes more than that, for example, and neighbors and at the shops...Of course the children went by here too (the elementary school was right down the street). So even the people on the other side (of the neighborhood) I saw a lot of. I think that the only people I didn't see (daily) were the Electric Company employees who lived over there, since they would go the other way in the morning.

Mrs. A about the neighborhood before the Pacific War.

Those employed in the neighborhood like the shopkeepers, might see the males leave in the morning and return at night. The concentration of shops insured the shopkeepers seeing each other frequently. Since there were no refrigerators, the women in the neighborhood went shopping at least once, sometimes twice, a day. This brought them into contact with the shopkeepers and each other. The daily shopping was, in fact, something of a major social event.

Oh! you know, I used to look forward to shopping for food. The stores I went to were just over there, all within a few hundred meters, so it wasn't difficult. But everyone around went to about 11:00 in the morning and about 3:00 in the afternoon, so that when I went I could talk to my friends. Sometimes, if I didn't have a lot of work to do, I take a couple of hours or so to do fifteen minutes worth of shopping. Of course, we all knew all the shopkeepers and they would pass on any news.

Mrs. A about the neighborhood before the Pacific War

These neighborhood networks during this phase tended to have high density and, in Barnes' (1954) and Bott's (1957) usage, high closure. Further, the networks were characterized by durability which correlated with the long-term residence patterns of the neighborhood; intensity levels high enough for most of the residents to trust and, to some extent, depend on each other; and frequency patterns which reinforced the other characteristics.

One contribution to the frequency of contact, and thereby to the stability and depth of social relationships and the cohesion of the neighborhood, was the sheer physical proximity of housing, including the shops. Although Sapporo is considerably more spacious than other Japanese cities and building plots, particularly at this early stage, were considerably larger than average, the daily tasks of putting out washing or airing the bedding brought one into face-to-face contact with neighbors. Further, the close physical proximity of housing, as well as the rather open nature of Japanese domestic architecture, made the maintenance of privacy or family secrets difficult:

It sounds funny now but I came from a very small town in the mountains not far from Asahikawa. I wasn't used to people around at all. When we first moved here, it seemed like a lot of people--there were three other houses on the lane. When Mr. M built his house right next door, I felt like we were in his living room--or even worse, sometimes the bedroom--particularly that first summer when everything was opened up.

Mrs. A

One's neighbors soon knew all about one's personal life and it helped to ameliorate the negative consequences of such widespread personal knowledge if everyone got along amicably. As Dore phrased it for postwar Tokyo, "Privacy becomes impossible, intimacy inevitable, and no holds barred" (1958:263). If Roberts is correct, then, and it is the quality of available information that is crucial to effective group formation and action, then the Japanese city should be a tremendous spawning ground of effective social groups, which is, in fact, a generally accepted aspects of Japanese culture (Roberts 1973).

In some ways, the immediate neighbors became substitutes for larger family groups left behind in the migration to the city. Advice of all kinds--from how to fix one's house to raise one's children--business and political discussions along with contacts that might prove useful, and instant assistance if needed were all day-to-day realities, particularly in warmer weather. One feature of Sapporo that differentiates it sharply form other Japanese cities such as Tokyo is that for a good portion of the year, outdoor contact of any type is severely limited by the weather, although not to the extent that most Americans used to central heating would assume. Even so, one does not stand outside in Sapporo exchanging recipes at -10°C. The deep winter snow also functioned as an inhibiting element for this across-the-back-fence type of social interaction. Further, inviting a neighbor into one's house is not the casual gesture that it is in the United States, but rather a gesture of real intimacy to be seriously considered. Thus, while proximity and relatively small houses clearly were an important factor in the absorption of the newcomers into the neighborhood, they were probably not as crucial as they were for social interaction as in postwar Tokyo where, according to Dore (1958), proximity and small houses forced most of the informal social interaction into the street.

Formal Organization:

At the group level there were also formal and informal absorptive mechanisms. The formal aspect consisted primarily of the two levels of formal organization already mentions, the Neighborhood Association and the tonari gumi. In terms of relative importance for absorbing newcomers into the ongoing social milieu of Hanayama, the tonari gumi was by far the most important. The tonari gumi during this phase was composed of a subdivision of the neighborhood in what appear to be no particular patterns except for nonexclusive physical proximity. When the system was reorganized after the war, the tonari gumi were organized by blocks, but in the early period such blocks were nonexistent. Rather, Hanayama was composed of clusters of houses bunched behind the retail stores lining the neighborhood boundaries.

The tonari gumi was one of the basic social units of the urban environment. In Hanayama the tonari gumi was the organizational pivot for most group activities and for much of the diplomatic maneuvering which made the smaller sections of the neighborhood, the blocks or clusters, amicable places to live. Membership in the tonari gumi was universal and even, at times, enthusiastic.

The tonari gumi functioned on two levels. One was on the most formal level as the smallest official political unit of the neighborhood and, in fact, of the district and city of which it was a part. The tonari gumi appears to be the direct descendent of the Tokugawa five-household-groupings (go-nin-gumi) wherein each family was directly responsible for the actions of each of the other families in their group. As such, the pattern of social responsibility formally being delegated to the group for the actions of an individual is at least several hundred years old in Japanese society. Thomas Havens, in his excellent social history of Japan during World War II, says that this pattern in turn was derived from the Chinese *pao-chia* system of collective responsibility having roots in Japan going back to the seventh century, AD (1978:37)

On a less formal level, the tonari gumi functioned as a mutual aid society where the members were given a structure for performing various tasks necessary for the efficient function of the neighborhood (e.g., snow packing, litter removal, street maintenance), an opportunity for organizing for various life crises such as funerals, births, and weddings, and a framework within which informal social interaction could occur. The formal structure of the tonari gumi was built around an elected leader (*han-cho*) and the official membership. The election of the leader was usually of the Japanese type for small groups where everything is decided unofficially first, then the election is held to formalize the previous decision. A split, non-consensus decision was considered disruptive to group solidarity and unnecessarily harsh. At its best, this type of consensus decision making should be sharply differentiated from 'railroad' type decisions where a small, highly organized faction can ram decisions through over serious objections. Informal discussion before formal interaction gave most members of the group at least some idea of the issue at hand and the range of opinions held by other members of the group. The role of the chair in such meetings was twofold. First, to allow for full expression of all the various points of view, if necessary prodding the reluctant or bashful. Secondly, after the range of opinion had been expressed, the chair would seek to articulate what appeared to be an emerging, generally acceptable position. This position would then be refined, through further discussion, into a consensus that the chair made clear, albeit through indirect methods (direct expression of a personally held opinion by the chair would have been considered poor form) so that everyone present would be conscious of the emerging position although there would still be no formal vote or any other direct confrontation of differing opinions. At this point, those who had expressed positions diverging from the emerging consensus position could verbally move toward the consensus, a sort of mild recant. Finally, when it was clear to the chair that everyone was in agreement of what the final position should be, a final, usually unanimous, vote could be called. In this system, everyone was encouraged to voice their opinions and group solidarity, perceived as being more important than any specific issue, is maintained and promoted. At the same time, a decision is made that is at least tolerable to everyone. Using this system even during the height of the war, elections were allowed in the neighborhood without overt external interference. However as one informant put it, "We always were careful to elect someone who was appropriate, if not the person that the district supervisor might have wanted."

The Neighborhood Association, composed of the tonari gumi at this time, had little direct impact on the actual living units of the neighborhood. It major functions lay in organization of neighborhood-wide activities such as New Year's and *Obon* (Festival of the Light, held in August) observances, and in mediating between the neighborhood and the larger organs of political power in the ward and the city. This mediating function varied significantly through time as the international situation prompted innovations on the national level, which then filtered down through the

Neighborhood Association to the tonari gumi. In the prewar period (1925-33) the City of Sapporo and its various wards and neighborhood enjoyed considerable autonomy. In part, this autonomy was the result of what could be termed a policy of benign neglect. During these years, the development programs for Hokkaido were stalled and the urban area of Sapporo, being the most developed in Hokkaido, was ignored. The extremely sparse population of the Northern Territories also contributed to the lack of attention on the part of the national government. The prewar period in Japan was extremely turbulent and most of the government's attention was focused on the core areas of Japan and the far richer and more densely populated imperial possessions of Korea and Taiwan. The workings of the Neighborhood Association in Hanayama was left almost totally up to the local residents with few, if any, restrictions placed on them. This rather easy going period was, unfortunately, short lived.

During the China War period (1933-41), two factors played a large role in the functions of the Neighborhood Association in Hanayama. While the war in China had resulted in the tightening of the social order in all of Japan including Hokkaido, the increasing control of the national governmental apparatus by the militaristic right wing involved pressures transmitted through the political hierarchy down to the neighborhoods. The primary effect of these two interrelated forces was a formalization of a set of duties for the tonari gumi to be transmitted through the Neighborhood Association. These duties involved "social watch dogging," control of social thought, in both of which people were supposed to report anti-social or unpatriotic acts or thoughts to the local police, and implementation of increasingly detailed national policies involving such activities as civil defense and consumer goods rationing. A principle means of increasing the regimentation and mobilization of the Japanese civilian population for the war effort was through the tonari gumi and the Neighborhood Associations. During the early phase of the war, this mobilization was only beginning with policies such as the growing militaristic instruction of social ethics in the schools (cf Havens 1978).

During both the China War period and the Pacific War period, various locations in Hokkaido were of great strategic importance as a jump off point for military activities such as those in Manchuria and later in the Aleutians; this caused greater attention to be focused on it. For example, the military activities centered around Nomonhan in the late 1930's and as a take off point for the deceptive move at the Aleutians to cover the attack on Pearl Harbor in 1941. As a result, there was always a large military force stationed in Hokkaido and other parts of the Northern Territories, its size peaking during the China War period. This force was not as large as those stationed in the crucial military areas near Tokyo and in Kyushu, however, and there seems to have been a strong distinction drawn between direct military and nonmilitary control zones. The major military base for the Northern Territories was about 8 kilometers south of Hanayama, which seems to have had some effect on the formal workings of the district government and the Neighborhood Associations.

> You know, with the army right down the road in Makomanai, we were a bit more cautious than we might have been. I know of people who lived in Asahikawa who openly brought in food from the farms; we couldn't do that--at least not openly...We were also very careful with our record keeping. The district head was very concerned that all the Neighborhood Associations had proper records. I don't think anyone ever looked at them, but he thought that--well, maybe toward the end of the war, that the army would take over the city, perhaps, and then all the records would be examined.
>
> Mr. A, Neighborhood Association head
> during part of Pacific War

During this period as part of its mobilization effort, the prefectural government released propaganda for mass consumption which played up the military traditions of the Tondenhei, picturing them as being far more militaristic than they actually ever were. For example, posters appeared on Tondenhei wearing full military uniforms of the early Meiji period, something which may never have happened in reality. The Tondenhei were not allowed to wear regular uniform although there might have been some special event in which this was allowed (or even required).

The effects of all this on the Neighborhood Association and the tonari gumi least officially, performed the functions expected of it. The rationing system in part went through the Neighborhood Association, and much of the civil defense system was organized or implemented by the association. On the informal level, it appears to have been ineffective. The thought-control aspects of the national policies seem to have been left up to the higher organs which, in Hokkaido, were not zealous efforts (Hokkaido *Keisatsu Honbu* 1968). Even the civil defense implementations were limited and, if tested, would likely have proved ineffective. For example, the idea of bamboo spears in half-trained civilians against American or Soviet armored divisions does not appear to have been one of the better tactical concepts of the war. The efficiency of the Neighborhood Association is, however, a secondary consideration. What is important is that the Associations were entrusted with these tasks and were officially functioning, in this respect, as an organ of the government by implementing national policy. One must assume, therefore, that the policy makers at the national level saw the neighborhood organizations as strong enough to do the job.

Another facet complicating an analysis of the mediating functions of the Neighborhood Association with the higher organs of government is that while the effects of the Pacific phase of the war intensified for Japan as a whole they decreased for Hokkaido. During the Pacific War the emphasis of national policy was clearly to the south, while the northern areas were denuded of troops by the end of the war. Even in Manchuria, the crack army facing the U.S.S.R. was virtually stripped of its best troops and equipment. The troop strength in Hokkaido was drastically reduced for the first great push into Southeast Asia, the effect of this shift being to de-emphasize the direct war effort in Hokkaido. While Old Japan suffered tremendous destruction in the final period of the war, Hokkaido was virtually untouched (U.S. Strategic Bombing Survey, Over-All Economic Effects Division 1946). The civil defense measures were rarely implemented in any form, although there were some false air raid alarms in Sapporo. The rationing system and its connected attempts to restrict or repress the black market was even less rigorously enforced in Hokkaido than in the rest of Japan.

connected attempts to restrict or repress the black market was even less rigorously enforced in Hokkaido than in the rest of Japan.

Therefore, the war's effect on the Neighborhood Association was one of slightly increased formal activity along nationalistic lines but of little or no increase in informal activity. The Neighborhood Association was extremely powerful and used by the urban, prefectural, and national governments as a means of implementation, but in fact, the policies that it was called on to implement appear to have been ineffective. The tonari gumi, which in the south may have had some effect as a means of social thought control, seems to have been far less important in the implementation of nationalistic aims in Hanayama.

That one does see, however, is the rise of tremendously powerful formal structures--both in the Neighborhood Association and in the tonari gumi--which were closely associated with the national policies of the war period. These two organs, patterned after previously existing Japanese village social forms, provided formal structures, sets of primary intermediary functions, and informal arenas that allowed the social dynamics of Japanese cultural forms to operate. It was mainly on this informal level that immigrants were incorporated into Hanayama and through which the ongoing social life functioned. Most of the community activities were carried out on the informal level, with or without an umbrella of formal structure. In some cases, such as street maintenance in winter, the formal organization was adopted long after an informal process had evolved. The formal structure evolved primarily to satisfy the higher levels of governmental bureaucracy.

The dominant analytical feature of the neighborhood social organization was thus the interplay between the formal and informal levels of social interactions. The social networks of the people in the neighborhood during this time define the boundaries of informal interaction which, in turn, is overlaid by the formal structures of the Neighborhood Association and other constructs derived from larger systemic units such as the city or the prefecture. The directives issued by the larger units were mainly processed through the formal organizational elements, so that they impinged on the informal levels only in a form that could be absorbed. That is, one of the major functions of the formal neighborhood levels of social organization was to mediate between the ongoing informal neighborhood social organization and the larger social units of which the neighborhood was a part. For example, the war-time rationing regulations, supposedly enforced by Neighborhood Association, strictly prohibited the buying or selling of non-rationed foodstuffs. Yet the Neighborhood Association was not only able to turn a blind eye to such gray and black market activities, but was in fact one of the means of organization of the distribution of gray-market food in the neighborhood. Thus the governmental directive was adjusted or adapted to fit the specific needs of the neighborhood.

Conclusions:

Conditions in the neighborhood during Phase I relate to the questions concerning the impact of immigration on social relationships and behavior and, second, by an examination of the relationship between behavior in the neighborhood and the processes of change occurring in the city. The impact of migration on Hanayama between 1925 and 1945 was that it stimulated the application of a series of absorptive mechanisms which acted, on the whole, as cohesive forces in the neighborhood. The migration process was slow and even, with little disruption. The net result of immigration, aside from population growth, was the reinforcement of the white-collar dominance of the social order of the neighborhood and the transition of the neighborhood from semi-urban to fully urban. The important variables in this process were the speed of migration, the characteristics of the migrants, and the absolute size of the neighborhood throughout the migration process. The migrants were white-collar employees, blue-collar employees and self-employed shopkeepers. All of these groups were already represented in the neighborhood, so there were no drastic changes in type.

Most of the migrants came from urban areas, which allowed the shock of migration to the city of Sapporo to be alleviated because of previous experience. The shock of migration was also mitigated by the traumatic conditions of World War II, which had forced many of the migrants to leave heir former homes. Given their exits form their previous homes, their entrances into Sapporo were easy. Further, all of the migrants into the neighborhood during this period shared a value which perceived extensive and high quality webs of social relationships to be extremely positive, those relationships being the basic building block of social life. finally, the neighborhood was very small and dominated by face-to-face patterns of social relationships which were admirably adapted for the absorption of the new immigrants.

The relationship between the social behavior and the ideological, social, and ecological processes of change in the city is more difficult to assess than the impact of migration on the neighborhood. The neighborhood was, on the whole, fairly well insulated from the more drastic social and political effects of the economic and demographic growth of the city by its physical, social, political, and economic isolation. The autonomy, perceived by the residents and apparently actually existing, during this phase meant that the neighborhood changed but disruptive effects of this change were cushioned. In addition, the isolation of the city from the rest of the country served to minimize the most drastic effects of World War II. The changes that did affect the city were filtered through local apparatus, which altered them to fit local conditions before they were able to affect the neighborhood. Thus, the patterns of social behavior remain constant, with a strong pattern of continuity with the patterns of behavior from previous periods, throughout the phase in spite of the significant changes in the urban environment of Sapporo.

CHAPTER IV

Phase II: 1945-1965

> After the war, we moved into the neighborhood when I got a job with
> the railroad. I had been in Manchuria doing the same kind of work....
> When we got here (1948) everything seemed very normal, as if there
> had been no war. We built this house then. Quite a few other people
> were moving into the neighborhood at the same time. We all came
> together.... It wasn't as full as it is now, of course, but there were
> soon rows of houses here, with the shops over on Stone Mountain
> Road and Colonial Militia Road. We were very glad to be here.

In 1945 Hanayama was sparsely settled but distinctly urban. The two major
boundary streets to the east and west were almost solidly lined with shops, while the
interior of the neighborhood, where there were once vegetable fields, was crossed
with several small lanes with wooden single-family detached houses clustered along
them. These lanes were only a couple of meters in width. All of the streets were
unpaved, even Stone Mountain Road, the major north-south artery. In summer the
streets had large pot-holes and were mud when it rained, which was often. In winter,
the surface was packed snow, which formed a solid sheet of ice.

The pattern set during the previous periods--the filling in of the residential area
between the shop dominated boundary streets--continued during the 1945-65 phase.
The dominant theme of this phase--one of continuity with the patterns of the past--is
indicated by the absorption of new migrants, the maintenance of extensive and strong
webs of social relationships, and a strong sense of neighborhood identity; all this
continued in spite of the effects of a major war, an economic boom, a decrease in
perceived neighborhood social and economic autonomy, and a massive population
expansion. However, the migration and absorption process of the phase were not
steady. Rather, there were a number of periods within the phase, reflections of events
and trends occurring on a national basis, which had marked affects on the social order
of the neighborhood.

This phase can be divided analytically into three periods: the occupation
period (1945-1952), the transition period (1952-1960), and the economic boom

period (1960-1965). These three periods are distinctive in terms of population growth rates and economic conditions but manifest similar social patterns and patterns of change. The first, the period of occupation, had a rapid population growth rate as a result of postwar repatriation and demobilization. The city of Sapporo absorbed many of the repatriates, even though national policy was to disperse the repatriated population throughout Hokkaido. Even in the earliest stages, however, there was a rapid primary and secondary movement of population into the larger urban centers. Sapporo was particularly important in this respect because it was the largest undamaged urban area north of Tokyo and the second largest undamaged area in the country, the largest being Kyoto.

During the transition period (1952-1960), the population growth rate of the neighborhood stabilized at a fairly low growth rate reminiscent of the prewar and early war periods of Phase I. The migration rate again increased to a high growth rate during the economic boom (1960-1965).

Effects of World War II:

Before beginning a detailed discussion of migration and growth in Hanayama during this phase, at least a brief sketch of the various effects of the Second World War on Hokkaido and on the rest of Japan is necessary. These differing effects of the war have significance later on the social relationships and growth patterns that are the main concern of the rest of this chapter.

Although it is impossible to summarize completely the impact of the war and the American occupation on Japan, there are some observations that should be made concerning the different effects of the war on Hokkaido and Old Japan. First and most important, Hokkaido suffered very little direct war damage. This meant that the physical plants of the primary, secondary and tertiary industries underlying the island's economy were basically untouched. The lack of destruction of housing, for example, meant that the dislocations occurring in the more southern sections on a vast scale did not exist for the Hokkaido population although there was clearly pressure on existing housing because of the immigration of repatriates. Further, particularly in the primary and secondary plants, the scale of physical destruction in Old Japan and the dislocation of populations, even from rural or semi-rural locations, meant that Hokkaido temporarily assumed a position of disproportionate importance.

Secondly, both in its physical presence (i.e., numbers of troops) and its sociopolitical emphasis, the American occupation stressed the more southern core areas of Old Japan with decreasing emphasis moving north from Tokyo. Since Hokkaido had not had an important military significance, at least at the end of the war, it was held to be relatively unimportant in military terms except for its proximity to the USSR. Because the overall population was low and the population density sparse, it was not considered an area of potential trouble. The number of occupying troops was minimal and the focus of the Supreme Commander for the Allied Powers (SCAP, MacArthur's occupation headquarters) on Hokkaido was low key. What SCAP attention was directed toward Hokkaido was more with a view toward possible trouble with the USSR than with the Japanese population because the Soviets had declared war on Japan in August of 1945 and swept across Manchuria and the Kurile Islands. Therefore, with one major exception, Hokkaido was left much to its own devices.

The major exception, the third major point, was the Hokkaido's sparse population and temperate climate was perceived to make it the best area to repatriate much of the Japanese national population from the now defunct empire, especially the Japanese nationals from the more northerly areas of the empire; Manchuria, Sakhalin, the Kuriles including the northern islands. These repatriated populations, plus the returning members of the demobilized armed forces, comprised one of the highest repatriate-to-resident ratios of any Japanese prefecture. The impact of this repatriation and demobilization is complex but two points seem clear: the repatriates as migrants had somewhat different social characteristics than had previous migrants to Hanayama and the number of repatriates had some influence on the attitudes of the Japanese in Hokkaido toward the Soviet Union. The social characteristics of the repatriates, a point that will be dealt with in somewhat more detail later, different from those of the non-repatriate/non-demobilized migrants because of the different experiences of the repatriates. Most of the repatriates that came into Sapporo were from the Soviet occupied Northern Territories or Manchuria with a scattering of repatriates from other areas of the now defunct empire such as Korea, Taiwan, and the Pacific Islands. There were, in this group, also demobilized soldiers and sailors who had seen combat or garrison duty throughout Southeast Asia, the Western Pacific, and East Asia. As a group, the repatriates had had a difficult recent past, being on the losing side in a world war and then the processes of repatriation and demobilization *per se*. As a result of these experiences, this group tended to be extremely capable and independent as well as highly motivated to deal with whatever problems migration might present.

The influence of the repatriates on the attitudes of the people of Hokkaido toward the Soviet Union was to increase the fear and distrust that already existed. Because of the USSR's actions at the end of the war--the invasion of Manchuria and the Northern Territories which the Japanese perceived as a betrayal of the non-aggression treaty--the Soviet occupation of the Northern Territories has remained a major stumbling block to the creation of a USSR-Japan peace treaty (cf. Ministry of Foreign Affairs 1970 & 1986, Mock 1989, Nimmo 1988). Many of the repatriates had had direct, and negative, experiences with the Soviet Union. The repatriates exacerbated the Hokkaido Japanese memory of the Soviet invasion of the Northern Islands, the expulsion of the Japanese population, and the designs that the Soviet armed forces had on Hokkaido itself. The USSR desisted, in late 1945, from an invasion of Hokkaido itself apparently only because of the threat of direct opposition by American Armed Forces.

The overall attitudes of the people of Hokkaido toward the Soviets has been one of distrust, fear, and lack of understanding relating to almost everything that has been Soviet policy in the Far East since 1945. Because of these continuing territorial and other associated questions; the negative and distrustful attitude toward the USSR is so pervasive that it has been maintained, generally speaking, even by people who hold otherwise pro-left political beliefs. The repatriation of a substantial number of persons who had experienced the direct actions of the invading Soviet forces in Manchuria, Sakhalin, and the Northern Islands has helped maintain the pervasive anti-Soviet attitude.

A final point is that because of the isolation of Hokkaido from the circles of power at the national level, the attitudes of the Hokkaido people are, on the whole, somewhat different from those held by other Japanese. The war is sometimes seen as something that the Japanese as a group must accept part responsibility for, but in some sense, the powerlessness, lack of participation in, and lack of effect on, seem to have made people in Hokkaido feel somewhat less responsible or perhaps more detached from the very emotional response that most Japanese have toward the war, particularly in their dealings with Americans.

The impact of the war, or rather the lack of direct affect, distinguished Sapporo from other Japanese urban centers during and after the war. There are several distinctive features that differentiate the postwar phase from the previous periods in Sapporo's history.

Growth of Sapporo:

The city of Sapporo grew very rapidly during this phase. Between 1945 and 1965, the population of the city of Sapporo increased almost 300% from 220,139 to 794,908, and, perhaps more important, the area of the city increased by more than a factor of ten--from 76.3 square kilometers to 1,008.7 square kilometers. This expansion had several implications. The neighborhood of Hanayama shrank, in perceptual terms, from a significant if small section of the city to an insignificant and extremely small section of the city. With the expansion of the population, the core (business and entertainment) area of Sapporo also expanded, primarily in the direction of the neighborhood. This meant that Hanayama was much closer to "downtown" than it had been. Finally, the city of Sapporo was undergoing a transition from a relatively small, unimportant frontier capital to a major city, both in economic and perceptual terms.

During this period the attitudes of the people of Sapporo underwent significant shifts; they had previously seen their city as a minor urban center, therefore focusing on their neighborhood as an important social entity, to seeing themselves as residents of a major cosmopolitan center where traditional modes of thought and social activity, such as maintaining the neighborhood as a viable social entity, were not only inessential for a good life but, in some cases, not *modan* ("modern"--in the sense of progressive and non-feudal--used primarily by younger people).

Second, the physical growth of the city also changed the points of contact between the neighborhood and the city. As the population density of the core parts of the city and the neighborhood increased, transportation routes to and from the neighborhood were constructed--a bus system in the occupation period and later streetcar routes. Because of its proximity to the downtown area, the neighborhood became an attractive area for upper echelon white-collar workers able to afford to build or buy single-family houses. In fact, the nicest existing homes in the neighborhood were built during this phase.

Many of the group of older white-collar employees living in the neighborhood in 1975 had entered between 1950 and 1960, buying land and houses. The main road running south from the core of the city, a boundary of the neighborhood, was paved in the late 1950's, expanded, and soon was lined with light industry as well as the previous retail establishments. The opposite boundary, the old Colonial Militia Road, no longer important as a major street, became almost exclusively a shopping street crammed with retail establishments. These changes meant that the neighborhood was simultaneously in closer communication with downtown Sapporo and more isolated from it. The closer communication came about with the improved transportation. The isolation occurred when the neighborhood was, in effect, by-passed by the improved means of transport direct to areas farther away from downtown. Stone Mountain Road became a four-lane major artery that tended to slide traffic past the neighborhood rather than channel traffic through it. The decline in importance of Colonial Militia Road also reduced the amount of incidental traffic through

Hanayama. In sum, the neighborhood of Hanayama was different during Phase II from what had existed their previously because the changes were simply adaptations to altered social conditions.

Formal Social Organizations:

The changes in formal social organizations of the neighborhood reflected these social conditions. The Neighborhood Association and the tonari gumi were both officially banned by the occupation forces in 1945 because of their involvement, or perceived involvement, in right-wing, militaristic-totalitarian (thought-control) activities. Ironically, the actual efficiency or interest of the Neighborhood Association or the tonari gumi during the war was questionable at best in Sapporo and possibly throughout Hokkaido and the occupation bans in general were ineffective. On the whole, the SCAP forces had little idea of what they were doing or how they should go about doing it. Although there were some excellent people in the occupation forces in one role or another, the general level of understanding of Japanese society and culture was extremely low. For instance, the official banning of a whole groups of organizations was circumvented since, in the case of the Neighborhood Associations and the tonari gumi, they were immediately reconstituted in Hanayama and, as far as I can tell, throughout Japan. There was almost no gap between the dissolution of the old organizations and the appearance of the new ones performing precisely the same functions. Also, the same people were in positions of power in both sets and they appear to have performed virtually the same activities, only the names sometimes being altered to appease the occupation forces. Finally, for the purposes of this analysis, it is the informal structures that most concern us, rather than the formal structures with which they are associated.

The Neighborhood Associations, during the occupation period, were reconstituted as the next to the bottom level of civil government in the city of Sapporo. The Neighborhood Associations together made up District Associations, which in turn were combined into higher levels of the urban political structure. The Hanayama Neighborhood Association was composed of thirteen tonari gumi or Block

Associations, which had some real social efficacy during the occupation period. The immediate problems of the postwar period were primarily dealt with on the local level--the only level on which they were dealt with much at all--by the Neighborhood Association and the tonari gumi. The primary function of the Neighborhood Association during this period was to coordinate the functions of the tonari gumi, which appear to have been the focal point of social activity. The needs of the period for housing, food, and consumer goods of all types made for a considerable banding together of neighbors in the tonari gumi to counter the numerous shortages. This function was, in effect, a continuation of the war-period cooperation which had tightened the social bonds of the neighborhood and forged it into a functioning social and, in some respects, economic entity.

It should be remembered that during this period, the neighborhood was a homogeneous place with only the same four socioeconomic groups as before represented: the older white-collar group, the younger white-collar group, the blue-collar group, and the shopkeepers. The migrants to the neighborhood during this period followed the same patterns as those of the previous phase, including the migrants during the occupation period already having social connections in Hanayama prior to their moving in. Thus, the absorption of the migrants was facilitated, as it has been with those of the earlier phase.

The other important function of the Neighborhood Association, similar to that of Phase I, was mediating between the neighborhood and higher levels of the urban sociopolitical organizations. However, during the occupation period, this was primarily a function of dealing with the occupation forces indirectly through the indigence urban organs. That is, rather than dealing with the policies filtered down from the national government in Tokyo, the Neighborhood Association was the point of contact between the people of the neighborhood and the occupation policies as they were modified by the national, prefectural, and urban bureaucracies. The extra layer--the occupation forces--applied at the top made for some significant changes in the position of the Neighborhood Association *vis a vis* higher levels of the Japanese sociopolitical organization. For one thing, the Neighborhood Association could use the either overt or covert threat of approaching the highest level of social control, the American forces, directly rather than passing back up through the chain of command. For example, if the Neighborhood Association felt it was being pushed in an unacceptable manner by the higher levels of government, it might appeal directly to SCAP or its representatives. As the then-head of the Neighborhood Association, Mr. A., put it:

> There was quite a change in attitude from the war period to the postwar period concerning the place of the Association. After some initial confusion, I like it much better afterwards. The District Association head was much less likely to just send down an order, and we almost never got direct orders from higher up. Part of that was, I think, because many of us got to know the Americans who were here (in Sapporo). I think that there was always a fear (on the part of the city bureaucrats) that we would talk directly to the Americans. I never did, not about official business anyway.

Whether Mr. A.'s perception is accurate or not is impossible to assess, but other people involved in the association at the time agreed that the higher urban official were much more polite after the war than they had been before.

Another important item was that there were a number of SCAP policies directly focused on small local units such as the Neighborhood Associations and the tonari gumi. These were occasionally implemented directly, without passing through the intermediate levels. The middle levels of the bureaucracy, therefore, had no direct way to modify the policies, although there were a number of effective indirect, bureaucratic means to be used.

From the point of view of the neighborhood, however, this semi-autonomy from the urban bureaucracy was seen as being real and, as such, probably had considerable psychological effect, primarily in establishing or re-establishing a strong sense of neighborhood identity. One reason for this was that the higher levels of urban government did very little to solve local problems. Policy implementation was conducted from the top down to the lower levels; rarely did lower level problems move back up the conduit to be solved at higher levels. Many of the social services (e.g., garbage collection, sewage) common in an American city, for instance were usually absent, particularly in a frontier city such as Sapporo or overseen by the lowest levels of political organization, usually the Neighborhood Association, at a measure of maintenance far below that of an equivalent city in the United States.

Although the Neighborhood Association was partly funded by the city, the city appears to have maintained little or not direct control over expenditures. The Neighborhood Association books, such as they were--the Hanayama books for that period are totally incomprehensible, even to a more recent head of the Association--were occasionally examined by the district offices but, except for gross personal abuses, there was little interest in how the various monies were spent. The Neighborhood Association thus enjoyed near autonomy from the higher levels of government. Equally important, however, is that the entire annual budget of a Neighborhood Association was extremely small and that the actual economic clout of such an organ was extremely limited except in the most narrow local sphere.

In the occupation period, then, it was the Neighborhood Association that was primarily the instrument for dealing with postwar problems on the social level. Although the situation is not altogether clear, it appears that SCAP did not fully comprehend Japanese political processes and mainly contented itself with controlling, with varying success, the higher levels of political organization, at least in the city of Sapporo. Also influencing SCAP's difficulty in managing Japanese domestic problems was that not only the practical elements of government differed between Japan and the United States, but also the basic philosophical principles upon which the Japanese government was based differed. there is some indication that SCAP had little idea of the extent to which national policy directives could be modified by the various bureaucracies as they passed through the levels of government. There is also some material indicating the lack of comprehension by the occupation administration of the flow of information up and down the various levels of the system. (cf. Montgomery 1949:10 for military attitudes toward Neighborhood Associations. Also, Dower, 1975 for a broader perspective). Thus, the Neighborhood Associations, supposedly under the legal control of higher levels of government, were in fact somewhat autonomous. Further, given the actual workings of the system, there was little or no way that certain local domestic problems, even if generalized throughout a region, could work their way up the system to be dealt with at higher policy levels. The philosophical differences manifested themselves in the ideas held by the occupation forces about the basic functions of government. One way to express this difference is to characterize the American view of governmental policy as legalistic and rigid, whereas the Japanese view of governmental policy can be described as relativistic and flexible. thus, the Americans wanted social problems managed at the highest level possible so as to standardize the solution for as many local units as possible. The Japanese felt that higher organs should be confronted with a problem only if it could not be solved in some way locally. Thus the American view would be to have one solution for one problem, and the Japanese view would have as many solutions to a given common problem as there were local organs dealing with that particular problem.

The manner in which the Hanayama Neighborhood Association and its tonari gumi dealt with the postwar problems was, in general, by extending the methods used for other problems in the past to cover the new situations. For example, immediately after the war approximately fifty adults were repatriated into the neighborhood. This group comprised about 15% of the total neighborhood population in 1950. Their absorption was viewed and dealt with as a problem of quantity, not quality. That is, the problem, absorption of the newcomers into Hanayama social patterns, was perceived as being the same problem that the neighborhood had always dealt with. The only differences were that there were more migrants and that the rate of migration was temporarily higher than normal. As mentioned previously, all of the new migrants already knew someone in the neighborhood and their absorption was similar to that described in the previous chapter.

On the other postwar problems that concerned the neighborhood, a few other examples should suffice. The food shortages, a major problem elsewhere in Japan, were minimized in the neighborhood and in Hokkaido as a whole. The wartime adaptations of personal gardens, personal contacts made with agriculturalists outside the city, black and gray market connections--and the strong economic position of the city relative to the rest of the country, with its concomitant assurance of full employment--made great changes unnecessary. Informally, the Neighborhood Association and the tonari gumi were one of the means of coordination for all of these various enterprises.

For example, one of the tonari gumi ran a successful exchange system, a gray market operation, utilizing four of the residents' agricultural contacts as a base to move foodstuffs into Hanayama in exchange for a variety of goods and services unavailable in the rural regions. This exchange network, begun on a small scale in the late 1930s to deal with the beginnings of various shortages, continued with an assortment of adjustments in scope and personnel, until the mid-1950s as an economic exchange system and up to the mid-1970s as a social entity. One of my better informants, in fact, assured me that if necessary, the whole system would probably be functional in very short order because they have continued to carefully maintain the necessary contacts.

This example of the working of a tonari gumi illustrates several things aside from simply how food shortages were handled, for example, of the important correlation between a formal and an informal social organization, how the tonari gumi, a formal structure, formed the basis of an informal organization to bring food into the city. The tonari gumi itself did not operate the food system but, rather, a group of people, all of whom not coincidentally knew each other because they were in the same tonari gumi made up the informal group to do the job. Incidentally, the person who was the prime mover in the food scheme was not the han cho, the leader of the tonari gumi.

Those relationships formed in both the tonari gumi and the food system were enduring ones that existed for more than forty years; the people involved with the groups continued to see themselves as having a special relationship with each other long after the immediate reason for the relationship had ceased to exist.

Finally, the formation of this food transformation system demonstrates a rather casual attitude toward the rules and regulations promulgated from the top of the political system. The anti-black market laws during and immediately after the war were strict. Although there seems to be no concrete evidence of anything illegal, there were some rather loose interpretations of the laws made by the Hanayama residents and considerable care was taken at the time to avoid the scrutiny of officials whose legal interpretations might have been less relaxed.

The housing shortages plaguing most of Japan were also less severe in Sapporo because the lack of war damage (particularly from bombing), but because of the limitations on material and labor housing in the post-war period was still a major problem. In Hanayama, the housing situation was good--relative to the rest of Japan where it was critical or even to other parts of Sapporo where, for a variety of reasons, it was severe. The Hanayama Neighborhood Association did not, of course, undertake to construct new housing, but informally it did provide an organization for the exchange of information about possible housing opportunities. Because of the physical situation in the neighborhood and its openness to migration, newcomers did move into the area in considerable numbers. Usually this involved staying with friends until some sort of housing arrangement could be made independent of the largess of friends or relatives. Many people in the neighborhood who had large houses rented out rooms or sections of their houses. This kind of solution to postwar problems appears to be a shift of the degree, not of the kind, of activity.

The functions of the Neighborhood Association, primarily dealing with the higher levels of governmental structures and coordinating the focus of real activity in the neighborhood, and the tonari gumi therefore were logically continuing functions performed in the earlier phase. During the transition period of Phase II (1952-60), the American Occupation forces were no longer present and the system of policy coming down from the national level to the neighborhoods resumed as before the occupation. Some informants said that they thought that there had been attempts on the part of the national and prefectural governments to tighten control over the local political organs, but there is no evidence to indicate that these attempts had an effect on the Hanayama Neighborhood Association or any of its activities. One explanation for this ineffectiveness was that Sapporo, from the postwar period on, experienced a growing rate of migration which meant that the main thrust of the civic administration was to be more concerned with growth than with established systems, rarely with those as small and relatively unimportant as the Neighborhood Associations.

From the perspective of Hanayama, the transition period was one in which the Neighborhood Association reached a highpoint ineffectiveness and power. With membership approaching one hundred percent of the households in the neighborhood and considerable prestige building up from the war and postwar periods, the older white-collar males who maintained positions of power within the association--and the younger men who did most of the work--enjoyed a period of little or no encroachment from the outside, few internal problems because of the slackening migration rate and a great deal of social capital accumulated over the years. From most points of view, this period and the boom period with its economic upswing were the high points in the social cohesiveness of the neighborhood. The tonari gumi functioned as the primary agents of this cohesiveness. The positions as heads of the tonari gumi, the han-cho, were held exclusively by older people, but not necessarily by members of the older white-collar group or even by men, although all of the significant positions in the Neighborhood Association were older white-collar males. The shopkeepers and the older blue-collar group were solidly established within the social matrix of the neighborhood. Many of the crucial functions such as crises and festivals in the lives of the neighborhood residents were approached through the organizations, the tonari gumi for personal affairs or the larger Neighborhood Association for events like national festivals. The problems of the Association and the *tonari gumi* had to solve were rather mundane after the turmoil of the war and the postwar years. Things such as preparing for neighborhood participation in festivals, the clearing or packing down of snow on neighborhood streets, and the execution of local festivals became major concerns.

There was, however, a significant change made during this period. Persons other than members of the older white-collar group began to move into positions of formal or informal power in the association and in the tonari gumi. This can be linked to the rise of "democracy" in Japanese thought which, as translated into action, meant only a minimal dispersal of formal positions, while the real power was maintained in the network of older white-collar males who tended to decide informally on important issues in advance of any formal meetings. The Japanese aversion to confrontation democracy, well documented elsewhere (Dore 1958; Nakane 1970; Norbeck 1954), prevailed in the Sapporo Neighborhood as well. Most of the decisions made by the tonari gumi and the Neighborhood Association were decided informally or in the course of discussion prior to a formal vote. As all concerned perceived split votes as detrimental to the solidarity of the group, the informal consensus forming process usually worked well. However, during this phase, individuals who were not older white-collar males slowly moved into positions where the informal consensus developed.

Thus far we have examined three aspects of Phase II in Hanayama. First, we have looked at the historical patterns of development that connect the neighborhood to Phase I and sketched the historical pattern of Phase II. Second, we have distinguished the prefecture's, city's, and neighborhood's experiences in the war from those of Old Japan, and we have identified some of the characteristics which distinguish Phase I from Phase II in the neighborhood. Finally, we have outlined the role of the formal organization in the neighborhood, the Neighborhood Association and the tonari gumi, and examined their most important functions for the operation of the neighborhood.

Economic Growth in Sapporo:

At this point, then, we can turn to an examination of the pattern of economic growth in the city and Hanayama that provided the basis for immigration during this phase. With this background material established, we will then turn to a discussion of the nature of the migrants who came into Hanayama, why they migrated, how they were accommodated, and the resultant patterns of social relationships.

Since the major forces which pulled migrants into the city were economic, an examination of Sapporo's economic growth during Phase II is necessary. Sapporo's temporary prominence in secondary industry at the end of the war, augmented by the SCAP policies that seized upon the undamaged industrial plant of Hokkaido as a stop-gap until the southern industries could be rebuilt, provided a catalyst for the great expansion of tertiary industries centered in Sapporo. This prominence encouraged the expansion of secondary industries on the entire Ishikari Plain. The increasing importance of Hokkaido's primary industries of agriculture, forestry, and fishing, along with the need to resettle a large number of repatriates, combined to provide a solid base for the secondary and tertiary expansion of the urban centers. The secondary cities on the Ishikari Plain, notably Mururan and Tomakomai, were the points of major secondary industrial expansion. Sapporo's expansion was primarily, even overwhelmingly, tertiary in nature.

There are two points concerning Sapporo's economic expansion and population growth that are very important. Such expansion and growth were very fast, even by Japanese standards. Wilkinson (1965:148) cites Sapporo as one of only five Japanese cities with average annual rates of population growth being more than 5% between 1920 and 1955. Glickman's (1979:42) econometric study of the Japanese urban system lists Sapporo as one of the fastest growing regional economic clusters between 1950 and 1970. Glickman also demonstrates that the other cities of Hokkaido, all of which function to some extent as Sapporo's economic hinterland, were also growing rapidly, as was the entire prefecture of Hokkaido. These trends are summarized by Tables 8, 9, and 10. Table 8 shows the growth rates for population and employment for the ten fastest growing individual regional economic clusters in Japan, a list including both Sapporo and the smaller Hokkaido cluster focused on the city of Kushiro. Table 9 shows the levels of growth rates of population and employment by industrial class, 1950-70, for Hokkaido indicating rapid growth of population and overall employment. Table 10 is included to give some idea, on a comparative basis, of what it means to be one of the most rapidly growing urban areas in Japan.

There are several aspects of the speed of economic and population growth which need to be examined. First, there is the correlation of economic and population growth *per se*. International comparison quickly shows that this is an unnecessary and uncommon correlation. Urbanization in Mexico City, Cairo, Calcutta, and Detroit are examples of employment and other crucial aspects of economic expansion not keeping up with population growth. In Sapporo, however, the correlation is demonstrated on Table 8. The key figures, for example for 1960-65, are the employment increase of 33.4%, with a population increase of 24.2%. This indicates a boom economy with more jobs than people to fill them. This imbalance creates a powerful force pulling new workers into the urban center as well as the social benefits of low unemployment.

Secondly, the long-term growth pattern is such that, over the course of several decades, Japanese migrants have moved from the hinterland into the large cities. This long-term pattern, particularly with the vast numbers of migrants involved, has allowed the development of mechanisms to facilitate the migration, such as relative or family-friend contacts (a nice parallel can be drawn to rural/urban migration in Taiwan as described by Gallin and Gallin 1974). As Table 11 indicates, the Japanese have been urbanizing rapidly for more than half a century.

Lastly, this speed of economic expansion and population growth meant that planners and others concerned with the facilities available to residents in the urban areas were always behind. The population growth of Japanese cities, including Sapporo, has taken place at such a pace that services of all kinds have been unable to meet the demand. Thus, there is always the stress of lagging services and the need, at the local levels to make do with whatever resources are available.

Table 8. Growth Rates of Population and Employment for Ten Fastest Growing Regional Economic Clusters

	POPULATION					EMPLOYMENT	
	percent change 1950-1955	1955-1960	1960-1965	1965-1970	1950-1970	percent change 1960-1965	1965-1970
Sapporo	18.6	18.2	24.2	19.0	77.0	33.4	23.1
Kushiro	24.4	25.2	12.3	7.8	88.5	20.7	15.6
Chiba	6.2	8.5	19.5	31.5	81.0	21.3	31.2
Tokyo	23.7	19.5	18.9	13.7	99.9	25.4	13.4
Yokohama	17.1	16.1	28.4	24.6	117.7	39.3	25.4
Hiratsuka	13.3	6.8	22.9	22.5	82.2	34.5	24.8
Nagoya	11.5	19.0	15.7	9.1	67.5	18.5	12.2
Toyota	18.6	9.7	17.1	22.1	86.2	23.1	25.9
Osaka	20.4	17.7	21.9	14.8	98.5	31.2	14.4
Hiroshima	11.9	10.5	16.5	14.8	65.5	18.6	18.0

Source: Glickman 1979;42-43

Table 9. Levels and Growth Rates of Hokkaido Population and Employment by Industrial Class, 1950-1970

	1950	1960	percent change 1950-1960	1970	percent change 1960-970
Population (1000's)	1185.9	1563.3	31.8	2079.8	33.0
Total Employment (1000's)		637.7		957.9	50.2
Percentage of Employment					
Primary		10.3		4.8	-53.5
Secondary		29.3		28.1	-4.0
Wholesale and retail		22.9		27.0	17.7
Service		16.4		19.7	20.5
Government		6.8		5.6	-17.5
Other Tertiary		14.4		14.8	3.2
Total Tertiary		60.5		67.1	10.9

Source: Glickman 1979:52

Table 10. Comparative Statistics on Worldwide Urbanization

	Percentage of Population in Urban Regions			Average Annual Growth Rates (Percentages)	
	1950	1970	1970/1950	1950-1960	1960-1970
Japan	37.4	83.2	2.22	6.6	3.7
France	54.1	67.9	1.26	2.2	2.2
Germany (FRG)	72.5	82.2	1.13	1.6	1.7
United Kingdom	77.5	79.1	1.02	0.5	0.7
Sweden	55.4	66.1	1.19	1.6	1.6
India	17.1	18.8	1.10	2.4	2.9
U.S.S.R.	42.5	62.3	1.47	3.5	3.5
Austria	49.0	51.0	1.04	0.4	0.8
United States	64.0	75.2	1.18	2.7	2.1
China (PRC)	11.0	16.5	2.14	6.4	6.0

Source: Glickman 1979:73

The second important point concerning Sapporo's economic expansion and populations growth is that the economic expansion has primarily been tertiary throughout both the preceding phase and this one. In his functional classification of Japanese cities, Wilkinson lists Sapporo as being primarily involved in services and transportation in 1920 and 1930. For 1950 and 1955, he classifies Sapporo as being mainly based in services, transportation, and commerce. At no time was Sapporo's economic base secondary industry (1964:179).

The nature of the economic base of Sapporo and the stability in type of base meant that Sapporo consistently drew the same kinds of migrants over extended periods of time. Further, the development of large-scale tertiary enterprises, the kind growing in Sapporo, requires a high percentage of well-educated, white-collar workers. In Japan, as elsewhere, the patterns of social behavior of white-collar

Table 11.   **Percentage of Population in Urban Regions: 1920-1970**

Ratio of Years

	1920	1930	1940	1950	1960	1970	1940 1920	1970 1950	1970 1920
Japan	18.1	24.1	37.9	37.5	63.5	72.2	1.93	1.93	3.99
India	11.2	12.0	13.9	17.3	17.9	19.9	1.24	1.15	1.78
Sweden	45.2	48.5	56.2	66.2	72.7	81.4	1.24	1.23	1.80
United States	51.2	56.1	56.5	59.0	69.8	73.4	1.10	1.24	1.43
U.S.S.R.	17.9	19.6	32.5	38.9	48.8	56.3	1.81	1.44	3.14

Source: Glickman 1979;71

employees is different from those Table 11 of other types of workers (cf. Cole 1971). The primary significant difference here was that the white-collar employees had on the whole more formal education than did other workers. Further, aside from their educations, the white-collar workers had had opportunities to make crucial social contacts in school, particularly in college or university, beyond those available to other types of workers. The importance of such social contacts holds in all countries, but in Japan, these "old school ties" are explicitly developed and scrupulously maintained to a degree far beyond those found in the west. As an anecdotal example, the Head of the Neighborhood Association was able, looking at his pre-war university graduation picture, not only to identify everyone in the picture (about 100 men) but also to state where they were living (or if they had died), and describe their jobs, their families and give other extensive, detailed information.

Tertiary industries also require other industries in order to function. Whereas primary and secondary industries require raw materials and markets, tertiary industries require either developed primary or secondary industries, plus transportation and communication facilities, themselves tertiary industries. During Phase II, Sapporo developed as an intermediary tertiary industrial center between the rapidly growing primary and secondary industries of Hokkaido and the rest of Japan.

Wilkinson's classification for 1955 lists twenty cities in Hokkaido, aside from Sapporo. Of these cities, seven are designated as primarily agricultural, four are considered mining, and two are primarily secondary industries. The other seven are regional (or sub-regional) transportation, communication, and commercial centers, most feeding directly into Sapporo. The exception is Hakodate, positioned on the extreme southern tip of Hokkaido, which is aligned directly with the southern cities of Sendai and Tokyo.

Finally, by their very nature, tertiary industries tend to force their employees to have contacts with people outside their specific concern. For example, a bank employee may have to deal with other people in Hokkaido, in Sapporo, and in the central part of the country, none of which are necessarily directly employed by the bank. Thus, the white-collar workers comprising the bulk of the tertiary industrial work force tended to have very large, if somewhat diffuse, networks unconnected with their place of residence but focused on their place of employment. The Japanese habit of exchanging *meeshi*, business cards with all socially necessary information, and keeping their for future reference, also augments this patterns of broad networks. This patterns is not as common for secondary and primary industry employees, although it certainly holds for white-collar males employed in secondary industries.

It is clear, then, that the nature of economic development in Sapporo, the steady and rapid trend toward tertiary industry, had a distinct effect on the patterns of social behavior of the inhabitants. In Hanayama, with its increasing domination of white-collar workers, this effect was especially significant and, in fact, reflected most aspects of the neighborhood social patterns.

Effects of Economic Growth on Hanayama:

In response to the rapid population growth and tertiary expansion of the city, the major shift that the internal economic structure made was to become totally dependent on the urban institutions beyond the neighborhood. Except for the shopkeepers, about one-third of the employed adults, all of the wage-earners in the neighborhood, worked outside of Hanayama, usually in downtown Sapporo. Most of the economic power in the neighborhood was held by the white-collar males. The blue-collar males, all of whom worked for either the local utility, a small pharmaceutical firm, or a food processing plant, contributed to the neighborhood's economic position but were isolated from the rest of the population.

The most important effect of the growth of tertiary industries in Sapporo on the internal economy of Hanayama was the shift in shopping patterns which begins in this phase. Most of the neighborhood shopping was done within the boundaries of Hanayama except for the regular patronizing of a farmer's market located some twenty meters outside the official neighborhood boundary. However, starting at the conclusion of the occupation period, the growth of department stores in central Sapporo began to divert shoppers from the neighborhood, at least for major purchases. The first department stores were small scale but economically successful and attracted competitors, including some of the great Tokyo concerns; the Mitsukoshi department store for example, opened a Sapporo branch in 1953. With the development of a massive downtown shopping area, the shopping focus of the neighborhood shifted in response. The day-to-day purchases were still done locally, but major purchases and an increasing amount of mundane purchases were done at the major department stores. While the local shops offered convenience and personal service, the department stores required a trip downtown. But at any given store and certainly in the group of department stores, there was a greater variety of goods than existed in the local shops. Each of the department stores had dozens of departments: supermarkets, restaurants, clothing, housewares, gifts, jewelry, furniture, and so forth. The department stores in Sapporo, like those in other Japanese cities, also had other important aspects. For example, most of the art exhibits were likely to be at one of the department stores. In fact, the stores commonly ran all sorts of displays and exhibits, sometimes devoting a good portion of an entire floor for this purpose. this promotional function also served to draw people away from neighborhood shops and into the big downtown stores.

The shift in shopping patterns from neighborhood to downtown had the important effect of weakening the economic base of the of the shopkeepers and the socially integrated neighborhood unit. Although by the end of the study period in 1988 there were still many different kinds of shops, the trend was definitely away from daily items, like food, and toward specialty shops and items like tofu (bean curd, which must be made fresh daily) shops, and liquor stores. This shift was slow, beginning about 1955. In 1975, about half the shops had converted from their original focus. As a local druggist put it in 1976:

> This shop is safe. I sell things that the department stores don't, but the shops on both sides.... When I first came here there was a greengrocer on one side and a butcher on the other. Now there is a restaurant and the tofu shop. The restaurant is very recent (about 1972) but the tofu shop came about 1960. When I first moved here, most of the shopkeepers had been here for a long time, but when the department stores and the big supermarkets like the one down the street opened, then many of the shopkeepers had to change jobs or the types of shop they owned. Some couldn't do it and left.

The second important effect on this transition is that the large department stores performed the economic redistribution functions efficiently enough, but they did not perform the same type of social functions within the neighborhood. In the beginning of Phase II, as in Phase I, most housewives would go shopping once or even twice a day since the shops were just down the street and storage facilities, especially refrigerators, were limited or nonexistent.

> We used to go just down the street, didn't we. Eve would meet at the fish market, then the butcher's or wherever. We all went shopping everyday since it was so easy. I like that. It was easier then. I still go there (to the local shops) but now I'm old fashioned. Then, everyone did, all the housewives in the neighborhood, so you got to see everyone and hear all the news.

> A Hanayama housewife who had been repatriated

During the transition period in the middle of Phase II, the trend was toward more downtown shopping and less local shopping, which resulted in loosening social contacts among the social groups within the neighborhood. The shopkeepers provided a social center for all of the neighborhood and, as contact with the shopkeepers became more limited, intra-group contact decreased proportionally. During this period, information about people, for example about marriages or deaths, was spread rapidly throughout the neighborhood. Further, this "grapevine" was explicit; people were aware of it and consciously maintained it.

> Back then, Mrs. Araya or Mr. Yamada (two shopkeepers) would always know who was thinking of getting married, who was engaged, who had done *O-miai* (the arranged marriage first meeting) but weren't quite sure. You always knew just where everyone was. You could plan ahead since you knew that so-and-so was thinking of marriage, you could start thinking about your budget (for the wedding gift). It was the same with other things. Mr. Susuki (the druggist) always knew when someone was very sick and you could plan for that (for the funeral gift of money and, possibly, for food and assistance).

> An older Hanayama housewife

> Well, everyone had time to talk a bit back then. They didn't just rush in and buy a fish like they do now. I could chat a bit with each person and they would chat with each other. It was very friendly. In the conversation, I would learn about things and pass them on, if they were important. [When told about the above comment] Oh! did she say that? It's true, you know. And that sort of thing make the

neighborhood easy (*yasashii* "easy," "amiable," "pleasant," "warm")
back then.

Mrs. Araya, referred to above

As the period progressed, this dissemination of information became more
limited, the trend being exacerbated by the rising affluence of the Japanese economy
and the individuals in the neighborhood. Starting with the transition period and
accelerating during the boom period of Phase II, the incidence of ownerships of
refrigerators that made once or twice daily shopping unnecessary had increased
drastically until, by Phase III, refrigerators were universally owned. The prestige of
buying from the department stores and the "label" effect, also had an impact on local
buying patterns. Having something, even just a piece of fruit, that came from
Mitsukoshi--the most prominent of the department stores because of its association
with Tokyo--gave the owner a bit more prestige than buying an identical piece of
fruit, possibly at a better price, from the fruit stand right around the corner.

The final effect was the expansion of the relatively narrow conduits through
which the neighborhood had had contact with the larger urban environment during
Phase I. In Phase II, these points of contact greatly expanded to include a number of
almost daily contacts even by those adults not employed outside the neighborhood.
Therefore, the insulating effects of the narrow points of contact, the minimizing of the
social and political impact of the economic links, were no longer as strong. As a
result, as the neighborhood became less insulated from the outside city; the sense of
autonomy which had been commonly held in the neighborhood began to decrease.
This perception of decreasing autonomy was aided by the increase of the rate of
migration into the neighborhood. In Phase I, the migration had averaged less than
two households per year. The rate more than doubled to more than five households
per year in Phase II. Although the pace is still not high, it is clearly a shift from the
pattern of the previous phase. On the other had, although there were more of them,
the migrants who came into Hanayama during this phase did not differ much from
those who had immigrated in Phase I.

<u>Migration</u>:

Like the migrants in Phase I, the migrants of Phase II were predominantly white-collar, relatively well educated, and most were from other urban areas. In the immediate postwar period (1945-50), Hanayama had a net migration of some twenty-four white-collar households but only two shopkeeper households and eleven blue-collar households as shown on Table 12. By 1965, there was a net gain of fifty-eight white-collar households as compared to a total of only sixteen blue-collar and shopkeeper households. As a result the composition of the neighborhood was strongly skewed toward white-collar households. By 1965 fully two-thirds of the households and the adult population of the neighborhood was white-collar (see Table 13).

As in Phase I, most of the migrants were originally from other urban areas as shown on Table 14. Of the eighty-four adults in the forty-one households for which there is reliable data, sixty-two (almost three-quarters) were from urban or sem-urban areas. Referring back to the discussion of White's argument that migrants with urban or semi-urban backgrounds would have less difficulty fitting in to the urban milieu, it is significant that these figures are not very different from those White cites from his Tokyo study (1978:96-98). If one accepts White's thesis of ease of absorption being correlated with proportion of urban origins, and I do, then one might predict that the Hanayama migrants of this period could adjust easily to the urban milieu in Sapporo and the neighborhood. As Table 16 shows, all of the social groups in the neighborhood appear to have roughly the same proportions of urban and rural origins. Further, most of the migrants shared a sense of group orientation that promoted easy absorption into the neighborhood social milieu. This sense of group identification, in this case based on residential proximity, combined with the previous urban experience, one reinforcing the other. Much of the migration into Hanayama during this phase, as mentioned above, was the result of either repatriation from the defunct empire of demobilization from the armed forces as listed by area of origin in Table 16. Almost one-third of the sample had come to Hokkaido at least in part through demobilization or repatriation.

> After the war, I went back to Tokyo but I couldn't find a job. Also, my family's house had been burned and there were six of us living in two small rooms. I heard from a friend who had been in the navy with me that there were jobs in Sapporo, so I came here (in 1948). I stayed with my friend and got a job. He helped me find it. After almost two years I was able to get married and moved here (into Hanayama).
>
> A former Navy pilot

Another account was the following:

> I came here because of marriage. At the end of the war, the Soviet navy came to Kunashiri and we had to leave. We were lucky; they made some people stay--they say in camps--and others, who left with us didn't have any place to go. I think that they went to a government (refugee) camp in Nemuro. We went to stay with my mother's sister in Asahikawa. Then I came to Sapporo and got married. We've been here since then (1947).
>
> Mrs. Kumada

There are three points about the processes of demobilization and repatriation to be emphasized. The first is that they occurred over several years. One of the shopkeeper who moved into the neighborhood during this phase and set up a butcher shop, left in army in 1946, worked for a while in Nemuro (a small town on Hokkaido's east coast), moved to Obihiro, a medium-sized city in the central part of the prefecture, and finally came to Sapporo and Hanayama in 1959. I list him as demobilized because he was originally from a medium-sized city in southern Honshu. His motivation for

Table 12.   Composition of Hanayama in Phase II

	1950				1965			
	Households		Adult Population		Households		Adult Population	
	#	%	#	%	#	%	#	%
Shopkeepers	20	22.7	54	24.9	25	19.4	53	18.9
Older White-Collar	18	20.5	44	20.3	36	27.9	77	27.4
Younger White-Collar	32	36.4	70	32.3	52	40.3	114	40.6
Blue-Collar	18	20.5	49	22.6	16	12.4	37	13.2
TOTALS	88	100.1	217	100.1	129	100.1	281	100.1

Table 13. Hanayama Migration: Phase II

1945-1950:	Shopkeeper	Older White-Collar	Younger White-Collar	Blue-Collar
IN				
Households	2	7	17	11
Adult Population	6	15	39	29
OUT				
Households	0	1	4	0
Adult Population	0	3	10	0
NET				
Households	2	6	11	11
Adult Population	6	12	25	29

1950-1965:	Shopkeeper	Older White-Collar	Younger White-Collar	Blue-Collar
IN				
Households	8	21	37	7
Adult Population	17	43	80	16
OUT				
Households	3	7	13	9
Adult Population	18	19	27	28
NET				
Households	5	18	20	-2
Adult Population	-1	33	44	-12

1945-1965:	Shopkeeper	Older White-Collar	Younger White-Collar	Blue-Collar
TOTALS				
Households	7	26	31	9
Adult Population	5	49	69	17

Table 14: Origins of Phase II Migrants: Proportions

	Males		Females			Totals	
	#	%	#	%		#	%
AREAS:							
Sapporo	0	0.0	2	4.7		2	2.4
Hokkaido: urban	9	22.0	14	32.6		23	27.4
Hokkaido: rural	3	7.3	7	16.3		10	11.9
Tohoku: urban	6	14.3	5	11.6		11	13.1
Tohoku: rural	1	2.4	1	2.3		2	2.4
Southern Japan: urban	11	26.8	6	14.0		17	20.2
Southern Japan: rural	3	7.3	4	9.3		7	8.3
Empire (urban)	5	12.2	4	9.3		9	10.7
Northern Isles (rural)	3	7.3	4	9.3		7	8.3
TOTALS	41	99.9	43	100.0		84	100.0

Proportions by Area

Area	Number	Percentage
Hokkaido	35	41.7
Tohoku	13	15.5
Southern Japan	20	23.8
Empire/Northern Isles	16	19.0
TOTALS	84	100.0

Table 15. Origins of Migrants in White's Tokyo Study

Migrated from	Prewar Generation	Interwar Generation	Postwar Generation
Other urban areas	23%	25%	35%
Semi-urban areas	43%	51%	37%
Urban and semi-urban subtotal	46%	76%	72%
Rural areas	35%	24%	28%
	101%	100%	100%
	N=1133	N=453	N=419

coming to Hokkaido was supplied by the demobilization process where soldiers and sailors were encouraged to come to the "frontier" in Hokkaido. Therefore, it should be kept in mind that demobilization had effects that continued long after the immediate postwar period. The secondary ripples continued to have strong effects throughout the phase and, one could argue, up to the present. For example, one contemporary effect of the high number of demobilized personnel in Sapporo would be the pervasive anti-Soviet attitude discussed earlier. What was true of demobilization was also true of repatriation, perhaps to even a greater extent, since the primary movements of repatriation was not completed until as late as 1949.

The second point is that the processes of demobilization and repatriation caused a pattern of migrant origins very different from those of either Phase I or Phase III, to emerge in Phase II. Both Phase I and Phase III migrants were primarily from Hokkaido. A plurality of the Phase II migrants were also from Hokkaido but almost a quarter were from southern Japan, significant numbers were from the Tohoku region of northern Honshu, and several came from the defunct empire and Soviet-occupied northern islands. As a result, these processes caused the distinctive pattern of migration found in Hanayama during this phase. One is tempted to speculate that the "shock" of migration that Tauber (1958:127) and White (1978:84) discuss would have been greatly reduced by the traumatic experiences immediately preceding the move. For those who had undergone the experiences of direct warfare

Table 16. Origins of Phase II Migrants: Numbers

	Shop-keeper m	Shop-keeper f	Older White-Collar m	Older White-Collar f	Younger White-Collar m	Younger White-Collar f	Blue-Collar m	Blue-Collar f	Land-ladies m	Land-ladies f	m	f	mf
Sapporo	-	-	-	1	-	1	-	-	-	-	-	2	2
Hokkaido: urban	2	2	1	5	4	7	1	-	1	-	9/2	14	23/2
Hokkaido: rural	-	1	-	2	2	2	1	1	-	1	3	7	10
Tohoku: urban	-	-	4	2	2	2	-	1	-	-	6	5	11
Tohoku: rural	-	-	-	1	1	-	-	-	-	-	1	1	1
S. Japan: urban	-	-	5	3	6	3	-	-	-	-	11/4	6/2	17/6
S. Japan: rural	-	-	1	-	1	-	-	-	1	-	3/3	-	3/3
Empire: urban	1	1	4	1	-	2	-	-	-	-	5/5	4/4	9/9
Northern Isles (rural)	-	-	1	1	2	2	-	-	-	1	3/3	4/4	7/7
TOTALS	3	4	16	16	18	19	2	2	2	2	42/17	43/10	84/27

Repatriated/Demobilized

	males	females	totals
Number	17	10	27
Percentage	41.5	23.3	32.1

or had been expelled from the country where they were living because their nation was on the losing side of the war, the impact of adjustment to an undamaged, economically viable city would have been relatively slight. Carrying this line of thought out further, White's argument would seem applicable to almost three-quarters of the migrants in my sample coming from urban or semi-urban areas as shown on Table 17. This point is discussed further later in the discussion of absorption of the migrants into the neighborhood, but here the important point is that these migrants were more worldly and certainly better traveled than their predecessors.

This leads to the third point. As mentioned earlier, the social characteristics of the demobilized/repatriated migrants differed from those of other groups of migrants. Although the sample in Hanayama was too small to give any sort of significant statistical measure, the memories of the residents, both those who were repatriated and those who were not, give some indications of at least perceived

Table 17: Urban versus Rural Migration

| | male | | female | | | |
	no.	percent	no.	percent	total no.	percent
Urban	31	75.6	31	72.1	62	73.8
Rural	10	24.4	12	27.9	22	26.2
Totals	41	100.0	43	100.0	84	100.0

differences. The major differences perceived were that the repatriates appeared readier to settle down, get absorbed into the community, and get on with a stable and quiet life than were other migrants. The rather grim experiences of the war appear to have left their mark. As one demobilized and repatriated navy pilot phrased it:

> When I got here I just wanted to live a normal and quiet life. I still do. My experiences in the navy were probably about average but to me, it was awful, particularly at the end. For a long time I did not want to do anything but work and be with my family--no problems, no trouble. Later, after the effects of the war had been reduced by time, I got involved in the Neighborhood Association and I enjoy it very much but at first...in fact for the first ten years or so here, I didn't want to do anything outside my job and family.

A then younger white-collar female who had been repatriated from Manchuria expressed similar ideas.

> My husband and I went to Manchuria in 1941. We had our oldest child in 1942 and another in 1944. Times were very difficult for us from about the time of the birth of my second child. Of course, when the Russians came it was very bad. My husband spent almost a year in a camp and we lived in poverty. Finally, in 1947, we were sent back to Japan and stayed for several months with my husband's family in Aomori-ken. Then, in late 1947, we came to Sapporo and this

neighborhood because my husband was given a job here. When we first came here, times were a little difficult but we were so glad to get her, with a job and our own house...we thought it was wonderful. We wanted very much to get along here in the neighborhood so we were careful to try to get to know everyone.

The other side was how the repatriated migrants were perceived by the people already in the neighborhood. As a then younger white-collar male who had moved into Hanayama in 1939 (on being discharged from the army on medical grounds) put it:

At the end of the war everything was difficult but as people moved into the neighborhood, you could tell who was from other parts of Hokkaido and who came from overseas. Those (who had been repatriated) were very polite to everyone and uncomplaining.... I suppose after what they had been through, the problems we had here in Sapporo were pretty easy.

Like the migrants of Phase I, most of the newcomers in Phase II moved into Hanayama because they knew someone in the neighborhood. Sometimes these relationships had been long standing; for example, three men who had served together in the Kwantung Army in Manchuria ended up in Hanayama because one of them had moved into the neighborhood--the wife knew someone already established there--and the other two followed with their families over the next three years. The crucial part of these contacts was social, not economic, although knowing someone to buy or lease from was important. By knowing a person or family in the area, the migrant felt that s/he had a means of entry and would be able to fit into the neighborhood. Without this means of entry, it was perceived to be extremely difficult or even impossible to be properly accepted.

We moved here because my husband worked with Mr. Yamada, who lives just down the street there. We looked for awhile; housing was scarce then, but we didn't want to live in a neighborhood with just strangers.

Mrs. Chiba, moved into Hanayama in 1954

The educational backgrounds of the postwar migrant sample were, like those of Phase I, high (shown on Table 18). Not surprisingly, the white-collar migrants were better educated than the blue-collar or shopkeeper migrants, the men tending to be better educated than the women. On the whole, this is what one might expect for an urban center with rapidly expanding tertiary industries. There are, as also might be expected, a few anomalies in this table. For example, the older white-collar male listed under speciality/trade had several years of specialized training as an accountant while he was serving in the navy. Because his current employment as a government accountant of some prestige is based on this training, I believe that it should be incorporated into the chart, even though his is not formal training in the usual sense.

Another anomaly is that there are three graduates of prewar universities and two postwar university graduates in a sample of only thirty-four persons (in 1975). This is more than double the national average, even though two of the graduates are from private universities lacking high prestige. As in the foregoing chapter, there is some significance in where the university graduates were employed. Two worked for private firms, two for public offices and one was employed by the U.S. State Department. In fact, the whole pattern of public versus private employment (eighteen graduates publicly employed, fifteen private, and one for a foreign country) suggests that there was considerable prestige attached to public employment. This perception was shared by my informants who agreed that employment in small firms had less prestige than employment in either large firms or in the public sector.

Employment in large firms or in the public section also commanded more economic weight--job stability and fringe benefits such as pensions and insurance--than did positions with smaller private firms. Unfortunately, informants tended to line up by their own employment as to whether larger private firms were more or less prestigious than public employment. There is also a certain fuzzy middle ground. It is very difficult, for example, to think of an institution embedded in the economy of the nation such as the Bank of Tokyo as a private firm. In this case, the Bank of Tokyo is a private firm acting, in many respects, as a national bank.

A more worthwhile distinction can be made, however, between secondary industrial and tertiary industrial employment. Of the thirty-four white-collar males in the sample, fully twenty-eight of the them were engaged in tertiary industries: retail

Table 18. Education and Occupations of Phase II Migrants

EDUCATIONAL
LEVEL

	Shop-keeper		Older White-Collar		Younger White-Collar		Blue-Collar		Land-ladies		White-Collar Male Totals
	m	f	m	f	m	f	m	f	m	f	
PREWAR											
Lower Primary (3 years)	-	1	-	-	-	-	-	-	-	-	-
Higher Primary (3 years)	1	2	1	5	1	1	-	-	1	1	2
Middle (5 years)	2	1	7	8	5	7	1	2	1	1	12
Special/Trade (5 years)	-	-	1	-	-	-	1	-	-	-	1
Higher (3 years)	-	-	5	1	4	2	-	-	-	-	9
Higher for Women (3 years)	-	-	-	2	-	4	-	-	-	-	-
University (3 years)	-	-	2	-	1	-	-	-	-	-	3
POSTWAR											
Middle (3 years)	-	-	-	-	2	2	-	-	-	-	2
Higher (3 years)	-	-	-	-	3	-	-	-	-	-	3
Junior College (2 years)	-	-	-	-	-	2	-	-	-	-	-
College (4 years)	-	-	-	-	-	1	-	-	-	-	-
University (4 years)	-	-	-	-	2	-	-	-	-	-	2
TOTALS	3	2	16	16	18	19	2	2	2	2	34

Table 18 (con't)

EDUCATION	Teacher (Primary)	Government	Other Public	Large* Private Firm	Private Firm	State Dept.
PREWAR						
Higher Primary (3 years)	-	-	-	1	1	-
Middle (5 years)	-	3	4	2	3	-
Special/Trade (3-5 years)	-	1	-	-	-	-
Higher (3 years)	2	3	2	1	1	-
University (3 years)	-	1	-	-	1	1
POSTWAR						
Middle (3 years)	-	-	-	-	2	-
Higher (3 years)	-	1	-	1	-	-
University (4 years)	-	-	1	1	-	-
TOTALS	2	9	7	6	9	1

*Large firms employ more than 100 people.

stores, transportation concerns including the then Japan National Railways (one of the employers of several of the blue-collar males in the neighborhood), financial institutions such as the aforementioned Bank of Tokyo, and government and public agencies. The secondary industries represented by white-collar employees in the neighborhood included a steel-producing plant, the headquarters of which--but not the physical plant--was in Sapporo, a small pharmaceutical firm (not the same represented during the earlier phase), two coal mining operations, and a paper mill. The shopkeepers in the neighborhood are, of course, all tertiary. The blue-collar employees appear to have been mixed. While the precise number of employees is difficult to ascertain, there were only three employers of blue-collar workers in the neighborhood: A food processing company, the local public electric utility, and a pharmaceutical company (mentioned in the previous chapter). All of these concerns operated company housing in the neighborhood. Roughly two-thirds of the blue-collar employees, then, were engaged in secondary industry, while about one-third was employed in tertiary industry.

The pattern of Phase II migration into Hanayama, then, is of migrants who are overwhelmingly urban in their backgrounds, well-educated, and heavily oriented toward tertiary industries for employment. This pattern is similar to that of Phase I with only the higher rate of migration and the more diffuse and varied background of the migrants distinguishing it from the migration pattern of Phase I. Further, as in Phase I, as these migrants entered the neighborhood, even in the very hectic immediate postwar period, they were readily absorbed into the social milieu of the neighborhood.

The absorption of the migrants into the social milieu of Hanayama during this phase was similar to that described for Phase I. As in the previous phase, there were individual mechanisms for absorption such as the O-hirome and group-level functions activated by the social organizations, the Neighborhood Association and the tonari gumi. The two major differences between the migrant groups entering the neighborhood during Phase II and those who had come into Hanayama during Phase I--the rate of entry and the variation of background--appear to have relatively little impact on the absorption functions of the neighborhood. The varied background of the migrants refers primarily to their area of origin, not the socioeconomic status of the migrants. As in Phase I, all of the migrants were of social categories already represented in the neighborhood. In other words, in important respects, the migrants were much like those already living in the neighborhood. The concentration of housing, a phenomena which developed during this phase, reinforced the effect of the homogeneity.

Neighborhood Growth Patterns:

During Phase I, the houses on the edges of the neighborhood had been inhabited exclusively by shopkeepers with the interior neighborhood being composed of a mixture of older white-collar, younger white-collar, blue-collar, and farmer households. During Phase II, the physical mixture in the middle of the neighborhood sorted itself out into relatively distinct territories. the shopkeepers, the only distinct group in Phase I, remained concentrated exclusively along the boundaries of the neighborhood. In the middle, the crucial shift that occurred quite soon after the war was to company-owned housing for the blue-collar families. As mentioned previously, three companies employed Hanayama blue-collar males and provided housing in the neighborhood. By the middle of the Phase, nearly all of the blue-collar housing in Hanayama was company owned.

The phenomena of company-owned housing is not unique to Japan. It is, however, highly developed in Japan possibly because of the high density of urban areas and the traditional shortage of housing, greatly exacerbated by the Pacific War. Simply put, in this arrangement, the company owns houses and makes them available to their employees at a nominal rent. This system has a number of advantages for both sides. From the employees' side, inexpensive and readily available housing in a country where housing is extremely expensive and difficult to obtain is the primary advantage. There are other benefits; the concentration of housing near co-workers is seen by most Japanese as a definite good, and it is an indirect form of income which can, to some degree, be shielded from taxes. From the employer's point of view, cheap, available housing makes for happy employees and for an increased degree of company control over the lives of employees, and, thereby, some insurance against workers leaving the company for other jobs. The insurance part works as follows: if an employee leaves Company A for Company B, the seniority which he had acquired in Company A is lost. Since either the eligibility for company housing, or the quality of housing, depends on seniority, the transferring employee will be either ineligible for housing or eligible only for poorer housing. Thus, the movement of employee from Company A to Company B, unless accompanied by an enormous raise in straight salary, will inevitably be accompanied by a decrease in the standard of living of the employee and his/her family.

In Hanayama, the major effect of company housing for the blue collar households was to concentrate those households into three places in the neighborhood and no where else. Thus, blue-collar households were grouped into three clusters; the shopkeepers lived along the boundary streets; and the white- collar households, both younger and older, were cluster in the rest of the area.

The physical isolation of the company-owned housing emphasized the distinctive nature of the blue-collar situation but, more importantly, the blue-collar group tended to identify more strongly with their respective companies than did other groups. In effect, there were three groups of employees--the drug company employees, the electric company employees and the food-processing employees--rather than one larger group, except in analytical or categorical terms. Any given blue-collar individual was far more likely to know and interact with a nearby white-collar individual than he or she was to know or interact, at least to any significant extent, with a blue-collar individual from one of the other companies. In the two cases where there were blue- and white-collar males employed by the same company, the company bond was more important than physical proximity. However, the clustering of company-owned housing, each cluster being distinct and usually not continuous with another company's, probably exacerbated the trend toward social isolation.

Thus, as a migrant family moved into the neighborhood, it was almost assured of being surrounded by families of the same social group as itself, possibly even by people employed by the same company, an association which Nakane (1970), Cole (1971) and Vogel (1967) all see as being more important, particularly for males, than common residence. The Japanese emphasis on group orientation and identification seems to apply in both instances but the employed males spent relatively little time in their area of residence and a great deal of their time with colleagues from work. The association through the common employment link was not limited to blue-collar households. In the early 1950's, for example, a food company built a cluster of four single-family detached houses in a rather isolated corner of the neighborhood expressly for rising young company executives, younger white-collar households.

There was also a cluster of three houses owned by a local bank inhabited by older white-collar households.

This cluster of like households continued throughout the phase into Phase III. From an analytical perspective, this clustering greatly aided the absorption of the migrants into the neighborhood.

> Moving here was much easier than where we had been before. We moved into this house, right between the Saguchi family and the Takata family. Since my husband worked with them (the husbands), we got to know each other right away. They helped us meet people on this street. Later, when the Takatas left (he was transferred) and the Yamadas moved in, we did the same thing for them.... Why did we do that? Well, you have to know your neighbors...and back then, everybody just did it...we all wanted to know each other and so we put time in (on the relationships).

The increase in the rate of migration, particularly the small flood of repatriated an demobilized people who moved into Hanayama immediately after the end of the war, placed stress on the mechanisms of the neighborhood to absorb them, but not to the extent that the overall effects, the degree of absorption, was seriously affected. The main reason for this lack of great effect was that, after the initial flood had subsided, the rate of migration was not high. It doubled over the slow rate of the previous phase but appears to have been no more than four to six new households per year, a rate that could be easily handled. Further, the concentration of similar households into clusters appears to have been more than sufficient as a counter to the increased rate. The crucial aspect, however, is motivation. During this phase, particularly in the high-stress period of the immediate postwar era but, to a lesser extent, throughout the phase, the value for intense and dense social networks was maintained at a high level. That is, for the great majority of people in the neighborhood, if not for all of them, the maintenance of extensive social relationships with other residents of the Hanayama neighborhood was a high priority task.

> It was easier then because everyone seemed to do it (maintain social relationships). But it did take time. You had to think about what you were doing, how so-and-so felt about something. The holidays were the most difficult because the old fashioned ways required gifts and

visits and such.... No, I liked it. (Back then) the neighborhood had a very strong spirit.... The spirit required work. We were not afraid of work back then; we spent the time and effort that we had to spend.... Why? Because we like the spirit and wanted to keep it. If you want something you have to work for it; it won't just happen.... Yes, we wanted that strong spirit and for that everyone had to get along.

As expressed in the above quote, the "strong spirit" of the neighborhood, the combination of a sense of identity as a resident of Hanayama and the strength of the web of social relationships built up in the neighborhood, was explicitly felt to be something work the investment of time, emotion, and money. the value on the maintenance of different types of social relationships, both singly and collectively, is not unique to Japanese society. This value is, however, an integral part of Japanese social organization. the various types of social relationship--political, kin, economic, friendship, or neighbors--make up the overall web of social relationships.

Social Relationships:

The existing relationships in the neighborhood during this phase closely resemble those found in the previous phase. The strong value on maintaining "broad faces," the mechanisms for absorbing newcomers into the neighborhood, and the increasing prosperity of the residents of Hanayama coalesced to make a tight social web within the neighborhood.

Although the patterns of social relationships for the entire study period will be discussed in the last chapter, there are several point specifically concerning this phase that should be stressed here. The first, and most important, is that throughout this phase, everyone in the neighborhood appears to have maintained at least a minimal relationship with everyone else. This extremely high density (in Mitchell's terms) or closure (in Bott's) remained, in spite of the turbulent postwar conditions and in spite of the greatly expanded total population of the neighborhood. The significance of the maintenance of these universal face-to-face relationships was that the neighborhood continued to function throughout this phase as a social entity. There was a sense of identification with the place of residence distinguishing it from other, non-residential, places. The people of Hanayama identified themselves and were identified by other people as members of a social group distinct from other groups. It will be argued in the next chapter that this high degree of face-to-face contact in the neighborhood was an essential element in maintaining the neighborhood as a social entity in any meaningful sense by providing a grouping to which individuals could orient themselves.

The second point, the degree and value of contacts of people inside the neighborhood to outsiders for the overall advantage of the entire neighborhood, relates to the first point, since with a high degree of density of intra-neighborhood relationships, these outside contacts would be much less valuable in their overall effect.

> When I wanted to find a job (for a nephew) I just asked around the street and my wife did the same. After a while, Mr. Yaguchi came and let me know that there was a job with his firm and that he would introduce my nephew.
>
> Mr. Yamada, about an event that occurred in 1956

> When my son broke his arm, I didn't know any doctors, but the neighbors did. In fact, he went with us to the doctor's office, introduced us and made sure everything was all right. Someone here knew someone else for almost everything we needed.
>
> Mrs. Shinoda discussing a 1959 event

The heterogeneity of the backgrounds of the people who migrated into the neighborhood during this phase greatly increased the number and types of informal social contacts outside the neighborhood. There were two effects of this increased range of extra-neighborhood contacts. First, those persons who had such contacts and utilized them for various purposes for people within the neighborhood increased their own prestige and local influence tremendously. The owning of a "broad face," numerous contacts through which various tasks could be done, was and still is probably the most effective means of social mobilization in Japanese society. These contacts could be either friends, individuals with whom some form of affection is maintained in the relationship, or acquaintances, individuals with whom no affection enters into the relationship. The distinction appears to be very similar to that expressed by the difference between the English words "friend" and "acquaintance".

The second effect was that these contacts to outside individuals gave the neighborhood an informal unofficial means of affecting public policy, particularly at the level of the city bureaucracy. These channels worked so well, in fact, that they were usually chosen over the more formal routes of contact. There was also a tendency in the formal Neighborhood Association to elect officers who had the necessary "broad face" to either working or honorary positions, thus combining the formal and informal channels in one and the same person. Aside from the relatively few extremely influential individuals there were others--particularly older white-collar males--who had specific contacts utilized in much the same manner. Usually these contacts had direct or indirect connections with the individual's place of employment which might, for example be within the city office where business needed to be done. An event demonstrating the effectiveness of this more limited contact system occurred in the early 1960s. One teen-age boy from the neighborhood got into some minor difficulty with the police. The boy's mother immediately asked the wife of a neighbor, a juvenile parole officer, to look into the case. Through the parole officer, approached through his wife, the problem was settled with minimal official proceedings , which was what the boy's mother wanted, but with maximum effectiveness since now the boy's whole family had an obligation to their neighbor to maintain the miscreant's good behavior.

> Well, we still owe a debt to Mr. Yamada and his wife. They were very understanding and helped when my son got into trouble. I don't know how we will pay it off.
>
> Boy's mother speaking in 1976.

As sort of an addendum, the boy's mother gave the parole officer a present of moderate value for his efforts, but the debt was still considered real and important in 1976.

It is important to note here that almost all of the older white-collar group had "broad faces," in comparison with the average resident, which was primarily a function of age as well as social status. The older white-collar contacts tended to be frequently in the civil service or other managerial echelons where various people might be more likely to need contact. However, while the white-collar contacts might be more important, the shopkeeper and blue-collar contacts were probably used more on a day-to-day basis, since almost everything from buying abalone to getting *zori* (shoes worn with formal kimono) repaired was done through personal contacts. The basic idea is expressed as follows:

> It is better to know the person you are dealing with. If you don't know someone personally, then you ask friends. Almost always someone you know will know the person you want to meet. Then the friend either calls up the person you gives you his business card with an introduction on it. Either way, you are then introduced to the person you want to meet and get to know him that way.
>
> An older white-collar housewife

Political contacts functioned in much the same way. During Phase II the Neighborhood Association, on many occasions, had to approach higher organs of urban government. According to a former head of the Association:

> Usually, if we had to do something with the district office or one of the other city offices, I would call up someone I knew in that particular office.... If I didn't know someone, someone else in the Association would and they would call.... When I called I would just say hello and mention whatever business the Association was going to have with that office. If it was a difficult matter, my contact (*sesshoku*) would introduce me to someone else closer to the problem. After I knew just what I needed to know, then we would send in the letter or form or whatever was officially called for. We always did that back then. Even now, usually Mr. S. (the current Association head) will telephone as well as send in the official forms. That kind of contact makes things go smoother and easier.

Even when the dealings were initiated through official channels, a practice more common as time passed, there were almost always unofficial contacts made with various key people along the way to ensure the successful conclusion of the endeavor. The advantage of the unofficial contact was that it allowed either party in the transaction to adjust or even refuse a suggestion without any official status riding on the actions. Only after everything had been unofficially--and very carefully--arranged would the official application be made.

Related to this question of informal contacts is the larger question of the depth or intensity of the relationships maintained with people outside the neighborhood. The social connections between individuals in the neighborhood and other people in the city grew more expansive but more diffuse during this period. With the rapid population growth of the city and the increase in the number of social and economic institutions with which the people in the neighborhood had direct contact, the range, in Mitchell's terms, of the social networks of the individuals increased. At the same time, because of the development of rapid industrialization in the city and the demands this made on individuals, the depth of contact often appears to have decreased. For example, although frequent contact with close relatives was still the rule rather than the exception, the frequency of contact decreased and the type changed. The close relatives were less likely to live in the same area or even nearby. This was particularly true, of course, for those in the neighborhood who were repatriated during the war. In fact, in computing the average frequency for contact of relatives for the neighborhood in 1940 and 1950, one finds a sharp drop in the average with kin-group members for all social categories in the neighborhood precisely because of repatriates. This pattern also held, however, between 1950 and 1965 when the frequency of kin-group contact continued to drop. There are two major reasons for this decrease in frequency of kin-group contact. The first is the distance of migration and the proportion of the population in the neighborhood who migrated. Looking again at Table 14, it is clear that many of the Hanayama residents migrated a considerable distance from their natal homes, aside from those who were repatriated from the dissolved empire or from the Northern Islands.

The second reason for the decrease in frequency of kin-group contacts is closely connected to the first. It was during this period that the major Japanese companies started transferring employees, particularly young white-collar males, with significant frequency. Among other things, this meant that one was somewhat less likely to live near one's family or larger kin group, old school friends, or even near older fellow employees with whom one had long-term relationships. This trend is particularly important if Nakane (1970) is correct in her analysis of the extremely hierarchical nature of Japanese business relationships. For most men during this phase, the contacts outside the neighborhood were primarily, if not exclusively, with occupation-related people, usually people employed by the same company (cf. Plath 1964; Vogel 1967). As the tertiary industries expanded, the networks of their employees also expanded. In contrast to the males, for adult women the major extra-neighborhood social contacts were kin, old school friends, and friends from their post-school premarriage employment. The family contacts were inevitably maintained, even at a distance, but the school ties tended to weaken if prolonged geographic separation occurred (cf. Nakane 1970).

Inside Hanayama, the web of social relationships reflected the alterations in the environment caused by economic expansion and population growth. While everyone still knew everyone else, the nature of the relationships had shifted somewhat. Because of the great increase in population in the neighborhood by 1965, the frequency of contact had diminished throughout Hanayama. Specific groups, such as the shopkeepers, had greatly diminished frequency with the neighborhood housewives as the shopping pattern adapted to changes in the retail structure of the city and increased household prosperity. The heightened physical isolation of various social groups, such as the blue-collar households in the company-owned housing clusters, tended to diminish frequency of contact. Further, the nature of the shopkeeper relationships, a peculiar combination of economic and social information brokerage with various other facts, developed through long-term relationships, were diminished and narrowed in scope and the frequency of social contact decreased; thus the durability of relationships was, on the whole, slightly reduced.

Other groups in the neighborhood were also affected by the increased population and changes in transportation routes, primarily by a decreased frequency of contact. Where in the previous phase, Mrs. A could see most of her neighbors on a daily basis, by 1965 this was not possible.

Oh no! By that time, most of the men took the busses and there were so many . . . that they went all directions. I could still see the little children and their mothers (going to the primary school) but not the older ones (middle school) because they built that new school over there (on the other side of the neighborhood). I'm old fashioned so even then I went shopping almost every day, even though we had a refrigerator and a freezer. That was still fairly common and I could see many people but, you know, a lot of them I just knew their names and just a little bit about them. Of course, the shopkeepers still knew everyone.

Mrs. A about the neighborhood in 1965.

The slight active decrease in durability of relationships caused by the increased transience and decreased average tenure of residence in the neighborhood (as shown in Table 7) is another aspect of this shift toward slightly weaker relationships.

As a result, there was a slight drop in average intensity of relationships throughout the neighborhood. The important point, however, is that the drop in intensity was not the result of a change in values of the population so much as an adaptation to the physical conditions--the increase in population and the clustering of

Table 7: Tenure in Hanayama (average years in the neighborhood)

	1940	1950	1960	1975
Older White-Collar	22	22	21	24
Shopkeeper	23	23	20	18
Younger White-Collar	6	3	8	5
Blue-Collar	12	8	7	9
Farmer	30	--	--	--
Entertainers	--	--	0	1
Landladies	--	--	0	5

housing--and the shift in frequency of interaction caused by economic changes in the city. The most important characteristic of this change in intensity of social relationships was that it took a slight drop. It became less likely, for example, for a younger white-collar male to feel that he knew an older white-collar male well enough to request an introduction or make some other request. Conversely, it became slightly less likely that the older white-collar male would be sufficiently cognizant of the needs of the younger white-collar male to act without being requested to do so.

Another major characteristic of this shift is that it was gradual. There was no point where the intensity of relationships can be said to have dropped suddenly due to one cause or another. The decrease, occurring over decades, was slow and slight enough that most of my informants perceived the neighborhood as being basically the same--in terms of the webs of social relationships--in 1950 and 1965. It was only in response to questions about details of social relationships from this period that this slight decrease in intensity was elicited.

The third point about the decrease in the intensity of the relationships is that it was probably causally linked to the decrease in the information-broker function of the Hanayama shopkeepers. It is my impression that to the extent the shopkeepers maintained the high information flow common in Phase I and the early periods of Phase II, the intensity of the social relationships remained, on the average, at the very high levels that existed in Phase I. When the information flow through the shopkeepers decrease, in response to the decreased frequency of shopkeeper interactions, the intensity of the social relationships decreased proportionately; this occurred because the relationships were deprived of a steady flow of the high quality information necessary for maintaining high intensity relationships.

A final characteristic of the decrease in intensity, frequency, and durability of social relationships in the neighborhood was the physical barrier to communications, in general caused by the house clustering of social groups. The blue-collar housing clusters are particularly notable in this respect. With the decrease in the effectiveness of the local shopkeepers as information brokers, this physical isolation became an analytically important feature.

Summary:

The web of social relationships in existence during Phase II was very like that existing in Phase I. There were some slight alterations of the patterns traceable to changes in the environment of the neighborhood, notably to population increase, physical clustering by socioeconomic group, and shifts in the economic structure of the city.

Although the web of social relationships remained similar to those of the previous phase, there were several differences between the impact of migration on the social behavior in Phase II and those in Phase I. While in Phase I, the impact had been minimal aside from activation of the absorptive mechanisms, in Phase II there are some very different trends. Two of the three basic variables had been altered: the rate of migration and the size of the neighborhood had changed. Only the characteristics of migrants remained basically the same. As in Phase I, the migrants into the neighborhood were white-collar employees, blue-collar employees, and self-employed shopkeepers. The immigrants were primarily from urban areas and many have undergone repatriation or demobilization, all of which minimizes the shock of urban resettlement. All of the migrants share the value of extensive social networks.

Unlike Phase I, the rate of migration more than doubles overall with strong spurts at the beginning and end of the phase. Perhaps more important, the size of the neighborhood doubles until, in early 1965, the adult population is almost three hundred and fifty people. The shift in the rate of immigration does not appear to have been significant, perhaps being not large enough, but the change in the size of the neighborhood is important. Although the pattern of face-to-face relationships is maintained, it was stretched to the point where additional expansion would have required some form of adaptation. Further, the changes in the city of Sapporo impinged on the impact of migration on the neighborhood, a distinct difference from Phase I when changes in the city did not greatly affect social interaction in the neighborhood.

The changes in the city, primarily population growth and a restructuring of the retail structure affected the neighborhood in a number of ways. The restructuring of the retail system and the concomitant shift in neighborhood buying habits undermined both the economic position of the Hanayama shopkeepers and diminished their value as information brokers in the neighborhood. At the same time, the increase in total urban population and the expansion of transportation lines allowed freer communication outside the neighborhood (see Table 19). Finally, the increasing practice of transferring employees and the expansion of company-owned housing decreased the tenure of residents in the neighborhood and created social barriers that split the neighborhood into sections. Thus, the impact of the migrants, coupled with the changes in the neighborhood caused by changes in the city, was far greater than it had been in Phase I.

Table 19: Location of Employment: Males and Females

	Inside Hanayama	Outside Hanayama	Unemployed	Totals
1925				
Number	49	26	46	121
Percentage	40.1	21.5	38.0	99.6
1940				
Number	53	40	61	154
Percentage	34.4	25.9	39.6	99.9
1950				
Number	54	80	83	217
Percentage	24.9	36.9	38.2	100.0
1965				
Number	57	167	122	346
Percentage	16.5	48.3	35.3	100.1
1975				
Number	98	384	222	704
Percentage	13.9	54.5	31.5	99.9

While the impact of migration on Hanayama during Phase II was to slightly loosen the cohesiveness of the formerly tight social relationships, the mechanisms for the absorption and incorporation of the migrants into the social milieu, a pattern of continuity, remained successful. The changes in the larger urban structures, however, were such that they slightly weakened the neighborhood's social relationships by initiating a dissolution of the physical and social aspects of its previous cohesiveness.

CHAPTER V

Phase III: 1965-1988

The neighborhood isn't very strong but it still is (a neighborhood). It
is about in the middle. The ways of the neighborhood are not as
strong as I would like. The old ways were better. When someone
came into the neighborhood, he learned the customs. New people
don't know or help each other. The relationships are poor. Being by
yourself isn't very good. There isn't a very good feeling in the
neighborhood.

The third phase of this study, 1965-1988, marks the culmination of many of
the processes that had been occurring throughout the six decades under discussion.
During Phase III, the rate of population increase for Sapporo held roughly constant,
but in absolute numbers more people were moving into Sapporo than ever before. In
the decade immediately following the war, the population of Sapporo increased by
93%. From 1956 to 1965, the population increased by 86%. During the third phase
of the study, it increased by 91% but that percentage of increase represents almost
three quarters of a million people. In the decade between 1965 and 1975, about
45,000 people per year moved into Sapporo. In the 1975-88 period, the average
annual number dropped to about 30,000. Given a significant rate of emigration from
Sapporo, primarily to and other large cities of the south, and a fairly low birth rate,
these figures represent a massive, steady migration into the city (Figure 11).

The migration into Sapporo during Phase III, as in the latter part of Phase II,
was primarily from the hinterland of Hokkaido. The exceptions to this were the few
migrants from the smaller towns and cities of the Tohoku region of Honshu and a
considerable, if often temporary, flow from the larger urban regions of central
Honshu. This latter group was inevitably white-collar, often professional, who moved
into Sapporo either as part of a transfer with a major corporation, most of which
maintain branches in Sapporo, or directly from the university into a Sapporo based
firm. There was also a fairly large number of temporary migrants; these were
businessman transferred to Sapporo for limited periods of time, usually one or two

years, then returned to the south. Since this group tends to balance itself out (that is, the immigrants roughly equal the emigrants), they do not effect the net increase in the population of the city, although they do have a significant social impact, primarily with respect to the growth and maintenance of Susukino, the entertainment district.

Thus, there was a situation at the beginning of Phase III of steady large-scale migration into the city of Sapporo, primarily for the outlying regions of Hokkaido. Another major factor to consider is that Sapporo in 1965 was no longer the small, backwater provincial capital that it had been in 1945. It was still not of the order of the two major metropolitan areas of the Japan, Tokyo and Osaka, nor even of the vary large cities of the southern "core" areas: Kawasaki, Yokohama, Nagoya, Kyoto, Kobe, and Kitakyushu. But Sapporo had one of the highest growth rates in the country for the period following the war and had risen, in terms of total population, to the ninth position in the population rankings of Japanese cities. Further, Sapporo was the only city north of Tokyo with a population nearing one million. Its isolation from the great southern cities--1,000 kilometers north of Tokyo--increased its overall economic, political, and social importance. Sapporo's growth rate was such that by 1975 it had become the seventh largest city in Japan and by 1986 it had become number five (Figure 17). At the beginning of Phase III, Sapporo had become a major Japanese city and was clearly on its way to becoming one of the biggest. While the people of Hokkaido had always more or less viewed Sapporo as the big city (in recent times, it had been the largest city in Hokkaido) but now this perception was beginning to penetrate outside of Hokkaido. By the end of the end of the study period, Sapporo had become, in all respects, one of Japan's more important cities (Figure 17).

The economic shift of the city, from an economic base of primary industries to secondary and then to tertiary industries, had been largely completed by 1965. The economic boom enjoyed by Japan until the "oil shock" of 1972, and then the recovery in the late 70's and the extensive economic growth of the 1980's, affected Sapporo primarily in that it became the clearinghouse, the center of commercial activity, for all of Hokkaido. The historical parallels between the pattern of Sapporo's evolution and

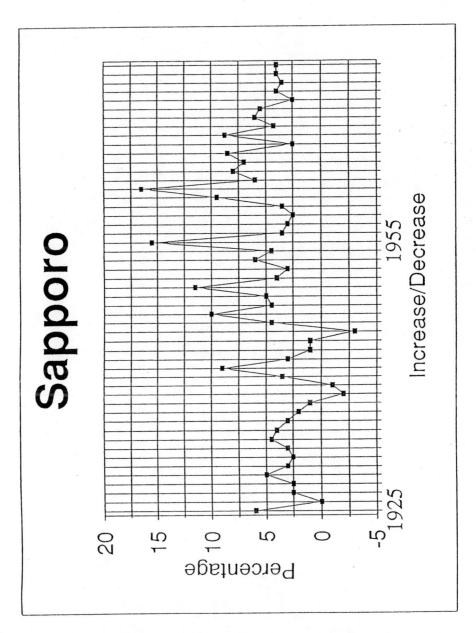

Figure 16.   **Sapporo--Percentage Population Increase, 1925-1998**

Figure 17: Ten Largest Cities of Japan: 1881-1988

Size Rank	1891	1908	1920	1930	1940	1950	1965	1975	1985	1990	1998
1.	Tokyo	Tokyo	Tokyo	Osaka	Tokyo	Tokyo	Tokyo	Tokyo	Tokyo	Tokyo	Tokyo*
2.	Osaka	Osaka	Osaka	Tokyo	Osaka	Osaka	Osaka	Osaka	Yokohama	Yokohama	Yokohama*
3.	Kyoto	Kyoto	Kobe	Nagoya	Nagoya	Kyoto	Nagoya	Yokohama	Osaka	Osaka	Osaka**
4.	Nagoya	Yokohama	Kyoto	Kobe	Kyoto	Nagoya	Kyoto	Nagoya	Nagoya	Nagoya	Nagoya
5.	Kobe	Nagoya	Nagoya	Kyoto	Yokohama	Yokohama	Kyoto	Kyoto	**Sapporo**	**Sapporo**	**Sapporo**
6.	Yokohama	Kobe	Yokohama	Yokohama	Kobe	Kobe	Kobe	Kobe	Kyoto	Kobe	Kyoto**
7.	Kanazawa	Nagasaki	Nagasaki	Hiroshima	Hiroshima	Fukuoka	Kitakyushu	**Sapporo**	Kobe	Kyoto	Kobe**
8.	Hiroshima	Hiroshima	Hiroshima	Fukuoka	Fukuoka	Sendai	Fukuoka	Kitakyushu	Kawasaki	Fukuoka	Fukuoka
9.	Sendai	Kanazawa	Kanazawa	Nagasaki	Nagasaki	Hiroshima	**Sapporo**	Kawasaki	Fukuoka	Kawasaki	Kawasaki*
10.	Nagasaki	Sendai	Sendai	Sendai	Sendai	Nagasaki	Hiroshima	Fukuoka	K-kyushu	K-kyushu	Hiroshima

Based largely on Wilkinson (1965:72)

*Tokyo, Yokohama and Kawasaki (numbers 1, 2, and 9) are contiguous making up the core of the largest conurbation in Japan

**Osaka, Kyoto and Kobe (numbers 3, 6 and 7) are also contiguous making up the core of the second largest conurbation in Japan

134

those of Tokyo and Osaka, the great tertiary centers, are striking; but not those between Sapporo and the important secondary industrial centers of Nagoya, Kawasaki, or Yokohama. Because of Sapporo's isolation from the prominent commercial centers, it emerged as the tertiary industrial focus of the north, rather than as a manufacturing center like many other large
Japanese cities whose tertiary focus was one of the two great southern centers.

Politically, Sapporo had come to dominate the region as it grew. Part of this dominance was a reflection of its greatly increased population, but its position as a central economic focus of the region was equally if not more important. It should be noted that Sapporo's national political strength, like that of all Japanese cities, was far below what might be expected given its population. It is the character of the organization of Japanese politics that urban centers are considerably weaker than their size might suggest, while sparsely settled rural areas are comparatively strong.

The social dominance that Tokyo held during the earlier phases now shifts slightly. Tokyo is still "The City" to most Japanese, but to Hokkaido residents, Sapporo comes a close second. Even cities such as Osaka and Kyoto, nationally far more important than Sapporo, were relegated to lower positions. In terms of behavior, this shift in the perception of Sapporo reinforced Sapporo's economic dominance over the rest of Hokkaido by adding social prestige to economic and political strength.

The position of Sapporo within Hokkaido was no longer one of first among equals, a fair description of its position at the end of the war. Rather it came to dominate Hokkaido in a manner parallel to the position of Tokyo *vis a vis* all of Japan.

Effects of Sapporo Growth on Hanayama:

The impact of these changes on Hanayama follows the trends discussed for the last phase. Almost no one in the neighborhood had any long-term experience living in a city as large as Sapporo had become. The physical location of the neighborhood, once on the fringes of the city, had now become the fringe of the downtown urban core. The previously sparse transportation through the neighborhood was now much more dense and, in the case of public transportation, runs were more frequent. Also, a new subway system was installed with a station within five minutes walk of the neighborhood, increasing the ease of communications. The expansion of the urban economic enterprises, particularly the move by the large national, Tokyo-based firms into Sapporo, increased the contact between Sapporo and the Tokaido megapolis to an extent unimagined in earlier periods. This trend toward closer communications was somewhat accelerated by the northern extension of the *Shinkansen*, the "bullet train" was completed but nowhere near as much as was predicted because, at least as of the end of 1998, the Shinkansen only goes as far north as Morioka in Iwate Prefecture although the tunnel between Hokkaido and Honshu has been completed. In local terms, this meant that the perceived distance lessened between families or friends in other parts of Hokkaido or even on one of the other islands. As the city grew, the Hanayama neighborhood became one of the core residential areas of Sapporo, and its inhabitants and others had to adjust their perceptions:

> When we first came here (1953), downtown seemed much further away. We even used to say "I'm going to Sapporo" when we had to go downtown. It's different now. Now this is Sapporo too, and all the other places around are also Sapporo.
> Young people don't use the old place names much anymore. This used to be Hanayama to everyone. Now they just give the street address as if it were near the station (downtown). Something is lost when one just says something-or-other street, something avenue. There is no color to it, no warmth. This was Hanayama (Nose Mountain), over there was Akebono (dawn, daybreak). I like those better than just numbers. How can one feel (have emotions) about numbers?

The neighborhood's specific large-scale changes primarily revolved around its and the city's great increase in population. The neighborhood population more than quadrupled during this phase, from less than 500 in 1965 to a little more than a thousand in 1975 to more than 2,000 in 1988 as more and more apartments replaced single-family housing. Because the neighborhood had been saturated in 1965 with single-family housing, the increasing in population within the neighborhood occurred through the replacement of single-family housing with multi-family units. The first two of these multiple units were built at the end of 1965. By the end of 1975, there were fourteen units of various sizes, with a total of 247 apartments accounting for more than half the adult population of the neighborhood. In 1988, there were 46 apartment buildings with a total of more than 700 apartments.

The multi-family units were different from the single-family units they replaced. There were two different kinds of multiple structure, those with "front" doors leading onto a central hallway and those with "front" doors opening outside, like an American motel. Internally opening apartments may or may not have *genkan*, the small entryway common to Japanese living units. If the individual apartments do not have genkan, then there will be a large one at the entrance to the building where shoes are removed and umbrellas stored. The apartments found in the early phases are smaller versions of the *danchi*, the huge apartment complexes found primarily in the southern urban centers but also in the suburbs of Sapporo. Later, much larger apartment buildings were also built in the neighborhood.

In Hanayama, the apartments are mostly small, ranging from a single six-mat room (each mat is about 3 feet x 6 feet; therefore, a six-mat room is about 12 feet x 9 feet) room with a shared toilet and no bath for the smallest and cheapest, to a four-room apartment (three six-mat and one four-mat), with a private toilet and bath for the largest and most expensive. Figures 26 and 27 show four examples of Hanayama apartments.

The two sets of floor plans (Figures 18 and 19) show apartments that combine modern and traditional features. In the first external door example, the combination of toilet (western style) and bath (Japanese style) is an attempt at space saving. While this combination may save space, it is an unfortunate innovation as the use of the Japanese style bath, where washing occurs outside of the tub, tends to soak everything in the room, including the toilet. All of the apartments of more than one room have a mix of *tatami* (straw pads more than an inch thick) and thin straw-mat

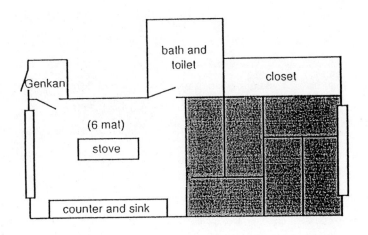

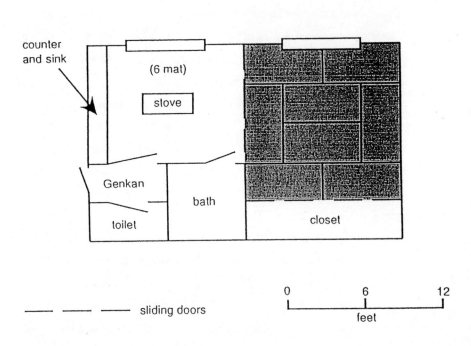

sliding doors

0   6   12
feet

Figure 18: Two Typical External Door Apartment Floor Plans

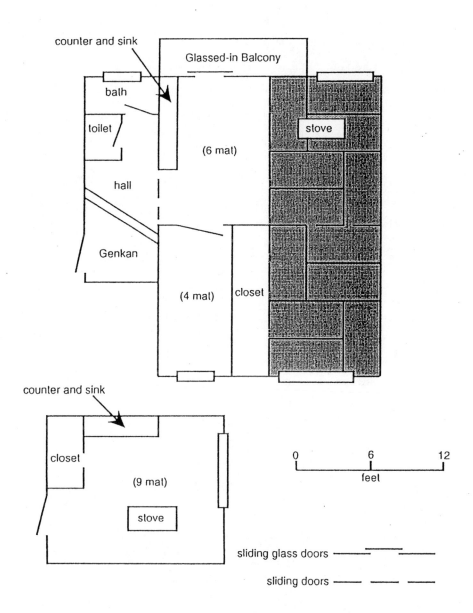

counter and sink

Glassed-in Balcony

bath

toilet

stove

(6 mat)

hall

Genkan

(4 mat)

closet

counter and sink

closet

(9 mat)

stove

0   6   12

feet

sliding glass doors ———

sliding doors ———

Figure 19: Two Representative Internal Door Apartment Floor Plans

covered floors. All of the windows are side-by-side sliding windows (as opposed to the western style over-and-under windows.) Often the internal sliding doors are removed semi-permanently to allow more space. The already rather limited floor space of these apartments is further curtailed by the stoves which, until recently, were the only winter heat source. In the summer, the stoves are dismantled and packed away. By 1988, most of the mid-floor stoves had been replaced by wall-hugging units. A further limiting element, not indicated in the floor plans, is the almost universal ownership of enormous, console model color television sets. Other internal features varied. Some apartments are furnished with western-style couches and easy chairs, others with traditional Japanese low tables and little else. Some of the apartments use western-style furnishings in the non-tatami rooms and traditional furnishings in tatami rooms. All of the apartments, and almost all of the single family houses, in the neighborhood have flush toilets, a feature far still far from universal in Japan, even in the cities. Other than the major furnishings, most of the apartments are crammed with the tenant's possessions as the apartments range from only a little more than 150 square feet to a little more than 400 square feet.

Heat is provided through kerosene stoves that tenants must provide from themselves. No hot running water or appliances (such as refrigerators or stoves) are provided. The structural features of the buildings (thermal and sound insulation) correlate somewhat with the cost of the apartments, but by U.S. standards these are generally shoddy. The poorly insulated inexpensive apartments allow serious droughts in winter. Also, one can distinctly hear normal conversations in neighboring apartments all year around; this is a feature with interesting social implications, to be explored later in some detail.

Because of the shift to apartments, for the first time in the history of the neighborhood, this phase experienced a serious demographic shift. Except for a brief and easily explained period during the war when younger men were scarce, the neighborhood had maintained a fairly standard age structure. During Phase III, this shifted. The primary reason being that the majority of the migrants into the neighborhood during this phase were not couples with children, but rather a socioeconomic group previously unrepresented in the neighborhood--the entertainers--a very large proportion of whom were without children. Further, the shift from single-family housing to multiple-unit housing lessened the possibility and incidence of the parents of young married couples living with their adult children. Thus, the demographic picture of the neighborhood shifts so that an age pyramid would have a large bulge in the 20 to 35 groups and sharply smaller numbers of children under 15 and older people above 60 (the 1965 and 1975 numbers are given in Tables 20 and 21). Part of the population shift can be explained by the sharply decreased Japanese postwar birth rate; the reduced number of children (0-15) is relative to the overall population (cf. Tauber 1958), but the population structure for the neighborhood goes beyond the overall pattern (see Table 22). Also, the increased birth rate would not effect the older population; in fact, it would do the opposite and push up the relative number of older people compared to the overall population. In fact, the relative size of this age group has decreased.

The economic connections between individuals in the neighborhood and the surrounding city shifted when its population shifted to one mainly (75%) made up of younger white-collar employees and entertainers. The entertainers worked in Susukino, the entertainment district lying about a kilometer from Hanayama. The nature of their occupations and life styles was such that they were mainly transitory, often shifting jobs and places of residence. The long-term, strong social bonding of the older residents, based on stable employment and residence, thus had to adjust to this shift in the neighborhood's population.

The economic situation also shifted in Sapporo during Phase III in that it was more complex than in Phase II and far more complex than in Phase I. The general trends in Sapporo's economy were a sharp decrease in primary industry, an overall slight decrease in secondary industry, and a strong, fairly steady increase in tertiary industries. By the end of the third phase, the primary industries had only about 4% of the total work force, the secondary industries employed only about 23% of the work

142

Table 20: Population by Age and Sex, 1976

	Males		Females		Totals		City Total
AGE	#	%	#	%	#	%	%
0- 4	64	6.1	77	7.3	141	13.4	9.2
5- 9	29	2.8	31	2.9	60	5.7	7.7
10-14	31	2.9	28	2.7	59	5.6	6.6
15-19	40	3.8	48	5.6	88	8.4	7.4
20-24	51	4.9	58	5.5	109	10.4	11.0
25-29	86	8.2	77	7.3	163	15.5	12.2
30-34	68	6.5	70	6.7	138	13.1	9.3
35-39	41	3.9	37	3.5	78	7.4	7.8
40-44	25	2.4	26	2.5	51	4.9	7.1
45-49	22	2.1	24	2.3	46	4.4	5.8
50-54	18	1.7	21	2.0	39	3.7	4.3
55-59	11	1.1	17	1.6	28	2.7	3.5
60-64	7	0.7	11	1.1	18	1.7	2.9
65-69	6	0.6	8	0.8	14	1.3	2.2
70-79	6	0.6	10	1.0	16	1.5	2.4
80-	1	0.1	3	0.3	4	0.4	0.4
	496	48.1	546	51.9	1052	99.9	

force, and the tertiary industries comprised about 73% of the work force. Throughout Phase III the tertiary industries reached about 76% of the work force in 1970, approached 79% in 1979 and had passed 82% in 1985, with equivalent drops in the proportions of the work force employed in primary and secondary industries. This increase in the tertiary-industry share of the work force combined with the rate of migration (discussed above) yielded an absolute growth of the work force which was very high, possibly one of the highest in the world, although specific comparable figures are not readily available. Many cities have a higher absolute migration rate than Sapporo. The major difference is that Sapporo's unemployment rate is low by

Japanese standards, almost non-existent by international standards. Thus, the total migration-to-industrial-growth ratio in Sapporo is markedly different than other high-growth-rate cities.

Table 21: Population by Age and Sex, 1965

AGE	Males #	Males %	Females #	Females %	Totals #	Totals %
0-19	99	18.5	105	19.6	204	38.1
20-29	48	8.9	64	12.0	112	20.9
30-39	43	8.0	39	7.3	82	15.3
40-49	26	4.9	29	5.4	55	10.3
50-59	23	4.3	21	3.9	44	8.2
60-	19	3.5	20	3.7	39	7.3
	258	48.1	278	51.9	536	100.0

Table 22: Neighborhood-City Population Comparison (Age)

	1965 Neighborhood	1965 City	1975 Neighborhood	1975 City
0-19	38.1%	38.1%	33.1%	30.9%
20-29	20.9	22.8	25.9	23.2
30-39	15.3	17.5	20.5	17.1
40-49	10.3	10.1	9.2	12.3
50-59	8.2	7.0	6.4	7.8
60-	7.3	4.5	4.9	8.1

Sapporo Industrial Expansion

Given the overall economic picture for Japan in the economic boom period from 1960 to 1972 and the high rates of growth that were re-established after 1976, the rapid industrial expansion of Sapporo is not surprising. What does seem unusual is that most of the expansion, in absolute as well as relative terms, was in tertiary industries. The impact of this tertiary expansion was that its attraction to migrants from the Sapporo hinterland seems fundamentally different from what it would have been had the expansion been in primary or secondary industries instead. With primary industrial expansion, it is difficult to see just how the city could have expanded to the degree that it did. The primary industries of Japan have been becoming increasingly mechanized, which means there is less demand for direct human labor. One clear indication of this is that while the number of persons employed in agriculture has decreased since the war, the agricultural production of Japan has increased through the expansion of high-energy technology, such as chemical fertilizers and machinery.

Secondary industries, which in Japanese statistical compilations include mining, require several supports that tertiary industries do not. First, given the dual nature of the Japanese economy, the existence of small-scale piece-manufacturing units may be necessary for the development of the upper level of large scale manufacturing units. These small-scale support industries did not exist in Sapporo to the degree that they were available in the south, and therefore large-scale manufacturing expansion in the historical Japanese pattern might have been unable to develop fully in Sapporo. In Hokkaido where secondary industries (except mining) have developed, they have been much more in the European pattern of single-level economic structures, rather than the dual pattern of southern Japan.

Secondly, for Sapporo to become a highly developed secondary industrial center, there would have had to have been a tertiary center available to support it, such as those in Tokyo and Osaka. Again, the isolation of Sapporo from the great centers of Old Japan may be at least partly responsible for the direction of Sapporo's evolution. Third, secondary industries normally require a high proportion of blue-collar workers than do tertiary industries. This does not mean that the migrants coming into the city would be all that different in their places of origin; one could argue that migrants would come from the various parts of Hokkaido into just as rapidly for blue-collar jobs as they do for the types of jobs that are available and take as supporting evidence the immigration patterns in the smaller manufacturing cities of Muroran or Makomanai. The primary difference, rather, is in their different social characteristics, which are corollaries of their educational preparation and perceptions or expectations for life. There may well be significant differences in the social patterns of blue-collar and non-blue-collar groups, that is, in areas such as neighborhoods dominated primarily by blue-collar or non-blue-collar groups. This study deals with a neighborhood totally dominated by non-blue-collar groups, so such a comparison is beyond its scope. And last, Sapporo's economic and geographic position, as a commercial and service center surrounded by primary and secondary industrial centers is not accidental. It should be remembered that this pattern of industrial growth was part of the original planning for the development of the Ishikari Plain and Hokkaido as a whole.

The postwar attraction of Sapporo has been as a social and economic pull primarily toward tertiary industries. For the purposes of this study, there are two basic types of tertiary industry, commercial and service: commercial tertiary industries are comprised of banks, wholesale and retail establishments, transportation and communication institutions, and other, often large-scale operation of this sort. Service industries are restaurants, bars, theaters, cabarets, and other entertainment-centered businesses with a central focus on those considered the "water trades" in Old Japanese usage.

For the purposes of this study, the major difference between commercial and service industries depends upon the types of employees. Commercial industries primarily employ members of the white-collar group and relatively few blue-collar workers. While there may be a few white- or blue- collar employees in the service industries, they tend to have as the bulk of their work force a third socioeconomic group, here called the entertainers. This group, as described earlier, have characteristics that distinguish them from all other groups.

Migration and Change:

From the perspective of the neighborhood, the influx of migrants seeking or having employment in the tertiary industries as occurred throughout its history. However, with a very few exceptions, the previous migration patterns had been those of the white- and blue-collar groups. Most of the few exceptions had been of the shopkeeper group who, in many ways, parallel the white-collar groups in their patterns of social interaction. During Phase III, the other kind of tertiary industrial employee makes his or her first appearance in the neighborhood and in massive numbers. The expansion of Susukino, the entertainment district from a small town strip of bars to a major section of a major city, had as a side effect a great increase in the number of persons employed there.

The entertainers traditionally lived in or immediately adjacent to the "gay quarters," the entertainment district of Susukino. At one time, even within the modest historical past of Sapporo, the entertainment district had been a walled section of the city complete with gates "guarded" by police. With a more modern attitude toward entertainment, the walls came down, but the entertainers still lived as close as possible to their places of employment. As mass transit increased the ease of living farther away from their places of work, many Japanese moved out, but the entertainers, possibly because of discrimination against them, tended to cluster at least near the "gay quarters." As Susukino grew, more and more people were employed in its establishments. As more entertainers moved into the city, the belt of entertainer residences around Susukino thickened until, in 1965, the district was about one kilometer thick, at least in the directions away from the "downtown" of the city. Thus the neighborhood of Hanayama, lying about one kilometer from Susukino, began to be a place where entertainers lived. (For a more complete discussion of this group, cf Allison 1994, Hane 1982, Mock 1996 and Plath 1964).

All of the migrants into Hanayama during Phase III were not entertainers although almost 80% were. The second largest group coming into Hanayama during this phase were younger white-collar families. The younger white-collar males worked in a variety of tertiary industrial concerns throughout the city (Table 23). For example, thirty-two of the younger white-collar male migrants were employed by Japan Railways and lived in a company-owned apartment building.

The change in migration pattern from Phase II, where migrants were mixed white-collar, blue-collar, and shopkeeper, to that of Phase III lies at least partly in the shift in types of available housing (mentioned above). When the neighborhood had been saturated with single-family housing, the continued growth of the city allowed the profitable expansion to multiple-family housing, primarily apartment houses. All the inhabitants of these new apartment houses were younger white-collar workers and entertainers. The move into the small apartments by the entertainers and younger white-collar workers was motivated by convenience and cost: apartments were far cheaper than single-family housing and in areas more accessible to their jobs and public transportation.

By the beginning of this phase, the area immediately around the central business core of the city had become very densely populated and any sort of housing was difficult to acquire. Unless one owned a car, a very expensive possession but one which became increasingly common throughout the phase, it was necessary to use mass transit in commuting from the outlying areas. While the mass transit system is excellent, quick and inexpensive, it is a bother and avoided by many people who prefer to live closer to their place of employment. The ride into Sapporo by bus or train or a combination of both from one of the outlying suburban areas took at least half an hour. Some train commuters lived so far out that it took them two hours to reach their jobs. The conditions on the commuter buses and trains were crowded and hectic during the morning and evening rush hours. At the beginning of this phase, just in time for the 1972 Winter Olympics, the city built a high-speed north-south subway system that relieved some of the neighborhood housing pressure by making travel more convenient. A connected east-west link, completed in the spring of 1976, completed a cross-shaped pattern of high speed access to the center of the city and, indirectly, to Hanayama. Thus, while the rate of construction of apartment buildings in old neighborhood slowed somewhat, continued migration into Hanayama was sufficient to ensure the profitability of additional apartment buildings. For example, two new buildings were erected in 1975, and others have been put up in 1976, 1978, 1983, and 1988 and the pattern appears to be continuing through 1998 when there were only about forty single-family houses left in the neighborhood.

The economic base of the neighborhood, exemplified in the individual economic connections between the inhabitants of Hanayama and the city, shifted somewhat during Phase III. While during Phase II nearly all of the employed persons in the neighborhood had worked for their various companies, or intended to work, permanently, giving the neighborhood population economic stability, the Phase III population became increasingly unstable. The average length of neighborhood residents' employment by a particular company was about 14 years in 1965, the same as the average number of years total employment. By 1975 the average had plummeted to about 6 years and by 1988 it seemed to be only a little more than 3 years. The major reason for this occupational destabilization was the entertainers' short-term occupational status. The next most important reason was the increasing transience of the younger white-collar males, who were more likely to switch jobs than in earlier years, a trend which appears to be continuing to accelerate. Further, the companies employing the younger white-collar workers were more likely to transfer them to other locations than previously. With the decrease in the residents' economic stability, the shopkeepers' economic positions became increasingly unstable, particularly in the face of the increasing competition from such larger concerns as the downtown department stores and a new phenomenon, the supermarkets.

The migration occurring in this phase had several features to distinguish it sharply from that of previous phases. First, the rate of migration, starting suddenly at the very end of 1965, accelerated to a peak rate of more than seven times that of Phase III, and more than seventeen times that of Phase I. Where Phase II migration averaged slightly more than five migrant households per year, Phase III averaged at least thirty-five new households per year. The actual Phase III rate was probably double the figure given, but the precise figures for the total number of entertainers households moving into and out of the neighborhood are unavailable (see Table 24). Further, this migration came in waves with the opening of the new apartment buildings, which leads neatly to the second distinguishing feature of Phase III migration.

Table 23: White-Collar Education and Occupations, Phase III

	PREWAR				POSTWAR						
	Prim-ary	Mid-dle	Higher	Univ-ersity	Prim-ary	Mid-dle	Higher	2-year College	Univ-ersity	Total	%
Younger White-Collar											
Males	-	2	2	2	-	5	26	9	5	51	
Secondary Industry											
Large Firm	-	-	1	-	-	2	1	-	-	2	(3.9)
Small Firm	-	-	1	-	-	2	1	-	2	5	(9.8)
Service/Commercial											
Large Firm	-	-	-	-	-	-	3	3	3	9	(17.6)
Small Firm	-	1	-	-	-	2	5	1	-	9	(17.6)
Transportation/											
Communication											
Large Firm	-	-	-	1	-	-	12	1	-	14	(27.5)
Small Firm	-	-	-	-	-	1	4	2	-	7	(13.7)
Government	-	1	-	1	-	-	-	2	1	5	(9.8)
Younger White-Collar											
Females	-	-	-	-	3	1	11	4	3	34	
Unemployed	-	-	-	-	3	11	8	2	1	25	(75.3)
Service/Commercial											
Large Firm	-	-	-	-	-	-	1	1	1	3	(8.8)
Small Firm	-	-	-	-	-	2	1	-	-	3	(8.8)
Transportation/											
Communication											
Large Firm	-	-	-	-	-	-	1	-	-	1	(2.9)
Small Firm	-	-	-	-	-	-	-	-	-	0	(0.0)
Government	-	-	-	-	-	-	-	1	1	2	(5.9)

The waves of migrants did not scatter throughout the neighborhood as had been the most common pattern during the previous two phases. Rather, they clustered together in the apartment buildings because the apartments were the primary locus of open housing. As new apartment buildings opened, the apartments filled with new migrants. These clusters ranged in size, directly correlated with the waves of migration, from a minimum of 6 households in the smallest apartment building to a maximum of 48 households for the largest. The apartment buildings acted as barriers in keeping the new migrants from intermixing with the older residents.

The third distinguishing feature of Phase III migration, a point already mentioned, was that the migrants were predominantly of a group previously

Table 24: Composition of Hanayama in Phase III

	1965				1975				1988			
	H-holds		Adult Pop		H-holds		Adult Pop		H-holds		Adult Pop	
	#	%	#	%	#	%	#	%	#	%	#	%
Shopkeeper	25	14.3	53	15.3	29	7.4	67	9.5	40	4.1	90	6.2
Older White-Collar	36	20.6	77	22.3	32	8.1	68	9.7	20	2.0	40	2.8
Younger White-Collar	52	29.7	114	32.9	89	22.6	189	26.8	300	30.4	500	34.5
Blue-Collar	16	9.1	37	10.7	9	2.3	19	2.7	50	5.1	100	6.9
Landlady	2	1.1	4	1.2	14	3.6	31	4.4	46	4.7	60	4.1
Entertainers	42	24.0	59	17.1	217	55.1	322	45.7	500	50.7	600	41.4
Others	1	0.6	2	0.6	4	1.0	8	1.1	30	3.0	60	4.1
TOTALS	175	99.4	346	99.8	394	100.1	704	99.9	986	100.0	1450	100.0

unrepresented in the neighborhood. Unlike Phase I and II where the majority of migrants had been white-collar households, the Phase III migrants were primarily entertainers, many of whom were single. Table 25 contrasts the categories by phase up to 1975.

The characteristics of the newcomers making up the Phase III migration into Hanayama in some ways continued the trends, such as origins of migrants, employment, and education, set by previous phases but with some important differences. The major trend of most migrants during Phase III being from other urban areas, mostly in Hokkaido, continued (Table 26 and 27). In fact, of the households from whom reliable figures are available, more than 70% were from Hokkaido and almost 75% were from urban areas as shown in Table 28. And as with two earlier groups of migrants, almost all of the newcomers were drawn to employment in tertiary industry. The white-collar groups show the same pattern as in the previous phases in that they were well educated and primarily oriented toward tertiary industries, with a relatively high proportion working in the public sector.

Entertainers:

The non-entertainer migrants were similar to the migrants of previous phases, but the entertainers occupational or economic stability, which resulted in their residential instability. Finally and most important, the entertainer migrants did not share the same values toward interpersonal relationships with the other Hanayama residents.

There are several points about the low educational levels to be stressed. The average reported formal education (Table 29), slightly less than nine years, means that the average entertainer terminated his or her formal education at the middle school. The entertainers had very little occupational or economic stability, which resulted in their residential instability. Finally and most important, a substantial number actually had not completed middle school. The completion of middle school is more important in Japan than it is in the United States because of the difficulty of written Japanese.

Table 25: Comparison of Migrants by Phase (to 1975)

NET GAINS

	Phase I 1925-1945				Phase II 1945-1965				Phase III 1965-1975			
	H-holds		Adult Pop		H-holds		Adult Pop		H-holds		Adult Pop	
	#	%	#	%	#	%	#	%	#	%	#	%
Shopkeeper	2	13.3	5	14.3	7	9.6	5	3.6	4	1.5	14	3.3
Older White-Collar	3	20.0	7	20.0	26	35.5	49	35.0	-4	-1.5	-11	-2.6
Younger White-Collar	8	53.3	17	48.6	31	42.5	69	49.3	37	14.0	75	17.9
Blue-Collar	2	13.3	6	17.1	9	12.3	17	12.1	-7	-3.7	-18	-4.3
Landlady	-	--	-	--	-	--	-	--	14	5.3	31	7.4
Entertainer	-	--	-	--	-	--	-	--	217	82.2	322	76.8
Other	=	==	=	==	=	==	=	==	3	1.1	6	1.4
	15	99.9	35	100.0	73	100.0	140	100.0	264	99.9	419	99.9
ALL WHITE-COLLAR	11	73.3	24	68.6	57	78.1	118	84.3	33	12.5	64	15.3

Table 26.   **Origins of Phase III Migrants (until 1975): Proportions**

	Males		Females		Totals	
	#	%	#	%	#	%
Sapporo	19	12.6	22	11.1	41	11.7
Hokkaido: Urban	64	42.4	76	38.4	140	40.1
Hokkaido: Rural	26	17.2	40	20.2	66	18.9
Tohoku: Urban	14	9.3	15	7.6	29	8.3
Tohoku: Rural	5	3.3	7	3.5	12	13.8
South Japan: Urban	20	13.2	28	14.1	48	13.8
South Japan: Rural	3	1.9	10	5.1	13	3.7
	151	99.9	198	100.0	349	99.9

PROPORTIONS BY AREA

	#	%
Hokkaido	247	70.8
Honshu, Shikoku & Kyushu	102	29.2
Tohoku (only)	41	11.7
S. Japan	61	17.5

RURAL/URBAN

Total Urban	73.9%
Total Rural	26.1%

Middle school in Japan is considered the point where students become minimally literate. At current educational levels, the ideographic nature of the Japanese language requires nine years for the acquisition of basic competency. Another point about the significance of the duration of formal education is that the time spent in formal education and the ability to pass school examinations are probably the most important considerations for upward social mobility in Japan. Far more than in the United States, Japan has evolved a merit system permeating all aspects of the society; it is based on formal education and examination and the credentials these provide. Thus, the significance of the entertainers' low levels of education is that they are limited in terms of enhanced social mobility. Without educational credentials, social movement is almost impossible (see also Mock 1996).

Finally, the entertainers were, on the average, the youngest group in Hanayama. Since the number of years of formal education available has been

Table 27: Origins of Phase III Migrants: Numbers in 1975

	Shop-keeper m	f	Older White-Collar m	f	Younger White-Collar m	f	Blue-Collar m	f	Land-lady m	f	Entertainer m	f	TOTALS m	f	mf
Sapporo	4	6	2	1	9	11	1	1	3	2	-	1	19	22	41
Hokkaido: Urban	2	1	-	-	15	13	-	-	4	6	43	56	64	76	140
Hokkaido: Rural	-	-	-	1	8	7	1	1	4	4	14	27	27	40	67
Tohoku: Urban	1	1	-	-	4	1	-	1	2	1	7	11	14	15	29
Tohoku: Rural	-	-	-	-	3	-	-	-	1	2	1	5	5	7	12
South Japan: Urban	3	4	2	1	7	2	-	-	-	-	7	21	19	28	47
South Japan: Rural	-	-	-	1	1	-	-	-	-	2	2	7	3	10	13
	10	12	4	4	47	34	2	3	14	17	74	128	151	198	349
Total Urban	10	12	4	2	35	27	1	1	9	9	57	89	116	140	256
Total Rural	-	-	-	2	12	7	1	1	5	8	17	39	35	57	92
TOTAL MIGRANTS	10		12	4	4	137		92	3	14	17	??	17	??	??

Table 28: Migrant Origins: Phase III (1975)

URBAN vs. RURAL

	Male		Female		Total	
	#	%	#	%	#	%
Urban	117	77.5	141	71.2	258	73.9
Rural	34	22.5	57	28.8	91	26.1
	151	100.0	198	100.0	349	100.0

HOKKAIDO vs. HONSHU

	Male		Female		Total	
	#	%	#	%	#	%
Hokkaido						
Urban	83	23.8	98	28.1	181	51.9 (73.3)
Rural	26	7.4	40	11.5	66	18.9 (26.7)
Total	109	31.2	138	39.5	247	70.8
Honshu						
Urban	34	9.7	43	12.3	77	22.1 (75.5)
Rural	8	2.3	17	4.9	25	7.2 (24.5)
Total	42	12.0	60	17.2	102	29.3

increasing steadily over the last half century, one would expect to find the youngest group to be the best educated. Yet the entertainers are the poorest educated of any of the social groups migrating into Hanayama in sizable numbers during this phase.

There are warnings that should go with these points, and with all of this material on reported years of education. There is a distinct possibility of sampling error that there is no way to control. Further, since formal education carries a great deal of prestige in Japan, far more than in the United States, there is a possibility that these figures have been upwardly inflated.

In particular, the instability of the entertainer occupations distinguishes the entertainer migrants from the non-entertainer migrants. The most common occupation of the entertainers was bar-hostess, a label that could be applied to most of the female entertainers in the neighborhood. The males worked as musicians (in cabaret or bar bands), bartenders, short-order cooks, bouncers (the Japanese term for this task translates literally as "assistant"), bar and cabaret managers, and other, less-easily labeled jobs. The term *hostess* appears to cover a variety of actual tasks such as would find females doing in any bar district in the world. Fairly representative, if not necessarily typical, of the motivations and job history of a bar-hostess is the following:

> I came to Sapporo because I could not find a job in Muroran. That was fifteen years ago when I was fourteen years old. I lived with my sister for a while, several years, and then I got my own apartment here about five years ago. I first got a job as an announcer in a cabaret. You know, announcing the various acts.... After I had worked as an announcer for about ten years, the owner said that he was going to cut my salary in half....because he wanted me to work for him as a hostess. I was angry, so I quit and went to work--as a hostess--at the small bar where I work now.... I usually work from about 7:00 p.m. to about 11:30 p.m. in the evening, sometimes later, sometimes less; it depends on how I feel.... Well (how much I make) depends, it is very changeable. I get paid every two weeks. My high was ¥800,000 but that only happened once. My low for two weeks was about ¥120,000....That is good for a hostess. There is a great deal of variation (among hostesses). I've been doing it for a long time and understand the job pretty well, so I make a lot. I did not make that much as an announcer.

This hostess had a savings account of about ¥5,000,000 in 1976 that she was planning to use to open a clothing shop, high fashion women's clothing. She appears to have been somewhat unusual, first because she only had two jobs in fourteen years and, second, because of the large bank account. More typical in these respects was a twenty-five-year-old bartender who made about ¥250,000 .

> I came from Mombetsu about four years ago and got his apartment. I've worked at the bar where I work now only about four months; before that I worked at X Cabaret for about two years. Before that I worked in two other places.... Yes, four places in four years.... Why? because I got more money.... I want to be a singer, but that costs money for publicity and such.... No, I have only a little saved up; I like to spend too much. If I didn't work most evenings, I wouldn't have saved anything. I make enough but I just spend it. I go to work about six and usually get home about midnight.

More of the entertainers were like the bartender than like the hostess, job hopping every year or few years for higher pay or some perceived benefit. Also like the

Table 29. Education of Phase III Migrants (1975)

| Group | PREWAR | | | | POSTWAR | | | | | | |
	Pri-mary	Mid-dle	High-er	Higher for Women	Pri-mary	Mid-dle	High-er	2-year Col-lege	Col-lege	Univ	Av.
Shopkeeper											
Male (10)	2	1	-	1	2	3	-	1	-	-	11.2
Female (12)	1	1	-	2	-	4	1	3	-	-	11.3
Blue-Collar											
Male (2)	-	-	-	-	-	2	-	-	-	-	9.0
Female (3)	-	-	-	-	1	2	-	-	-	-	8.0
Landlady											
Male (14)	-	5	1	-	3	3	-	-	2	-	10.4
Female (17)	6	7	-	1	-	2	1	-	-	-	9.2
Entertainer											
Male (74)	-	-	-	-	17	44	12	-	1	-	8.9
Female (128)	-	-	-	-	31	77	16	2	2	-	8.8
Younger White-Collar											
Male (47)	-	-	-	-	-	5	26	9	5	2	12.7
Female (34)	-	-	-	-	3	13	11	4	3	-	10.9
Older White-Collar											
Male (4)	-	2	2	-	-	-	-	-	-	-	12.5
Female (4)	1	-	-	3	-	-	-	-	-	-	12.0

Average male = 10.5 years   Average female = 9.4   Combined average = 9.9

bartender, most of the entertainers planned to save--often for some other career--but in fact had relatively small savings.

The economic instability exaggerated by the occupational instability correlates with residential instability. The entertainers were constantly moving, usually to what they believed to be a superior apartment, but sometimes for other reasons, such as the avoidance or termination of interpersonal relationships. The average tenure in the neighborhood for entertainers in 1975 was about one year (see Table 7), far less than that of any other group. In 1988, the number was slightly higher but still by far the lowest of any of the residential groups. The next lowest groups, the younger white-collar workers and landladies, averaged about five years in Hanayama in 1975.

By 1988, the landladies average was far higher. Part of the residential instability reflected by the very low entertainer tenure figures was a function of the place of residence, the apartment buildings. The entertainers all lived in apartment buildings

Table 7: Tenure in Hanayama (average years in neighborhood): 1975

	1940	1950	1965	1975	1988
Older White Collar	22	22	21	24	19
Shopkeepers	23	23	20	18	14
Younger White Collar	6	3	8	5	6
Blue Collar	12	8	7	9	4
Farmer	30	--	--	--	--
Entertainers	--	--	0	1	2
Landladies	--	--	0	5	11

which had existed in the neighborhood only since 1965. A portion of the younger white-collar group, on the other hand, had lived in the neighborhood for ten years or more in single-family housing, which brought the group average up considerably. That is, the entertainer who lived in the neighborhood the longest (in this sample) lived there for about 12 years. The younger white-collar household with the longest tenure in Hanayama lived in the neighborhood for some 25 years, then became an older white-collar household. The entertainers would have been hard pressed to build strong interpersonal relationships, even if they had so desired.

Entertainer Social Relationships:

The attitude of the entertainers toward building and maintaining strong, durable social relationships based on residential proximity was the most important distinguishing characteristic between the entertainers and most of the other migrants. Simply put, the entertainers did not want to build and maintain strong social ties based on residence. An extreme sample of the type of response to queries concerning the "traditional" social relationships existing among most of the other people in the neighborhood was that of a cabaret musician who commented:

> That's why I came here (to Sapporo). To get away from all that.
> That's what small towns are like, all sticky. Everyone knows
> everybody else's business. I don't like that and I don't want to do that,
> so I came to Sapporo. This is a big city. It is a modern place, not

feudal like (the town he came from). That kind of thing is all right for farmers in villages, but not for someone like me.

The hostess with the large bank account, quoted previously, had a more temperate but similar response:

> That's what the old people do. I suppose that it is very Japanese--I do it too, for business. I have contacts and friends, but not here. I don't think it's bad, it just takes a lot of time and effort and there is no need for that sort of thing anymore. I'd rather do other things. The only people I know here are Mrs. S (the landlady) and Mrs. I (the neighboring landlady who was a great friend of Mrs. S.). I don't even know the name of the hostess in the next apartment. I see the people I work with every day; I don't want to live with them. That is why I came here.... Yes, I think that I'm typical of the people who work in Susukino; a lot of them are like me.

The entertainers saw the construction and maintenance of strong, far-reaching social relationships--aside from business contacts and a few friends--as being old fashioned, "feudal," not worth the time and effort, and constricting their personal freedom. Most of them came to Sapporo not only to find interesting and relatively high-paying, jobs, but also to escape what they saw as the cloying nature of the smaller places they came from. Sapporo was perceived as being the "big city," and Susukino's entertainment district a "Little Ginza" (the Tokyo entertainment district): bright lights, good jobs, and modern social forms. Many of the migrant entertainers suggested that the older Japanese were "too polite" and "too constrained by custom." One of the entertainers, a college-educated cabaret assistant manager, drew a direct historical reference:

> We Japanese haven't really changed. Look as Mrs. Yamada and Mrs. Nakamura when they meet (two elderly ladies who used the very extensive polite forms of greeting and address). That could be in the old time, the Tokugawa era (17th-19th century). They are still old fashioned Japanese. Most of the people are like that around here. It's even worse, they say, in places like Kyoto and the other old cities. The only place that is more modern (modan) than Sapporo is Tokyo.

One of the important implications of this statement is the distinction drawn between "most people around here" and the speaker and his group, the entertainers. The non-entertainers are old fashioned. The entertainers are modern, contemporary.

Apartments Versus Single-Family Housing:

Some of these characteristics described for the entertainers also applied to the other group living in the apartment buildings. There was a distinct correlation between place of residence--apartment or single-family house--and the social orientation among the younger white collar households. This was particularly crucial since, during Phase III, almost all of the single-family housing is replaced by apartments with the concomitant shift is social behavior patterns.

The residents of single-family dwellings tended to be more conservative or traditional, more in line with the neighborhood social milieu and maintaining social patterns like those of the younger white-collar groups of previous phases. As a young Japan Railways employee phrased it:

> Right now, in my career, the important thing is to build a broad face.... No, not just at work, here in the neighborhood too. Not just because there are several Japan Railway employees here, although that is a very important factor... Well, it's that I don't know who will be important in the future. Maybe the Neighborhood Association head will introduce me to someone who will be very important, maybe not. But if I know as many people as I can, then my chances are better, aren't they?

This is almost a classic statement of why networks were built and maintained. About the only thing missing is a comment about how knowing everyone around makes life easier and more pleasant, a sentiment expressed by many Hanayama residents.

The apartment dwellers tended to be far less interested in blending into the social matrix of the neighborhood. The sentiments expressed were very much like those described earlier for the entertainers. The apartment-dwelling, younger white-collar group also felt that the construction and maintenance of durable and extensive social networks required too much investment of time and effort and were constraining on personal freedom. Even so, the younger white-collar apartment dwellers were occupationally and residentially far more stable than the entertainers, the implications of which are explored below in the discussion of interpersonal

160

relationships in the neighborhood.

The apartment dwellers were usually slightly less well educated than the single-family housing group (see Tables 30 and 31), having approximately a year less formal education. The apartment dwellers were also slightly younger than the single-family housing adults. Both of these features are probably a function of company housing policies where more senior employees tend to get better company housing. All but two of the single-family housing dwellers were living in company-owned housing. Of the two exceptions, one was a young partner in a prosperous trading company; the other, a married daughter (and her husband) of a wealthy, older Hanayama white-collar couple, who owned the house their daughter was living in. Of the other nine households, the males--younger white-collar employees--appeared to be senior to the males living in the company-owned apartments. Both blue- and white-collar workers living in company-owned housing

Table 30. Education of Phase III Younger White-Collar Migrants (1975)

	Single-Family		Apartment Housing	
	male	female	male	female
	(21)	(26)	(36)	(21)
Primary	--	2	--	1
Middle	--	4	5	9
Higher	4	6	23	7
Junior College	5	9	4	1
College	8	4	3	2
University	4	1	1	1

Average Years Formal Education
Single Family Housing:
       males   14.8   total 13.6
       females 12.5

Apartment:
       males   12.2   total 11.8
       females 11.1

invariably worked for larger firms than those who had to rent, at much higher rates, their own apartments on the open market. For example, one company-owned building charged about a third the rent of the equivalent, privately owned ones. The rent on single-family housing followed much the same pattern. The best deal in the neighborhood was a cluster of houses owned by a large food-processing company. Although small by American standards, they were large by Japanese urban ones

Table 31: Housing of Phase III Younger White-Collar Migrants (1975)

	Single-Family Housing						Apartments					
	Male		Female		Total		Male		Female		Total	
	#	%	#	%	#	%	#	%	#	%	#	%
Sapporo	3	23.1	5	33.3	8	28.6	6	17.5	6	31.6	12	22.6
Hokkaido: urban	7	53.8	6	40.0	13	46.4	8	23.5	7	36.8	15	28.3
Hokkaido: rural	-	--	1	6.7	1	3.6	8	23.5	6	31.6	14	26.4
Tohoku: urban	1	7.7	1	6.7	2	7.1	3	8.8	-	--	3	5.7
Tohoku: rural	-	--	-	--	-	--	3	8.8	-	--	3	5.7
S. Japan: urban	2	15.4	2	13.3	4	14.3	5	14.7	-	--	5	9.4
S. Japan: rural	-	--	-	--	-	--	1	2.9	-	--	1	1.9
All Urban	13	100	14	93.3	27	96.4	22	64.7	13	68.4	35	66.0
All Rural	-	--	1	6.7	1	3.6	12	35.3	6	31.6	18	34.0

with seven rooms plus a kitchen, a bath, a toilet for a rent of ¥10,000 per month. These were occupied by younger white-collar workers, rising young executives, who could have afford to pay higher rents but probably not the standard rent for the high quality housing they lived in. Unfortunately, some kind of standard for rents of single-family housing was impossible to establish. No one in the neighborhood rented a house without some sort of special arrangement.

Part of the distinction by place of residence is exaggerated because much of the single-family housing and some of the apartments lived in by younger white-collar households were provided by the companies. Therefore, those who lived in the single-family housing tended to have more senior positions in the company hierarchy than those younger white-collar employees living in the apartments. Nearly all of the apartment dwellers wanted to live in single-family housing, but it was too expensive and they were not of the categories entitled to company-provided or assisted housing. The interest in better housing is common in Japan, as indicated in a famous cartoon of a salary-man "life cycle" by Sato Sampei. In this cartoon, the first panel shows the young man, at the age of ten, dreaming of fancy cars. At the age of twenty, his dreams are of women. At thirty, married and with a child, he is obsessed with apartment buildings and houses (Skinner 1979:146-7). The pressure for housing in Sapporo is less urgent than in the great southern cities, a point discussed further later on, but it is strong enough to have some social effects. The most important effect of the housing pressure was to ensure that the residents of single-family housing tended to expect to remain in the neighborhood for a considerable time, staying until they could afford to purchase a house of their own, a very long-term proposition. As one employee of a large company put it:

> Now that we have our own house, I don't think we'll move again. There might be nicer houses, but this is pretty good and it's very cheap. I think that we might stay here until I retire and we have to move out (the speaker was not due to retire for almost thirty years); even they I'm not sure what we'll do, housing is so difficult now. Probably move to Teinei (the northernmost suburb).

The apartment dwellers, on the other hand, tended to be younger, less advanced in the company hierarchy, or they worked for smaller companies not as lavish with fringes such as housing. This group has far fewer expectations, justifiably, of living in the neighborhood for any significant length of the time. As a crude measure of permanence, the single-family housing, younger white-collar group averaged almost twelve years residence in the neighborhood, while the apartment, younger white-collar group averaged only a little more than two years. This difference is also reflected in the respective composition of households of the two types as shown in Table 32. Further, the apartment group was more likely to have lived in other parts of Sapporo, moving from neighborhood to neighborhood rather frequently, more often than the single-family residence, younger white-collar group.

Younger White-Collar Residents:

The economic position of the younger white-collar group correlated with the shifts in residential patterns. In Phase II most if not all of the younger white-collar group were employed by large establishments had economic stability , if very low incomes; and had stable prospects for the future. The Phase III situation of the younger white-collar workers was different. Without the prospects of a stable future, either financial or geographical, the economic position of the younger white-collar employee becomes tenuous. As a group, the younger white-collar employees were low wage earners. The average of the group was difficult to determine because of the normal patterns of pay in Japan tend to mask total compensation. Aside from the

Table 32: Younger White Collar Family Composition

	Single Family Housing (11 households)		Apartments (17 households)	
	Males	Females	Males	Females
Household	11	--	17	--
Spouse	--	9	--	17
Child	7	5	10	9
Parent	1	--	--	--
Other Related	1	--	--	--
Non-Related	--	2	--	--
	20	20	27	26

monthly, or base, salary, there are biannual bonuses, which together might equal the base salary but which are set sums, usually varying with either the company's success, union-negotiated formulae, or some other irregular factor. The younger white-collar annual incomes averaged about ¥2,000,000 to ¥3,000,000 counting salary, bonuses, insurance benefits, housing benefits, and other official fringe benefits. The median of my small sample was nearer the ¥2,000,000 end of the scale. The low pay of the younger white-collar workers, a remnant of the *tenryo*, permanent employment system, was supposed to be offset by the prospects of considerably higher pay as they gained seniority. But without permanent job security, this group found itself in a weak economic position. As a result, the infusion into Hanayama of the relatively unstable younger white-collar employees--those who lived in private apartments, were employed by smaller companies, had less formal education, and had limited economic or residential stability--undermined the economic stability of the neighborhood economy. The retail shops were less economically stable, for example, because the apartment-dwelling, younger white-collar households spent little money in the neighborhood. They did nearly all of their shopping in the department stores downtown or at the supermarket built during this phase just outside the Hanayama boundaries. Interestingly, the unstable apartment-dwelling group did not appear to be more conservative with their money than the more stable, single-family housing group; in fact, quite the opposite. The apartment dwellers appeared to have more consumer goods--stereos, short-wave radios, and tape decks--while the more stable, younger white-collar group, given their incomes, tended to have amazingly large personal savings.

The money saved by the younger white-collar group average, in my limited sample, more than a year's income: about ¥3,500,000 ($27,000 in 1975) per household. This pattern of substantial personal savings was also found with the older white-collar group, the shopkeepers, and the blue-collar group. The older white-collar group, nor surprisingly, had the largest savings, then the shopkeepers, followed by the stable, younger white-collar group. The large savings are the result of many things: perhaps the most important is the limited retirement pensions offered by Japanese companies, an almost nonexistent national program for the elderly, and the various traumas the Japanese have undergone in the last century or so. Because company and national retirement programs are lacking, one must fend for oneself, invariable with personal savings, insurance, and the help of one's family, if one is fortunate. As one younger white-collar housewife put it:

> We really don't know what to expect in the future. We are lucky to have a decent house and we have (health) insurance, which is very good, but what if one of our parents get sick or something really bad happens? I try to save ten percent of (her husband's) salary every month. That makes it very difficult but we use the bonuses to buy big things.

Another put it:

> This isn't the United States. Japan is a very poor country. We do not have a good system for old people here, so we must do it ourselves. It is one of the most important problems in the country, I think. In some ways it is better now; before people didn't have (the very broad coverage) insurance because they couldn't afford it. Now, my company pays for mine and it covers everyone in the family, even mother (who lives with him).

Returning to the economic positions of the groups in the neighborhood, much of what is true for the unstable younger white-collar group was also true for the entertainers. While the entertainers were better pain than the younger white-collar group, the flow of their money to the neighborhood establishments was almost zero, except for the apartment rent paid to their landladies. Whereas the younger white-collar group at least tended to purchase such basics as food within the neighborhood, the entertainers appeared to have almost no contact with the shopkeepers, usually buying what little food they used in their apartments near where they worked, rather than in the neighborhood. As a result, the entertainers had little economic contact with the neighborhood. The significance here is that in previous phases the neighborhood social relationships had usually been an intertwining of social, political, and economic ties forming webbed patterns. But the entertainers' limited economic ties with other individuals in the neighborhood is consistent with their limited social and political neighborhood ties.

Older White-Collar Group:

Historically, the socially most powerful group in the neighborhood, the older white-collar group, experienced an even greater increase in their economic, political, and social power outside Hanayama during this phase. The turmoil at the beginning of the previous phase, the period of the American occupation, and the rise back to economic affluence during the transition period brought the average economic position and power of the older white-collar group down from what otherwise it would have been. At the end of Phase II, the Japanese economy as a whole had phenomenal boom-period growth and, as far as Sapporo was concerned, this period of high growth (often more than 10% in real economic growth per annum) continued virtually unabated through the first part of Phase III in spite of the "oil shock," high inflation, and other problems and actually accelerated in the second part, up to the bursting of the "Bubble Economy". Given these conditions, it is not surprising that the older white-collar group, economically the most powerful in the neighborhood to start with, tended to rise with the economic boom. Unlike part of the younger white-collar group, the older white-collar group did not have to deal with any personal economic instability because of their seniority in various, usually large, economic concerns and, unlike the shopkeepers, their economic sphere was expanding rapidly. The resulting affluence of the older white-collar group tended to rise both absolutely and relatively during Phase III.

The ties of the older white-collar employees with the economy of the city as a whole also increased roughly in proportion to the expansion of the urban economy. Therefore, they provided a stable base for the retail economy inside Hanayama. The older white-collar group also owned most of the non-corporate single-family housing in the neighborhood, averaging slightly more than one house owned per older white-collar household, and they provided most of the cash flow for the neighborhood political organizations. In contrasts to the other groups already discussed, the older white-collar group's economic ties with the rest of the city had become even stronger and more stable. However, as the number of Older White-Collar households decreased, along with the deterioration of the Neighborhood Association, the relative influence of the Older White-Collar group actually decreased.

Blue-Collar Residents:

The blue-collar group maintained its economic stability but the number of workers in the neighborhood decreased radically during this phase. In fact, the the end of the Phase, there were only a few blue-collar workers living in apartments scattered throughout the neighborhood, the company-owned duplexes were gone. As relatively young people living in apartments, the blue-collar households provided some of the base for the internal neighborhood economy, the retail establishments; but with a total of only eight households in 1988, their contribution must be viewed as minimal.

Shopkeepers:

The shopkeepers' economic ties both inside and outside the neighborhood are the most difficult to assess. Although the number of shops increased during Phase III (in 1965 there were twenty-five shops in the neighborhood, in 1975 there were twenty-nine and in 1988 there were thirty-one), the types of shops shifted somewhat. Phase II shops were primarily run by small retailers such as grocers, butchers, and beverage dealers, with the shift to an increase in the proportion of service shops selling cosmetics and coffee, for example, in Phase III.

There were a number of other socioeconomic changes, some already mentioned here significantly affecting the shopkeepers economic position. Their major economic shift was a result of the wholesale market in the city of Sapporo changing from an unsophisticated, person-to-person business in the immediate postwar period to a more complex, but still network-based business in Phase III. The wholesale concerns continued their extremely rapid growth in Phase II through Phase III, decreasing proportionately the economic leverage of any given small shopkeeper. Also, in terms of particular goods (for example, foodstuffs), the small neighborhood shops increasingly came into direct competition with the large downtown department stores for both customers and "good" connections with the wholesalers. Continuing with the example of foodstuffs, the locally produced material was more or less equally available to both large and small establishments because this material could be purchased through the local, relatively small-scale network of wholesalers. But for material that was not produced locally, the larger department stores and the supermarkets had a tremendous advantage. The larger the concern, the lower the price per unit charged by the wholesalers.

It is true, however, that the very largest concerns, such as the great department store-chains, did their own wholesaling and ran their own transportation systems. Usually, the larger the store, the cheaper the product--although not always, because sometimes the small shops were willing to operate with far smaller profit margins. Accordingly, certain items came to be carried only by the larger stores, which in turn attracted customers away from the smaller, local, less well-stocked establishments. This cycle came into full swing during Phase III. The overall trend was for the eventual total domination by the large establishments and the extinction of the small ones. Unlike the secondary sector of the economy, the dual structure where the smaller companies feed into the larger ones providing them with a certain degree of elasticity to withstand economic fluctuations, the retail sales sector pitted the smaller shops against the larger stores in direct competition with the small shops having only the advantages of convenience and a "personal" touch.

The countervailing force against the trend toward extinction of the small, local establishments was the expectations and ground rules for the small establishments were different from those applied by the larger firms. In part, this explains why the local shops have not already become extinct. The large establishments ran on standard business principles of profit and loss. The small ones were largely realizations of a strong value in Japanese culture: being economically and social independent. Every one of the shopkeepers interviewed--almost half of those in the neighborhood--expressed some form of this sentiment. For example,

> I quit my job (with a large pharmaceutical firm) to open this shop twenty years ago, so I could be my own boss. It's no good working for a company where you're lost in the crowd, Here I do what I want when I want. I took enough orders during the war to last the rest of my life.

and,

> I work long hours, but I work for myself and my family, not for some rich owner. When I retire, one of my sons will run the shop. If I worked for some company, what would my children inherit?

Non-shopkeepers in Hanayama shared many of the same values toward independence but, on the whole, felt that the price paid by the shopkeepers was higher than they wanted to pay. Instead, the non-shopkeepers opted for lower-risk, higher security employment. In order to be independent, the local shopkeepers put in longer hours, drew lower incomes, and maintained low standards of financial security compared to employees of their larger counterparts. An informal sample suggested that the average large department store employee worked about 44 hours (full time).In the small shops in Hanayama, the average work week for owner/operators was about 61.5 with a high of well over 80 hours per week. In addition, full-time employees in the Hanayama stores worked fewer hours than did the owner/operators. Comparative pay scales were impossible to establish precisely but it was clear that the small Hanayama shopkeepers could have earned considerably higher incomes had they held equivalent positions in large retail establishments. Further, the financial security of the neighborhood shopkeepers was low, although the older shopkeepers seemed to have built up buffers of insurance and personal savings to enable them to weather minor fiscal reverses. Employees of the large department stores enjoyed the same financial security common in larger Japanese firms. This does not mean, however, that the small establishments have not had to adapt to increasing competition.

In adapting to the competition, the economic ties of the small local retailers in the neighborhood became increasingly a local (within Hokkaido) network based on personal contact and small-scale economies. This adaptation was found in retail stores only. The other adaptation made by the neighborhood--as a statistical group, not as individuals--was to shift the emphasis of the neighborhood shops from purely small-scale retail to a mixed bag of small-scale retail and, increasingly, service shops such as dry cleaners, coffee shops, and restaurants.

In the service-shop sector, the direct competition with large establishments (described above) did not apply so directly or devastatingly. The development of these service shops meant that the wholesaler network of the shopkeepers shifted somewhat to fit the service-shop requirements. thus, although the overall economic situation of the shopkeepers within the neighborhood could be said to have deteriorated somewhat, the range of the supply networks for the group as a whole increased significantly. This trend toward diversification of the Hanayama establishments also meant that the neighborhood will probably be able to maintain its shopkeeper population in spite of the possible direct competition with the supermarkets and the department stores.

The growth of the larger retail establishments outside the Hanayama neighborhood and the shift in population within the neighborhood has meant that the shopkeepers' previous economically stable ties with other groups in the neighborhood has deteriorated. The older white-collar group and the shopkeeper relationships, on the whole, have remained stable but the links with the younger white-collar group, the entertainers, and the blue-collar group has sharply declined. The transition from a retail-shop cluster to a mixed retail/service-shop cluster also produced two different types of shopkeeper. The older shopkeepers--all retailers--maintained economic ties with each other, even when directly competitive; this is seen in the example of the fruit sellers who would occasionally pool their resources to cash in on a wholesaler's bargain. There was also considerable gift giving at various times of the year to reinforce these links. The new service shopkeepers, somewhat younger in average age than the older shopkeepers as well as being newer to Hanayama, tended to have only limited economic contact, or none at all, with the retail shopkeepers or with each other.

The attitudes expressed by the newer shopkeepers indicated that they, like the entertainers and the apartment-living, younger white-collar employees, were more interested in being *modan* than in maintaining extensive neighborhood social bonds. the sentiments expressed were not as extreme as those of the entertainers quoted previously, but some of the ideas--particularly the concept of personal freedom unencumbered by sticky interpersonal relationships--were held in common.

Landladies:

The last group to be considered in terms of their economic position inside and outside of the neighborhood is a socioeconomic category new to Phase III: the landladies, who tended to have highly variable economic ties outside the neighborhood. The apartment houses were financed by small combines of which the manager-landlady was a principal. Specific data on what degree of ownership was held by which landlady was generally lacking. However, based on general conversations and two specific cases where the account books were accessible, there seemed to be considerable variation concerning finances. In the two cases where specific data was accessible, the ownership patterns were quite dissimilar. One landlady, with her husband, owned one hundred percent of the apartment house, a situation apparently unique in the neighborhood. The more common pattern was represented by the second landlady who owned a quarter share of her large apartment house. A second quarter was officially owned by her brother, and one-sixth each was owned by three unrelated people, all of whom she had known in her previous occupation as a *mama-san*. Although this was not clear, it appears that one of the one-sixth shares was, in fact, a mortgage held by a local bank through the president, who was the "official" shareholder. In informal conversations, sometimes the landlady would refer to the bank as a co-owner and sometimes to the individual. The whole situation was, in fact, quite confusing. Who owned what was arranged in a complex manner, at least in part, the landlady pointed out, to allow a "favorable interpretation" on taxes. The landlady and her brother then proceeded to buy out the other co-owners over about a ten-year period. The details about interest payments were not clear, but from the landlady's explanation it seems that the interest eventually would equal about ten per cent per annum, a not unreasonable amount; in fact, a very favorable one given the lack of collateral.

The economic ties of the landlady were primarily to her backers--including a bank if it were involved--and to suppliers of goods and services required in maintaining the apartments. In this respect, any given landlady normally had various services performed by the same person or persons over extended periods of time (e.g., *tatami* maintenance, plumbing, painting). Often the people who serviced the apartments were previously known to the landlady. For other services connected with the apartments (e.g., laundry and kerosene) there were regular deliveries, usually by the same companies used by all the tenants in the building, often arranged through one of her financial backers and with some sort of kickback arrangement to the landlady. An individual landlady might also have other outside business interests involving various contacts primarily economic in nature. The landlady who owned her own buildings, for example, also owned part of another apartment house in an adjoining neighborhood in addition to a farm in the rural district south of Sapporo. The other landlady, who had started with a quarter of her apartment and with her brother had bought out the other principals, had shared in a long list of enterprises, including bars, two fishing boats, a farm, and a small trucking firm. Some of these enterprises were in connection with the same group that owned shares of the apartment house she managed, and some were not, although her family seems to have been involved in all but one of the bar connections.

The sum of the landlady-economic connections with the outside city were such that the landladies, after the older white-collar group, had the widest outside connections. Often many of these contacts were, in effect, brought into the neighborhood with the landlady when the apartment building was constructed. Thus the landladies, like the older white-collar group, provided access to outside economic contacts for people--usually their tenants--in the neighborhood. In this respect they acted as information or introduction brokers, as did the older white-collar group, a position of some social power in Japanese society or any other.

The primary economic ties of the landladies in the neighborhood were with their tenants. The tenant-landlady relationship was usually wholly economic with social aspects being held to a minimum but there were exceptions, particularly with tenants who had lived in the apartment buildings for several years. With these exceptions, the landladies developed deep ties. The landladies also developed strong economic ties with the shopkeepers and, in some notable cases. with members of the older white-collar group. The ties with the shopkeepers were just what might be expected: the landladies slowly but steadily built up regular economic and concomitant social bonds with the retail shopkeepers. Having looked at the individual groups, it is now possible to extract some of the overall patterns.

Neighborhood-City Ties:

The economic ties between the neighborhood and the city were more broadly based and diffuse in Phase III than they had been in previous phases. Part of this broadening was a result of the increase in population of the neighborhood and the city, which meant more links from the neighborhood to the outside. The other major factor was the introduction of two new socio-economic groups, the entertainers and the landladies, into the neighborhood with their own external economic links.

The contrast with the earlier phases is marked. Whereas in Phase I the ties with the larger city were through limited conduits, the Phase III ties were very extensive and covered nearly all possible areas of urban economic life: manufacturing, construction, transportation, service, entertainment, retail and wholesale marketing, communications and government. Taken as a whole, then, the neighborhood of Hanayama had a greater potential economic range, a number of contacts, and thus potentially greater leverage than ever before. The reasons why this potential leverage was not exerted to the fullest was more a function of political and social factors than economic ones, but it is important that the economic potential existed. If it had been a cohesive political and social body, as it had been in Phases I and II, Hanayama had the political and economic contacts to exert considerable leverage within the district and even the city political and economic organs. It did not do so, not because the means were not there, but because the neighborhood lacked the cohesiveness necessary to develop the interest to exert such leverage.

The growth of the neighborhood's economic base was important for another reason besides giving Hanayama potential political leverage. With the increasing affluence of the Japanese since the war, the economic structure has had a variety of changes, adequately described elsewhere in terms of their impact on social life (e.g., Dore 1958; Cole 1971; Vogel 1967 and 1979; Reischauer 1977; and Bestor 1988), covering virtually all forms of modern Japan. These changes are reflected in the increased range of economic ties within the neighborhood, and in the lessening of the overall leverage of the individuals in the neighborhood; the reason for the diminished individual leverage lies directly in the decreased cohesiveness of the neighborhood as a social entity. In effect, while the economic network range has increased through time, the intensity--the willingness to use the network links--has decreased. The overall trend of the economic situation of the neighborhood during the study period was from a state of relative autonomy, with internal primary industry wherein the economic ties to the rest of the urban area were limited, to a state of total dependence and widespread, intensive economic ties to the city outside the neighborhood. The transition from farms to small shops, apartment buildings, and white-collar employees making a residential area indistinguishable from the surrounding urban terrain. Economically, the neighborhood became a far less distinctive and autonomous unit within the urban sphere.

The social connections between people in the neighborhood and the outside city continued the trend noted for the last phase, becoming more expansive, more contacts established outside the neighborhood, but shallower in that the average intensity, durability, and frequency of the exterior relationships appeared to decrease. The enormous growth of the city and neighborhood populations (see Table 14) contributed to the trend toward network diffusion. The social contacts of the neighborhood, in total, were far more extensive during Phase III than in Phase II. Part of this diffusion can be accounted for by the increase in the heterogeneity and number of socioeconomic groups in the neighborhood; these increases thereby enlarged the relationships maintained with groups and individuals outside the neighborhood.

Another significant contribution to heighten outside relationships is the increased incidence of telephones, which allowed easier communication and aided in the frequency of contact. Telephones were, however, quite expensive. At the beginning of Phase III, they were relatively rare although valued. By the end of Phase III, telephone were universal. Ownership of a telephone line cost about ¥60,000. However, despite the cost, the value of the telephone was recognized in maintaining social relationships. As one of the landladies, a rather elderly woman, commented:

> I think it's wonderful. I can just call people up instead of having to visit them. It's very good here in the city because it's hard for me to get around, but I like to know how my family is doing, and my children just call me up every day or so. I even talked to my brother in Hakodate. We never had anything like this before.

She had lived on an isolated farm and was more enthusiastic about the telephone than some of the more sophisticated residents of the neighborhood, but the ideas were those expressed by many people. All of the older white-collar, shopkeeper, and landlady households had telephones. By 1975, almost all of the younger white-collar households in single-family housing had phones, some of which were paid for by the individuals and some by the companies that owned the houses. I only found two younger white-collar households in single-family housing without a telephone. In both cases, expense was the only objection, and they intended to acquire telephones as soon as possible. In the event, they did. Both households got telephones in 1979. However, in 1975 fewer than half of the apartment dwellers had their own telephones, a figure which had risen 90% to by 1988 and since has become literally universal with the spread of cellular phones.

One of the services provided in the apartment houses was access to a public telephone. The landlady or someone in her household would answer the phone, then buzz the apartment wanted on a complicated buzzer system. The telephone was always centrally located and calling out was done like any pay telephone in the United States. That one could use the public telephone instead of a private one and the prohibitive costs probably contributed to the scarcity of apartment telephones. However, the transience of the apartment dwellers was also an important consideration. With an average of only a little more than one year in an apartment, the ¥60,000 fee loomed even larger although the line could be transferred to another nearby residence or sold, usually for about what one paid for it.. For whatever reasons, however, the differential access to telephones would indicate a difference in access to an important channel of communications, which appears to correlate strongly with socioeconomic category.

The most easily measured unit of social linkages was family contacts. Table 33 shows the frequency of reported contact among family members by geographical distance and category. The figure indicates a correlation between proximity and frequency of contact (including telephone calls and letters). There is also an age correlation. The older residents of Hanayama have more frequent contacts with their families than do the younger residents. The proportion of people in the neighborhood whose families lived in or near Sapporo steadily decreased throughout the study period. Almost all of the entertainers, for example, came from outside Sapporo but inside Hokkaido. Although everyone in the neighborhood appeared to maintain some

Table 33: Frequency of Family Contact (1975)

	White-Collar n = 33	White-Collar n = 31	Shop keeper n = 21	Blue-Collar n = 9	Enter-tainer n = 30	Land-lady n = 14	Totals
Sapporo	(17)	(2)	(4)	(3)	(4)	(19)	
Once/year*	--	--	--	--	1	--	1
3-4/year	--	1	--	--	--	1	2
once/month	1	--	--	--	--	1	2
once/week**	16	1	4	3	3	17	44
Within 100 km.	(5)	(7)	(9)	(2)	(11)	(17)	
once/year*	--	1	--	--	6	--	7
3-4/year	1	4	3	--	2	2	12
once/month	3	1	3	2	2	2	13
once/week**	1	1	3	--	1	13	18
Hokkaido	(7)	(29)	(18)	(7)	(21)	(22)	
once/year*	2	19	--	1	17	--	39
3-4/year	3	4	--	4	--	14	25
once/month	1	5	16	2	3	5	32
once/week**	1	1	2	--	1	3	8
Other	(23)	(13)	(11)	(7)	(21)	(19)	
once/year*		16	4	--	4	11	136
3-4/year	5	7	9	1	7	13	42
once/month		1	1	1	1	3	310
once/week**		--	1	1	1	--	2 5

* or less
** or more

sort of contact with his or her family of origin, the quality of contact was perceived to have steadily decreased. What is called quality here is what Mitchell calls "intensity," the willingness to respond positively to requests and needs, but also included are frequency of contact and the individuals perception of the quality of the relationship. Again, the telephone was an important means of maintaining frequency of contact, but the other aspects--the intensity of the relationship and the perceived value of the relationship--appear to have deteriorated; this is true particularly among the younger people who are also more likely to be geographically separated from their natal families. In part, this shift is a conscious one since many of the younger people came to Sapporo, among other reasons, to isolate themselves from their families. As a bar hostess put it:

> Why did I come to Sapporo? I suppose to find a job, but also to get out of (a small town on Hokkaido's east coast). I just couldn't stand the small town prying into everybody's business. And my parents. My mother and I don't get along very well. I don't see them much; the last time was more than two years ago now. I do see my sister who lives in Otaru occasionally. I send my parents a New Year's Card. Sometimes my father will call but not much, he's too stingy.

Looking at generational differences, it seems that it is much more likely that an older person's adult children will be living in Sapporo than that a younger person's parents are living in Sapporo (see Table 34). The secondary linkages yielded by familial primary contacts of course, are also affected, decreasing in direct proportion to the decrease in family contact. That is, if a person's family lives in

Table 34. Parents/Children in Sapporo (1975)

	Couples with Adult Children (n= 42: 93 children)	Adults with Living Parents (n = 81)
Live in Sapporo		
Number	37	7
Percentage	39.7	8.6
Live within 100 km of Sapporo		
Number	12	11
Percentage	12.9	13.6
Live in Hokkaido		
Number	16	49
Percentage	17.2	60.5
Other		
Number	28	14
Percentage	30.1	17.3

Sapporo, he or she is more likely to have a number of contacts traced through family members. Persons whose families do not live in or near Sapporo were less likely to have contacts directly derived from their families (Table 35).

The same patterns that were true for families also existed for school ties, particularly with white-collar employees and entertainers, but also for other groups. A common perception through held by nearly all informants was that those who

Table 35.   Family Contacts and Distance

	Have Direct Family Derived Contacts in Sapporo	Do Not Have Direct Family Derived Contacts in Sapporo
Kin live in Sapporo (n = 13)	13	0
Kin live in Hokkaido (n = 163)	6	157
Other (n = 24)	1	23

attended the University of Hokkaido, one of the old Imperial universities and located in Sapporo, or even any other Sapporo college had larger and more important social networks outside the neighborhood than those who did not have the school ties. People who attended school in Sapporo also perceived their school ties as more important, on the whole, than those who went to school elsewhere (Table 36). There also seemed to be a strong correlation between the amount of education and the

Table 36.   Perceptions of Importance of School Ties (n = 63)

FELT THAT SCHOOL TIES WERE:	University of Hokkaido	Other Sapporo College or Jr. College	Other Sapporo School	Outside School
Very Important	2	11	2	1
Important but Other Contacts Equally so	0	7	13	17
Not Very Important	0	1	4	5

perceived importance of school ties. That is, university graduates were most likely to see such ties as very important, while primary school graduates, at least those few in Hanayama, had not maintained school ties at all. Returning to Table 36, the one individual who had gone to school outside of Sapporo but stressed the importance of his school ties had attended one of the great private universities in the Tokyo area. Two of the "outside Sapporo" group to whom school ties were important but who thought that other ties were equally important also were highly educated. None of the five respondents in the final category, outsiders who thought that school ties were unimportant, were highly educated.

As the number of people in the neighborhood whose families were elsewhere and who attended school outside of Sapporo increased, the incidence of deep, durable contacts developed from these sources decreased. The secondary contacts derived from the primary family and school contacts also decreased. This decrease was perceived by one older white-collar male as a crucial shift in the social pattern of the neighborhood. As he put it,

> Before, a young person would move into the neighborhood with introductions --from his family, family friends, school people, or employer. You had something to hold onto until you got to know the people. Not now. Now nobody knows who they are or where they came from. How do you deal with people like that?

The decrease in family and school contacts was perceived by most of the older residents as a serious problem, not only in the neighborhood but possibly for Japanese society as a whole.

If these basic, very durable linkages have decreased, particularly with their important function of generating secondary contacts, the question arises, where did the increase in overall network ranges necessary come from? The first answer is from increased population, both in terms of absolute numbers and relative density. The white-collar groups represented were usually employed by large concerns of various types, usually tertiary (Table 23). the absolute size of these concerns tended to be steadily growing, thus opening new avenues for social links. The density of the neighborhood doubled and, except for the apartment dwellers, the customs of the neighborhood--and Japanese society in general--demand at least superficial contact with one's immediate neighbors. As density increased, therefore, the total number of persons known at least minimally tended to increase.

Overall, the social position of the neighborhood--as opposed to the social linkages enjoyed by persons living in the neighborhood--followed the pattern of the economic connections within the larger urban environment. The neighborhood had been viewed as a distinct social unit in Phase I, separate from Sapporo, even though technically part of it. That is, the neighborhood and the district were still seen as distinct units, but they were not then perceived as being as autonomous, as they had been viewed in Phase I. The area was usually discussed by its name, Nose Mountain Village, rather than street names (Japan's equivalent to addresses in the United States is an area, streets are usually not named and houses not sequentially numbered). During Phase III, the autonomy and distinctive features of the neighborhood were blurred into the surrounding area. The old district name, Hanayama, was no longer used much, except as the name of a post office branch, and even the technical boundaries of the neighborhood were not know to most of the inhabitants. The native perception of the neighborhood was that of a social entity as the beginning of the study period. By the end of the study period in 1988, the neighborhood as a social entity has been dismissed by the great majority of inhabitants.

These perceptions correlated with the social groupings and types of residences in the neighborhood. all of the entertainers; the apartment-dwelling, younger white-collar employees; and the newer landladies were ignorant of the formal boundaries of the neighborhood and the old neighborhood name. Conversely, all of the older white-collar and shopkeeper informants, including the newer shopkeepers, were aware of the location of the formal boundaries of the neighborhood and its old name, Nose Mountain Village, which some of them still used. The older landladies--those in the neighborhood for several years--also tended to know the boundaries and almost all used the old name for the neighborhood regularly in normal conversation, even more than the older white-collar or shopkeeper informants. Thus, the social patterns of the neighborhood tended to parallel economic patterns.

Political Organization:

The formal and informal political organization of the neighborhood fit into much the same patterns. Looking first at the formal political organizations, the Neighborhood Association had enjoyed great power and prestige at two earlier times--the later war period of the early 1940's and the late 1950's. At the end of Phase II, in 1965, the Neighborhood Association enjoyed considerable power and had the membership of most oif not all the neighborhood inhabitants. the political control of the Neighborhood Association was mainly in the hands of the older white-collar group, but the shopkeepers and the younger white-collar males were making inroads, at least partly as the result of the efforts, grudgingly or otherwise, of some of the older white-collar males to "democratize" (*demokurashii*) the Neighborhood Association.

During Phase III, the Neighborhood Association deteriorated rapidly in all respects. With the migration into the neighborhood of the entertainers and many younger white-collar households (see Table 37), the universal membership that the association had enjoyed in the previous phases declined within a period of ten years to a formal membership of less than 70% of the households of Hanayama. By the end of the study period, membership was less that 50%. Almost all of the single-family housing households continued to belong to the Association, but considerably less than half of the apartment households maintained even formal membership. That the membership might be only formal for some of the apartment dwellers is expressed in the following comment from a hostess:

> Yes, I belong to the Neighborhood Association, but I don't do anything. You see, Mrs. S., the landlady, is the head of the block association (*han-cho*). It doesn't look good for her if I don't belong. Look (pointing to the list of Neighborhood Association members)--almost everyone in the apartments here are members, but I don't think thatanyone goes to the meetings or anything. In fact, I don't really know when or where the meetings are.

Similar sentiments were expressed by most of the apartment dwellers, entertainers and younger white-collar employees alike. Further, a quick glance at the list of association members shows that the three landladies who have been perennial block association heads have recruited most of their tenants. The apartment houses whose landladies are not block association heads are poorly represented, except for two cases where the landladies are great friends of the landladies who are the block association leaders.

During this phase, virtually all of the formal functions of the Neighborhood Association appear to have been abandoned or taken over by other organs, except for the liaison function with higher organs of the urban government. For example, the annual festival (*matsuri*) and neighborhood wide clean-up projects have been dropped and resident registration is now done only by the police, without Neighborhood Association assistance. Although the skeleton of the association survived to the end of Phase III, its only real functions appeared to have been a limited input into the district organization; a basic framework for what is left of the tonari gumi; and certain "social club" type activities such as the annual dinner to elect new officers.

Looking at these surviving functions, the District Association was made up of the Neighborhood Association heads (*chōnaikaichō*) representing the seventeen neighborhoods comprising the district. From the point of view of the residents of Hanayama, the District Association had as its primary function a rather vague input into larger city organs concerning specific district requirements such as street repairs, police functions, and school maintenance, all of which were duplicated by other agencies and organizations. According to the head of the Neighborhood Association and other informants working with the District Association, the major function performed at the district level was to act as a coordinating and liaison agent between the neighborhoods and the city organs. Most of the Hanayama residents, however, appeared to have very little idea of how these various levels of government worked, nor did they appear to have much interest in learning more about them. There were perceived, on the whole, as being unimportant, particularly by the younger migrants

Table 37: Hanayama Migration: 1965-1975

	IN		OUT		NET			
	H-holds	Pop.	H-holds	Pop.	H-holds		Pop.	
	#	#	#	#	#	%	#	%
Shopkeepers	7	22	3	8	4	1.5	14	3.3
Older White-Collar	4	8	8	19	-4	-1.5	-11	-2.6
Younger White-Collar	108	229	71	154	37	14.0	75	17.9
Blue-Collar	2	5	9	23	-7	-2.7	-18	4.3
Landladies	14	31	--	--	14	5.3	31	7.4
Entertainer	???	???	???	???	217	82.2	322	76.8
Other	3	6	--	--	3	1.1	6	1.4

who displayed the greatest ignorance in this area.

 The annual banquet and other less formal get-togethers for the officers of the Neighborhood Association and the heads of the tonari gumi were the places where association "business" was transacted, but with the replacement or abandonment of its former functions, the business of the association became increasingly social and decreasingly businesslike. The social functions were important, however, especially on the lower level of the tonari gumi.

 There was a direct correlation between the proportion of the older white-collar group involved in the formal neighborhood organizations and the degree of effectiveness these organizations had. During Phase II, the majority of the various officeholders were of the old white-collar group. There were seven officers elected annually by the Neighborhood Association. During Phase II, about twenty-five different people held one of these seven offices at one time or another. Only two (of those known) were not of the older white-collar group, both being older shopkeeper males. By the middle of Phase III, the older white-collar group was only a plurality of the associations membership, while most of the offices were held by members of the younger white-collar, landlady, and shopkeeper groups. At the same time, both persons who had served as association head during the phase were older white-collar males, but of the seventeen people who had served in the other six positions, only nine were of the older white-collar group. In addition, by 1975, only two of the thirteen tonari gumi heads (han-cho) were older white-collar and one of them a woman. By 1988, the Older White-Collar group was only a fragment and the residual neighborhood association was pretty much a younger-white collar function with a fair number of shopkeepers also active.

The final function of the Neighborhood Association was to serve as a framework for the functioning of the tonari gumi. Since the effective remaining internal functions of the neighborhood lay in the informal aspects of the organization grouped around the tonari gumi, the Neighborhood Association's providing them some structural support and legitimacy had some value, but it appeared to be rapidly decreasing. Because the association continued to have a neighborhood-wide formal structure above the formal block association, the tonari gumi informally kept going some continuity with the past. Thus, a certain ease of neighborhood entry remained useful for some of the migrants. Since the Neighborhood Association several structural steps away from the effective functional arena, however, it is difficult to ascribe much real value to it.

The effective functional arena, the informal efforts of the tonari gumi, primarily involved interpersonal relationships within the neighborhood and, to a lesser extent, the absorption of migrants into the social milieu of the neighborhood. In the past, the absorption of new migrants had been a primary function of the informal workings of the tonari gumi. In Phase III, this function continued but on a limited scale. The limits were basically that only the residents of single-family housing were absorbed in ways similar to the mechanisms so successful in previous phases. As mentioned above, the major differences in the patterns of migration between Phase III and the two previous phases were the attitudes of many of the migrants and the physical geography of the settlement--clustered company-owned housing and apartment buildings.

The absorptive mechanisms of the neighborhood, based on the development of close interpersonal ties, could only operate with those individuals who wanted to be absorbed and who were accessible to their new neighbors. The company-owned clusters of single-family housing presented some problems in that they were physically isolated from the rest of the neighborhood. There was a tendency to "get to know" only other people employed by the same company. Less extreme forms of isolation involved younger white-collar, single-family housing that was contiguous to other single-family housing. The people who moved into these dwellings established contact with others outside their own group and were, in time, absorbed fairly well. The cluster of housing did pose some difficulty. As one young housewife put it:

> When we first move here, we quickly got to know the people (living) nearest; our husbands all work together, so they knew each other to start with, although not very well. For the first months we were here, we got to know them (the fellow employees) better, but didn't meet anyone else...except the block association head. We joined the Neighborhood Association.... After a bit, we got to know some of the other people but it took more than a year before we knew who most of the people on the street were. I still don't know some of them, although I do say "good morning" when I see them.

Most of the younger white-collar migrants quickly joined the Neighborhood Association after moving into Hanayama, and most of them introduced themselves to their immediate neighbors. These were, however, a distinct minority of the total number of neighborhood migrants. The majority during Phase III moved into the new apartment houses and toward the end of the phase, there were almost no single-family houses, all of the migrants moved into apartments. Not only were the apartment residents physically isolated by the nature of the buildings from the single-family housing neighbors, but they tended to move into the buildings in waves, at least at first when the buildings first opened.

The major consideration, however, in the development of the social absorption of the apartment migrants was that most did not want to be drawn into the social milieu of Hanayama or into any other similar system. As discussed above, most of the entertainers and many of the apartment-dwelling, younger white-collar adults had come to Sapporo to avoid the kind of social interaction that being absorbed into the neighborhood's social patterns would involve. Some, in fact, were actively hostile to the idea, holding themselves aloof, even to the point of angering people like their landladies who felt snubbed.

This self-inflicted social isolation of the apartment dwellers was not universal. There were a few apartment people, mostly younger white-collar employees, who were interested in establishing social roots in the neighborhood. The process of their introduction into the social milieu of Hanayama was different than that of the single-family housing, younger white-collar migrants. Instead of O-hirome and the spread of pertinent social information through immediate neighbors, the landladies acted as social brokers for the apartment dwellers.

All of the landladies had acted immediately and forcefully on moving into the neighborhood to make themselves accepted socially by the Hanayama inhabitants. They had introduced themselves to their neighbors, sometimes to everyone on their street, to the other landladies, and in a few cases to all of the officers of the Neighborhood Association. They had joined the Neighborhood Association as quickly as possible. By 1975, three of the thirteen block association heads were landladies. By 1985, almost half, six of thirteen, were landladies. All of them expressed strong agreement with the value of building and maintaining strong relationships in their place of residence. All of the landladies identified themselves as being a member of a group, "the landladies." That is, part of their identification of themselves was the group identity. They were all Hanayama landladies. The landladies were the only group in the neighborhood to unanimously identify themselves as a distinct category. The only other individuals to sometimes make a similar identification were the older shopkeepers. The readiness of the landladies to label themselves with a group identity seems to fit with their eagerness to fit into the neighborhood social milieu in a rather traditional way. This sentiment was do doubt reinforced by the neighborhood also being their place of business.

To return to the absorption of the apartment migrants, the landladies not only introduced those interested to other people in the neighborhood, some of the more socially active landladies literally recruited what they called "good people" for introduction into the social sphere of the neighborhood. The landladies' introductions were usually made in the halls or the courtyards of the apartment buildings. Recruiting, a kind of special entrepreneurial activity, usually occurred inside the landladies' quarters, usually in the living rooms. This is a noteworthy point because such casual visiting of one another's living quarters was rare. The pattern of such recruiting appeared to be that the new migrants would get to know the landlady rapidly. She would then start introducing them around, and if they responded favorably--that is, appeared to enjoy it--the process continued; if not, it stopped. The following quote from a landlady indicates what benefits she received from her introducing people:

> Well, its fun and I like to do it. Young people (she was well over 60) are so shy. Of course, I wanted to be useful in the association, so you might say that I became block association head that way, but I wouldn't say that. There is one other thing. My business depends on the "good spirit" (*yoi ki* "good emotion", "good feeling") of the apartments. If I have a good reputation, then good people rent my apartments. If good people are happy in the neighborhood and feel comfortable, then they will stay longer. That's just good business.

Because most of the apartment houses were run on very narrow financial margins, vacancies could be disastrous, and steps must be taken to avoid long transitions between tenants.

Although the landladies began acting as information brokers during this phase, the trend toward a decreased information flow and less durable and intense social networks continued from the previous phase. The role of migration and the changes in the city of Sapporo in affecting these trends are discussed later. First, we should look at the networks as they evolved during Phase III.

There were four types of social networks employed inside the neighborhood by the residents of Hanayama at the end of Phase III. The social networks most closely approximating the previous phases in Hanayama were the relationships build and maintained by the older groups in the neighborhood, the older white-collar employees and the older shopkeepers. Although the density of the networks--the number of people known in the neighborhood--was low, these residents maintained durable relationships reinforced by frequent, often daily, interaction. The intensity of the relationships--the willingness to respond positively to requests or needs--was maintained at a high level, primarily because this aspect of social relationships was seen as being of paramount importance. the maintenance of strong neighborhood relationships was possible because their number, proportionately, was greatly restricted. The older white-collar residents and the older shopkeepers knew each other; and individuals in each group would know a few of the younger white-collar residents, usually those living in single-family housing, and most of the landladies. The shopkeepers knew the blue-collar females and some of the younger white-collar females. In all, a limited web was maintained, a sharp contrast to the "broad face" situation found in the past among these older groups.

The next most conservative groups were the single-family housing, younger white-collar residents and the newer shopkeepers. these people also had relatively small networks compared either to those of the older residents or to those of their own categories in time past. While the older shopkeepers and older white-collar residents knew from 100 (for the older white-collar residents) to 200 (for the older shopkeepers) adults in Hanayama, the single-family housing, younger white-collar residents and the newer shopkeepers knew an average of about 75 other adults. The single-family housing, younger white-collar residents knew most of the shopkeepers (older and newer) and some of the older white-collar residents, as well as a few of the other single-family housing, younger white-collar adults. If they were living in company housing, the most common situation, they knew everyone else in the same company-housing cluster. the newer shopkeepers knew some of the older shopkeepers, a few of the other newer shopkeepers, and a scattering of the younger white-collar and entertainer residents who patronized their establishments. For both groups the relationships were of low durability, reflecting their short tenure in Hanayama; of highly variable frequency, ranging from several contacts a day to one every few weeks; and of moderate intensity. The intensity of the relationships depended primarily on who the relationships were with. For example, the newer shopkeeper-customer (of whatever group) links were of low intensity, while the younger white-collar male to older white-collar male relationship would probably have as high an intensity as the younger white-collar male could make it. Another example of high intensity relationship was found among the company-owned, housing-cluster residents where the residential proximity was reinforced by the power bond of mutual company employment, employment being for many of the males the primary emotional focus of their lives.

The *modan* ("modern," "hip") groups, entertainers and younger white-collar apartment dwellers, had networks that were extremely small. What few relationships they had in the neighborhood lacked significant durability, frequency, or intensity. The only exceptions to this rule were the rare tenants who stayed in the neighborhood for several years and had built a few networks through their landladies, as discussed earlier. These network-building apartment dwellers were a very small minority; out of a sample of 67 apartment adults interviewed in 1975, only 3 knew more than 20 other people in the entire neighborhood. Thirteen out of the thirty-seven entertainers interviewed knew no one in Hanayama except the landlady from whom they rented their apartments. The average tenure in the neighborhood for these thirteen was about sixteen months. In sum, therefore, the networks of the apartment residents could be said to be almost nonexistent.

The final group, the landladies, form something of a residual category. The group was quite small and their approach to social interaction was conservative. Their networks were as large as they could make them. Possibly because of the coexistence of residence and business (a point examined further in the next chapter), the landladies spent a great deal of time and effort building up and maintaining their social networks. In 1975, with an average neighborhood tenure of only 5 years, the landladies knew an average of more than 150 adults in the neighborhood, excluding their own tenants. The exclusion of the tenants is necessary to avoid a skewing effect. The landladies new all of their own tenants, sometimes more than 60 people, which would make for a rather large network immediately. It would be even more exaggerate if secondary contacts were included, because all of the landladies knew each other; therefore literally every tenant in Hanayama was in the secondary network for every landlady. The 150 was for primary, non-tenant contacts only. With the more conservative groups in the neighborhood, the older white-collar and shopkeeper residents, the landladies tried to build strong relationships. With most of the younger white-collar residents and especially the entertainers, the quality of the relationship or even the relationship itself, including those with their tenants, were not so important with the exception of those few cases mentioned above where the tenants were "taken under the wing" of their landladies.

Summary:

The face-to-face, everyone-knows-everyone-else nature of the social relationships that had existed in the previous phases was gone. The closure, to use Bott's (1957) phrase or density (Mitchell 1969) averaged between 10 and 20 percent for the entire neighborhood. The various social groups in the neighborhood had adjusted their webs of social relationships to fit their new residential circumstances.

Unlike the shifts in the patterns of social relationships occurring in Phase II, the Phase III changes were quite sudden, dramatic, and appraised as important by those residents whose social networks changed. The older residents of Hanayama saw the changes in the social life of the neighborhood as being the direct result of the entertainers moving into the neighborhood. As one older white-collar housewife put it:

> This used to be a neighborhood with a strong spirit. That was before the apartment buildings were built and the hostesses and such started moving in. They (the entertainers) don't know how to be polite; they

have no manners--like many young people.... Since they came, the
neighborhood has become a cold place to live.

In the eyes of the older white-collar residents and the older shopkeepers, the
entertainers were to blame for what they saw as the deterioration of the
neighborhood, the disintegration of its social fabric.

There was clearly a change in the degree of the impact of migration on the
social behavior of the neighborhood from what had occurred in the past. All three of
the variables--the rate of migration, the characteristics of the migrants, and the size
of the neighborhood--were different from previous situations. In fact, about the only
major similarity between Phase III and the earlier phases was that the majority of
migrants into Hanayama had urban backgrounds.

Looking at the differences in probably order of importance, the most radical
shift that distinguishes the migration of Phase III from that of previous phases was the
characteristics of the migrants, specifically the younger white-collar residents and
entertainers who lived in the apartment buildings. Unlike previous migrants, the
majority of these migrants into Hanayama during this phase did not have a positive
value on the building and maintenance of strong, durable social relationships within
their area of residence. They had less formal education and far less occupational and
economic stability than other residents of Hanayama or previous migrants. For the
most part, they consciously held themselves apart from each other and from the
neighborhood residents.

Secondly, the rate of migration was far greater than the rate of immigration
in previous phases. Even if these later Phase III migrants had actively sought to blend
into the social milieu of the neighborhood, their success would be questionable. The
number of people coming in, in batches as new apartment buildings opened, physically
isolated from older residents by the structural nature of the apartment buildings,
seldom sharing similar occupational or social backgrounds, would have put a stress
on the social mechanisms of the neighborhood perhaps beyond their absorptive
capacity. In combination with the disinterest and sometimes active hostility of the

new migrants toward being absorbed, especially with the concomitant decline in the effectiveness of the formal Neighborhood Association, the rate of migration made the successful incorporation of more than a very small minority of the new migrants impossible.

Finally, in addition to all of the above, the growth of the neighborhood may have reached the point where the old patterns of social interaction were simply swamped by numbers, a trend which seems to have begun at the end of the previous phase. With the population doubling yet again in Phase III, there were probably more adults in Hanayama than anyone could keep in touch with.

The impact of migration on Hanayama during Phase III was to continue to break up the cohesiveness of social relationships which had bound the neighborhood into a social entity in the previous phases. These processes had continued to the point where, in 1975, the neighborhood was no longer considered by most of its inhabitants as a social entity in any sense of the term. The mechanisms of absorption and incorporation of immigrants into the patterns of social interaction in the neighborhood had been swamped by a flood of migrants who, on the whole, had no desire to be incorporated or in any way involved in its activity.

CHAPTER VI

Constraints and Continuity:

Patterns of Social Change

The last four chapters have described the historical sequence of the development of the neighborhood of Hanayama. During the colonial period of the late nineteenth century, the national government initiated serious migration into Hokkaido, set the stage for the evolution of the small hamlet of Sapporo into a modern metropolis, and granted land that would become the neighborhood of Hanayama to three militia families. In the first quarter of the twentieth century, colonization of Hokkaido progressed at a steady if not spectacular rate, the neighborhood grew as shopkeepers and white and blue-collar employees settled, and a web of social networks was woven binding the residents into a highly integrated social fabric.

The prewar (1925-1932), China War (1933-1941) and Pacific War (1941-1945) periods saw the emergence of Hokkaido as the only surviving colonial territory and the least physically damaged part of Japan. The economic boom of the postwar phase (1945-1965) triggered rapid population growth in Sapporo and in the neighborhood of Hanayama. The migration into Sapporo included large numbers of demobilized service personnel and civilians repatriated from the former colonies. In spite of the disparate backgrounds of migrants, Hanayama maintained its social cohesion throughout the phase. The final period, 1965-1988, saw the continued economic and population growth of Sapporo and the neighborhood. This is also when the dissolution of the neighborhood as a social entity occurred as the forms of social organization that had maintained social integration in the past were weakened by the rapid influx of the entertainers, a social group with a different and incompatible adaptation to its environment, and by changes in the physical geography of the neighborhood. The pattern of growth thus portrayed is first one of gradual growth over many decades with the maintenance of strong social articulation, followed by the sudden dissolution of the social fabric coincident with the flood of entertainers into the neighborhood during the final period.

This final chapter discusses the question of representativeness, shows how each group was adapting to its environments, social and physical, using Barth's concept of constraints in the context of a cost-benefit model of individual choice making, and points out some of the implications that this material may have for the study of cities.

Analytical Perspective:

The previous chapters have presented a view of social relationships in Hanayama that shift through time but which, at any given point, can be seen as static, a web of nodes and linkages. This view is inherent in the network model. Were one to be tied to this model exclusively, it would make explanations of change, as opposed to descriptions of change, difficult. In order to examine change itself, we must shift our paradigm, in Kuhn's (1962) sense and examine the same material from a different perspective. The shift in paradigm is akin to shifting from Firth's idea of social structure to his view of social organization (1964). The shift from networks to another perceptual framework, like Firth's structure and organization, "[is] primarily [a matter] of emphasis. They represented different ways of looking at the same material; they are complementary, not opposed concepts." (1954; 35)

Patterns of social relationships will change where changes in constraints have made existing patterns impossible, improbable, or unprofitable. The concept of constraints, taken from Barth (1965:196), is that they are strategic barriers defining and delimiting the range of possible behavior by individuals. This is done by making some choices desirable, practical, and profitable and others undesirable, impractical, and unprofitable. Individual members of a social category will attempt to optimize their positions by choosing the favorable choices and rejecting the unfavorable ones. For example, a migrant moving into Hanayama will not find it profitable to spend time and effort building up a large, residence based social network if it is likely that he or she will be transferred away from the neighborhood within a short period of time. However, a migrant expecting to remain in the neighborhood for a decade or more can afford to spend the time and effort necessary to build up a large social network as he or she will be able to reap the benefits. Thus, the length of time of expected stay in the neighborhood constrains the behavior of both migrants, channeling their behavior into divergent patterns.

The networks discussed previously are the result of a great many decisions made over time and categorized by the socioeconomic status of the individuals making them. The changes in social relationships observed in Hanayama can be understood, not as the result of changes in the ultimate goals of the population, but rather as adaptations by various sets of people to shifting social and physical constraints.

One of the advantages of using the concept of constraints to behavior is that it avoids an argument for social changes based on posited shifts in the ultimate life goals or basic values of the population. There are several important points here. If a value shift is posited, then it must be demonstrated for each of the social sets through time. There are methodological problems involved in such a demonstration. How can one test the value structure, in an objective manner, of the residents of the neighborhood in 1925? Therefore, explanations that avoid such a problem are superior. There is also an application of Occam's Razor. Positing the value shifts is an extra step, a more complex solution but one not giving a better answer than the more simple solution. Given the equality of the solutions, the simple one is preferred. Thus, it would be adequate to disallow the value shift argument on the basis of simplicity alone. However, in addition, the informants' perception of the neighborhood was that the values had not significantly changed. Further, in the discussion of various socioeconomic groups, it will be suggested that if the ultimate life goals had shifted, other shifts peculiar to each group would have been expected but did not in fact occur.

Types of Change:

The various characteristics of the networks of the groups discussed show three logical possibilities: significant change in a consistent direction, no significant change, and variation which may or may not be significant but which is not consistent in direction. The problem is not only to explain the significant shifts but also to explain those characteristics showing minor change, no change, or inconsistent change. It is the pattern of continuity and change that needs to be explained, not just the big shifts.

The four major categories of constraints that have shifted are: 1) the physical geography of the area including the shape and structure of the city, population density, and the relative positions of places of employment relative to places of residence; 2) the amount and types of resources available for individual allocation reflected in land or building ownership and tenure in the neighborhood; 3) the types of socially acceptable behavior and the kinds of sanctions imposed for violations; and 4) the type and degree of influence exerted on the neighborhood from higher political systems such as the city, the prefecture, and the nation.

Unfortunately for the clarity of this discussion, there are no clear one-to-one cause-and-effect relationships among the categories of constraints and shifts in the social networks. The constraints act on social behavior in combination, not individually. Thus the visible results, the shifts in the social networks, are the result of various changes in the constraints, even to the possibility that a shift in one constraint might have its effect canceled out by a shift in another. For example, the social effect of increased ownership of private telephones may well have partly counteracted the effects of steadily increasing population density and increased distance from natal areas during Phase II (1945-1965). In spite of this complexity, there are some adaptive patterns discernible in the network shifts of the various socioeconomic groups. For example, the older white-collar group has withdrawn from most of the other residents in the neighborhood in response to the ever increasing numbers of entertainers and the shopkeepers maintain high density networks only with other older residents of the neighborhood.

The value, as expressed in interviews, for maintaining large social networks of long durability and high intensity remained unchanged throughout the study period;

it also remained for ultimate life goals such as economic security, social relationships that were stable and rewarding, including family relationships, and occupational success. What altered were the social and physical conditions in which the older white-collar residents, male and female, had to operate. The greatly increased adult population in Phase III, with its migrants who did not share the value of large, residence-based social networks, made it impossible to maintain either the density or, more importantly, the intensity of the social relationships which had been the norm in previous times. The intensity of the social relationships of the older white-collar females was not as affected as that of the males, because the female networks were much more limited.

Thus, the older white-collar females could and did maintain networks similar in content, that is, durability, intensity, and frequency, to those which they had always had. The only major change for females was that their networks incorporated proportionately fewer people within the neighborhood. The increase of frequency of contact reported was a function of the increased incidence of private telephones in the neighborhood, particularly in the homes of the older white-collar households and the shopkeepers' stores.

The question, then, is why the other shifts in the social and physical environment that had such marked effects on other social groups did not affect the older white-collar group. The answer lies in the position of the older white-collar group in the economic, political, and social order. To a large extent, the older white-collar group is much more insulated from change than are other groups. This is the most wealthy group, the only one, for example, where a large majority of the informants owned their own dwellings. This group also had the most local political power and social prestige. During the study period, the amount of money and time, which are key resources in the formation and maintenance of social links, increased substantially. This is also the group least involved with, and affected by, the changes in the socially accepted behavior constraint. The older white-collar group's ideas about socially acceptable behavior changed very little compared to that of other groups, as might be expected for an older, relatively wealthy group.

Finally, the older white-collar residents employed a concept of friendship or neighborliness based on a degree of mutual trust not shared by the other groups. The older white-collar adults had access to more information due to the strength of their relationships with each other and to the other long-term residents of the neighborhood, notably the older shopkeepers. This appears to be support for Robert's (1973:9-10) argument that it is the information exchanged that determines the strength of the social relationships. It is the exchange of information that leads to the trust necessary for strong social relationships. The older white-collar residents adapted to the decrease in available information caused by the shopkeepers' decline as information brokers by reducing the relative size (density) of their networks within the neighborhood and lowering the intensity (obligations) of the less important or more recent contacts.

Shopkeepers:

The shopkeepers, on the other hand, were forced out of their social patterns by what were primarily economic forces. Here again, we must divide the shopkeepers into older and newer groups. The older shopkeepers, those whose networks actually changed, had to change or close. The interesting feature is not that they changed, but that they changed as minimally as possible and still operated viable businesses. Where the old patterns still worked, as in the links with the other older shopkeepers, the older white-collar group, and the landladies, they were maintained and new links forged. Where the old patterns became increasingly dysfunctional, as in the case of the entertainers and the younger white-collar group, the shopkeeper networks show large shifts such as the decreases in durability, density, and intensity.

Part of the reason for the shifts in network patterns is found in the economic environment of Sapporo. In the previous periods, the competition from the large "downtown" establishments had not directly impinged upon the small neighborhood retail establishments. With improved transportation within the city and the growth of the "downtown" department stores, there was increasingly direct competition.

Further, the small, local neighborhood retailers had another major source of competition. Supermarkets, small by American standards but far larger than the traditional food markets, began spreading in Sapporo in the early 1960's, with one going up in the adjoining neighborhood in the early 1970's. The supermarkets, like the department stores, carried a larger variety of goods than did the neighborhood stores. It is impossible to assess the precise amount of money lost because of the nearby supermarket, but it was seen as a serious threat by those shopkeepers whose shops stocked the same or similar goods which the supermarkets carried and, in fact, many of these stores either went out of business completely by 1988 or radically shifted their products. The old shopkeepers whose businesses were threatened by the supermarket thought that the best way to compete was by means of applying a "personal touch" with their customers. In this way the older shopkeepers were able to continue strong networks of regular customers among the older neighborhood residents, who preferred such an approach over the impersonal variety of the supermarkets or the department stores. However, when asked if this approach was successful, the shopkeeper tended to give a rather dismal gesture indicating that no great success was achieved. Pressed further, the shopkeepers said that it worked well with older customers, but that the younger people "didn't care about that any more."

The older shopkeepers also gave discounts in the form of extra goods. This was the practice of adding extra goods at no extra cost or rounding a bill down for regular customers, for example, selling eleven pieces of fruit for the price of ten or charging ¥200 instead of ¥218. It has been suggested that the shopkeepers also may have extended short-term credit to their customers, reinforcing their customer's sense of obligation to them but this was not possible to verify, even upon examination of one set of accounts. However, it was clear that the shopkeeper had received considerable short-term credit from his suppliers, which would have strongly reinforced that relationship. All of the shopkeepers interviewed said that they gave no credit (an illegal activity under the leading laws), but two long-term neighborhood residents said that at the end of the war and during the occupation and reconstruction periods, small amounts of credit were commonly allowed in the form of permitting favored customers to delay payment of their bills.

The new shopkeepers, operating services rather than the small retail establishments of the old shopkeepers, were not in the neighborhood long enough to experience the shifts in social networks found among the older shopkeepers. The newer shopkeepers did not attempt to build up the extensive networks like those that the older shopkeepers had kept up in previous phases and still saw as the best way to do business. The newer shopkeepers looked to "modern," impersonal business methods for their approach. The newer shopkeepers did try to build a habitual clientele, but they did not try to maintain relationships outside business transactions. As the newer shopkeepers operated services--restaurants, bars, and coffee houses--catering primarily to the younger residents in the area, their approach appeared to mesh with what their customers expected and wanted.

The newer shopkeepers appeared to be successful. Their clientele was made up of regular younger residents of the nearby areas, plus a small drift-in trade. The newer shopkeepers, like the older shopkeepers, gave small discounts to favored, regular customers. The newer shopkeepers were impersonal only in relative terms. Americans, used to extremely impersonal relationships in shops, would find the newer shopkeeper interactions with their customers personal. For example, the shopkeepers tried to learn the names, company affiliations, and other personal information about their regular customers. They would be solicitous of the comfort of the customer, whether the coffee was strong enough or the brand of beer was the one the customer preferred. This personal care was one of the attractions of this type of shop. As a younger white-collar employee who worked nearby said,

> It's nice to go for lunch to a place where they know you, isn't it? I come here every day with my friends about 11:30. When we walk in the door, the owner greets us by name; there are always seats saved for us, and our lunches have already been started so we don't have to wait very long.

This kind of service is rare in the United States except in certain old and quiet bars.

On the other hand, the newer shopkeepers limited their relationships with customers. One of them said:

> When I close, that's it. I don't want to be a cook twenty-four hours a day, just while the restaurant is open. This (kind of) restaurant is good for that; people who eat here don't live nearby, so I don't see them except when they come in to eat. That's a nice part of the work, isn't it?

This attitude contrasts sharply with that of the older shopkeepers who made little distinction between working and non-working time.

Thus the shift perceived in the shopkeeper networks was the result of a selective shift in the older shopkeeper networks and the intrusion into the shopkeeper category of a subgroup with an adaptation radically different from that of the older shopkeepers. However, while the approaches of these two subgroups differed, their economic and social goals were similar. All of the shopkeepers conceived of themselves as independent, not tied to an economic and social web of "working for someone else," the way they perceived the white- and blue-collar employees. The shopkeeper goals in life were modest: enough income for a modicum of consumer goods, the ability to educate their children, and to attain a comfortable level of economic security, enough to sustain themselves in their old age. None of the shopkeepers wanted to build their establishments into large enterprises. The universally expressed goal was to maintain their independence.

The gender differentiation found in the networks of the older white-collar group was also present in the networks of the newer shopkeepers, but not in the networks of the older shopkeepers. The older white-collar residents and newer shopkeepers developed different social environments for males and females. The newer shopkeeper females were more likely to be employed, always in the shop, than were the older white-collar females, but their position in the shop was subservient to that of their husbands. Further, about half of the newer shopkeeper females were not directly employed at all. That is, they would "help out" on an extensive basis but without remuneration. The social and physical environments of the male and the female older shopkeepers were identical except for some variation common to Japanese gender roles. For example, the males were more likely to handle that part of the business dealing with suppliers and wholesalers, while the females were more likely to do the books. Even in interactions with the same people, the females would use the more polite--and more subservient--speech patterns, while the males would use the more informal and egalitarian forms. Thus while there was some variation among the older shopkeepers, it was minimal. For example, the females knew the suppliers and if necessary, as in the case of illness of the male, could take over that aspect of the business. For dealings with regular customers, the females might drop into informal speech patterns and, for strangers, the males would use the polite forms. One possible reason for the difference between the older shopkeeper female networks and those of the older white-collar and newer shopkeeper females was the older shopkeeper females had considerable economic power because of their constant, even equal, involvement within the family business. The older white-collar and newer shopkeeper females had no equivalent economic leverage and were more traditional in their social interactions.

Summary of Older Groups:

These two groups--the older white-collar group, and the shopkeepers both of whom lived in the neighborhood from 1925 to 1988 (see neighborhood tenure chart, Table 7), displayed adaptations to changing social conditions, but both of them have adapted minimally to the shifting conditions in the neighborhood. The older white-collar group had their primary economic ties outside the neighborhood and were, in a social sense, well established with high job security and stable prestige. The shopkeepers displayed two patterns: the older shopkeepers adapted to the new economic conditions by trying to reinforce the old social networks, and the newer shopkeepers established different social patterns suitable for what they saw as modern life. The older shopkeepers had stable prestige but little economic security, while the newer shopkeepers had neither, at least in the neighborhood of Hanayama. The size of the store did not appear to be important.

To return briefly to a point raised at the beginning of this chapter, the possibility of a shift in ultimate life goals or values in the Japanese population over the sixty-year period of this study, the minimal shift of the older white-collar residents and the shopkeepers appears to indicate that a value shift has been minimal or has not occurred at all. If a significant change in the basic values or ultimate life goals had occurred among these groups, then one would expect something other than absolute minimal adaptation to shifting conditions. The minimal shift that actually occurred then, is evidence--albeit not proof--that the value shift has not occurred.

Younger White-Collar:

The group living in the neighborhood throughout the sixty-year period was the younger white-collar group. The least economically well off but the most upwardly mobile of the three groups, white-collars displayed a pattern of network shifts that most clearly demonstrate the idea of network shifts that most clearly demonstrate the idea of network patterns reflecting adaptations to shifting physical and social conditions. The network patterns of the younger white-collar group have been affected by almost all of the constraints mentioned for the other groups.

The change in the physical geography of the city and in the neighborhood prevented the maintenance of high density networks; it isolated the individual younger white-collar families from both other younger white-collar households and non-younger white-collar households and, because time could be spent by employed younger white-collar adults in the neighborhood, the intensity and reachability of relationships decreased, especially for the younger white-collar males. The aspects of physical change involved were population increases, the intrusion into the neighborhood of apartment buildings where many younger white-collar families lived, and the extension of places of employment to a progressively greater area requiring more time for commuting to and from work. The constraining effects of increased neighborhood population density and decreased time, one of the major allocatable resources of employed younger white-collar workers, is clear, but the impact of the apartment buildings is more complex.

There is much literature on the design of housing and the social interaction patterns that correlate with various designs in the United States (cf. articles by Milgram, Rainwater, Yancy and Swartz in Helmer and Eddington 1973). Here the task is to show how the changes in physical geography of the neighborhood prevented patterns of previously existing behavior from continuing. By 1940 all of the housing in the neighborhood was single-family housing or duplexes. This situation remained until 1965, albeit with increasing housing density, when the first apartment buildings were constructed in Hanayama. The Japanese pattern of traditional neighborliness includes contacts with the three houses opposite and the house on either side. These houses in particular were the ones where one introduced oneself on moving into the neighborhood and with whose residents one tried to stay on good terms. As the housing density increased, the physical area of this "inner sphere" contracted, but the basic pattern could remain unbroken. That is, the houses on either side might be closer than in the previous generation, but they were still single-family houses or duplexes where the same pattern could be and was maintained. Much of the social interaction of Hanayama involved informal interactions in the area outside of the houses, although somewhat less so because of the climate than in Old Japan.

The apartment buildings broke up this pattern of formal and informal social interaction in two important respects. The first was physical: the apartment buildings had little or no exterior space wherein social interaction could occur, (Cf. Mock 1988), unless the middle of the street was used. The neighbor on the apartment-building side became a huge edifice, not a family with whom one can interact. The "family" next door became up to forty-two separate households. The second important aspect was social and involved the perception of the apartment resident. The apartments were of two major types, company owned and privately owned. In the only company owned apartment building Hanayama, there was something in common among the tenants: they all worked for Japan Railways. This one apartment building was also homogeneous in its make-up, all of the residents being from younger white-collar households. These elements allowed interaction somewhat similar to those found among single-family housing households, but were not found in the privately owned apartment buildings. The privately owned apartment buildings had heterogeneous populations that were, furthermore, extremely short term. Finally, many of the apartment residents were entertainers who did not share the neighborliness necessary for the maintenance of the kind of previously valued social interaction patterns. From this, it was clear that the "three houses across and one on each side" rule did not translate to "Three apartments across and one on each side."

A cautious parallel can be drawn between the residents of small apartments in that started appearing in Hanayama in the middle 1960s and the white-collar residents of the more famous danchi, the blocks of apartment houses found in the great southern cities. The Hanayama apartments are similar to the danchi in the amount of interior space (250 to 300 square feet) and in the physical arrangement of exterior space. Keifer, in a study of a white-collar Osaka danchi (1976), found a lack of communality and an apathy toward developing social relationships with other people in the area. He thought that "the non-communality of the typical danchi resident stems from a lack of any stake in the future" and the nature of the Japanese white-collar employee, "who works in a highly structured social environment remote from the community both in space and values." The work environment makes demand on time and loyalty because Japanese bureaucracies still retain an ethos of personal dedication and self-sacrifice for the interest of group goals (Keifer 1976:20). The Hanayama younger white-collar residents displayed a similar pattern because of their short-term involvement and the demands on the males by their places of employment. Like Keifer's danchi residents, the Hanayama apartment residents

> ...not only scoffed at the idea of their neighbors telling them how to run the community, but also considered the responsibility for leadership to rest outside the community--usually with the local and national government . . . (Keifer 1976:21).

Nearly all of the Hanayama apartment residents expressed sentiments of unconcern and disinterest in community affairs and activities. By the end of the period, there were two very large apartment buildings, danchi in any sense of the term.

There were a number of features that might contribute to the difference in attitudes between the apartment and single-family housing residents, but they are complex. The apartments, on the whole, were much smaller than the single-family housing. The privacy allowed by the inexpensive construction methods was far less than that in the single-family houses. By American standards, there was almost no privacy in the apartments. Conversations, in normal speaking tones, could be heard in adjoining apartments during the day and often, in the quiet of the night, conversations could be clearly distinguished from as far as three apartments away. Other noises, flushing sounds, water in pipes, doors opening and closing, could be heard for most of the nearby units. Does the lessened domestic privacy increase the need for social privacy? Certainly this is not true across cultural boundaries. For example, the Japanese tend to have far less domestic privacy and appear to need less social privacy than do Americans. But within a given culture, it might be an important consideration.

Another element that would be important in the United States, ownership versus tenancy, was not crucial in Hanayama. Most of the single-family housing residents in the neighborhood did not own their own houses. Perin (1977) argues that American perceive home ownership as an almost essential part of respectable living. This does not appear to be true in Hanayama. Home ownership was a mark of wealth and the one younger white-collar family who owned its own house was unique because of the unusual wealth. However, even among the wealthiest group in the neighborhood, the older white-collar residents, only about half owned their own homes, and all of these had bought them before 1955. As houses and land have become increasingly expensive, home ownership remains a dream, but it is becoming a rare reality and disappeared entirely in Hanayama. However, housing on the outskirts of Sapporo remains somewhat less expensive than housing in the great urban centers of Japan.

Of the allocatable resources that the younger white-collar residents had, there had been several changes, but only two acted as severe constraints on their social relationships. Their incomes had increased greatly in real buying power over the previous half century and job security was high; thus the younger white-collar adults had more money to spend. The effect of this change was the opposite of constraint; it opened up new possibilities.

The other two major resources, however, had decreased. The primary decrease had been in time, both in absolute and in relative terms. Although they spent fewer hours at work than their counterparts had fifty years before, they spent more time outside of the neighborhood in work and work-related activities (e.g., work, commuting, after-work activities) than their counterparts had. Also, more younger females were employed outside the neighborhood than previously had been the case, a trend that appears to be increasing. The third resource, emotion, was closely tied in with time. Previously, the amount of time and emotion that a younger white-collar male was expected to and did invest in his relationship with his family was minimal (cf. Vogel 1963). Although a precise measurement of emotional investment is not possible, the perception of the neighborhood informants strongly suggested that the younger white-collar males were investing far more time and emotion in their families than had previously been the case. One younger white-collar male expressed this idea forcefully:

> I lived here (in Hanayama rather than a suburb) so I can see my children sometimes. If I lived out in the suburbs, I would never see my children--or my wife. I don't want to be a "lodger papa" (*geshukunin papa*) like some of the people at work.

A similar situation had evolved for the younger white-collar females, who tended to focus on their families to the exclusion of almost all other considerations. This trend toward an exclusive family orientation, particularly among younger white-collar housewives, had been noted nationwide in Japan. There is even a term, partly borrowed from English, used in the popular and academic press to label this orientation: *mai homu shugi* ("my homism" or, more literally, "the principle of my home"). In Hanayama, "my-homism" is such that some of the younger white-collar females knew no one else in the neighborhood, even their landladies. One of the more important sources of information concerning both the male and female shifts came from older white-collar informants. On the whole, the older white-collar residents seem to have approved of the male trend, although the older white-collar males often warned that the younger white-collar males' careers would suffer. The trend toward "my-homism" in the younger white-collar females was viewed ambiguously. The focus on children was generally considered good, but the disinterest in her neighbor and the social life of the community was looked upon with disfavor, sometimes even seen as selfish.

Another element involved was the increasing geographical distance between the younger white-collar males and their natal families as shown in Table 27. Although communications had become easier because of the post office and the telephone, face-to-face interaction between the younger white-collar males and their natal families was decreasing because the younger white-collar males' families were more likely to live away from Sapporo than they had in previous times as shown in Table 33.

The result of all these features had been to reduce the resources available to the development of neighborhood relationships, particularly for the younger white-collar males. The females' situation was somewhat similar but with some major differences. The effect on the females of working outside the neighborhood has obviously diminished the average amount of time available for constructing neighborhood links but has greatly increased the extra-neighborhood possibilities. Relatively few of the younger white-collar females have employment outside of the neighborhood (only four out of twenty-eight informants, probably not more than fifteen out of a total of eighty-nine younger white-collar females in Hanayama in 1976), but their network patterns are sufficiently different to skew the group averages.

The difference between the male and female pattern shifts is mainly a function of gender roles. By investing more time and emotion into their families, the males were moving closer to what has traditionally been the role for younger white-collar females. In Hanayama, the females' exclusive focus on their children has been reinforced by the geographical proximity of their natal kin, with whom a great interest in the children is shared. The females' kin were slightly more likely to live in Sapporo than were the males' kin. However, the figures for the neighborhood, less than 20% for the males and about 33% for the females, were far lower than those found by other analysts looking at kin networks in the south. For Tokyo, for example, Koyama (1970) reported 40% of the kin living in the immediate area, and Nojiri (1974) reported 48%.

The younger white-collar group was, not unexpectedly, one of the groups (with the entertainers) who had to adapt most readily to shifts in generally acceptable social behavior. The three most noticeable features have been shifts in company policies with respect to transfers of employees, the gradual decrease in some traditional customs, and the decrease in the incidence of living units with more than one adult generation represented. The increased incidence of company transfers reduced the tenure in the neighborhood--the stake the younger white-collar residents felt they had in Hanayama. The decline of customs such as O-hirome had inhibited the information flow essential to the establishment and maintenance of strong interpersonal relationships. The decline of multi-generational household, at least to 1975, shown on Tables 38 and 39, a trend most strongly marked by the rise of single-person households from none in 1925 to almost 15%(a total of 59 households) in 1975 indicates a loss of multi-generational lines of communication.

The younger white-collar group was particularly affected because they were at the most vulnerable stage in network development. Long-term residence in a given area, traditional customs build around network-building transactions, and the presence of an older generation were all paths through which networks could be expanded and maintained. The shifts that made all of these less likely or less frequent made the forging of new relationships more difficult and therefore, as a general principle, less

Table 38. Family Composition in 1925

GROUP (n)	Head	Spouse	Child and G'child (minor)	Child and G'child (adult)	Spouse of Child	Parent	Other Related	Other Non-related
Farmers (2)*								
Male (9)	2	-	5	2	-	-	-	-
Female (6)	-	1	3	-	2	-	-	-
Younger White-Collar (13)*								
Male (20)	13	-	6	-	-	1	-	-
Female (24)	-	13	8	-	-	3	-	-
Older White-Collar (7)*								
Male (13)	7	-	4	1	-	-	1	-
Female (15)	-	6	5	2	-	1	-	1
Blue-Collar (5)*								
Male (13)	5	-	6	1	-	-	1	-
Female (14)	-	5	7	-	1	1	-	-
Shopkeeper (16)*								
Male (35)	15	-	15	3	-	1	1	-
Female (40)	1	14	17	2	2	2	1	1
SUBTOTAL								
Male (90)	42	-	36	7	-	2	3	-
Female (99)	1	39	40	4	5	7	1	2
PERCENTAGE								
Male	46.7	--	40.0	7.8	--	2.2	3.3	--
Female	1.0	39.4	40.4	4.0	5.1	7.1	1.0	2.0
TOTAL (189)	43	39	76	11	5	9	4	2
	22.8	39.4	40.2	5.8	2.6	4.8	2.1	1.1

Number of Households in Sample.....43
Number of Households in Hanayama...43
* number of households in this group

Table 39. Family Composition in 1975

GROUP (n)	Head	Spouse	Child and G'child (minor)	Child and G'child (adult)	Spouse of Child	Parent	Other Related	Other Non-related
Younger White-Collar (28)*								
Male (47)	28	-	17	-	-	1	1	-
Female (46)	-	26	14	-	-	4	-	2
Older White-Collar (23)*								
Male (28)	23	-	1	2	1	-	1	-
Female (28)	-	23	-	1	2	-	1	-
Shopkeeper (16)*								
Male (26)	15	-	6	1	-	1	1	2
Female (29)	1	14	6	-	1	3	1	1
Blue-Collar (9)*								
Male (15)	9	-	6	-	-	-	-	-
Female (19)	-	9	7	-	-	1	-	-
Landlady (14)*								
Male (18)	6	-	7	2	1	-	2	-
Female (26)	8	7	3	1	2	-	1	4
Entertainer (19)*								
Male (20)	19	-	1	-	-	-	-	-
Female (20)	-	19	1	-	-	-	-	-
SUBTOTAL (109)*								
Male (154)	100	-	38	5	2	2	5	2
Female (164)	8	9	98	31	2	5	8	3
PERCENTAGE								
Male	61.2	--	27.3	3.6	1.4	1.4	3.6	1.4
Female	6.0	55.7	20.8	1.3	3.4	3.4	2.0	5.4
TOTAL (318)	109	98	69	7	7	10	8	10
	34.3	30.8	21.7	2.2	2.2	3.1	2.5	3.1

Number of Households in Sample.....................109
Number of Households in Hanayama...................394
Number of single family households (not counted)...54

* number of households in this group

likely. The values of the younger white-collar group toward the advantages of building an extensive network did not appear to have changed significantly. Almost all of the younger white-collar informants, 32 out of 37, both male and female, thought that extensive networks were not of the best ways to "get ahead," but an even higher number cited one or more of the reasons discussed here, in one form or another, as factors making it difficult or impossible to emulate the path of current older white-collar groups:

> I should know my neighbors but with the children, I really don't have the time. If we lived in an old fashioned way, with grandparents then I could get out sometimes. Of course, then I would have to live with a mother-in-law in the same house.
> younger white-collar housewife

> I've only lived here for six months and I don't know anyone (around here). Why should I? I'll probably be transferred again soon. I want to live in Tokyo if I can.
> unmarried younger white-collar male

In almost all statements of this sort were mixed comments expressing sentiments about modernity, the value of individual freedom and economic independence.

The comments on modernity were both positive and negative. Although almost all the younger white-collar informants expressed positive attitudes towards what they perceived as personal independence, most of them also expressed reservations about what they perceived as too much freedom. In spite of their concern for personal freedom, most of them were locked into what most Americans would see as oppressively structured work situations, and all of them expressed strong sentiments on the value of stable family life.

If the values toward building extensive networks had significantly shifted, some concomitant behavioral shifts could be expected. Perhaps the most important of these would be away from building up networks anywhere, not just in the residential area. That is, if the values had shifted, then we should not find younger white-collar residents building networks not only in their areas of residence but also at their places of employment. Further, we would expect to find a reduction in the degree of maintenance of kin networks. If fact, none of these expectations are met. The younger white-collar residents of Hanayama are quite vigorous in building up networks at their places of employment and in maintaining their kin networks. A crucial point to remember is that those younger white-collar residents who had prospects of remaining in the neighborhood for extensive periods, such as those living in the company owned single-family housing, did make efforts to build up networks based on residential proximity. It was those younger white-collar residents who were operating under external constraints, usually that of having only a short period in the neighborhood, who did not seek at least minimally to expand their social networks based on residential proximity.

Under these circumstances, the decline of the formal organizations, the Neighborhood Association and the tonari gumi was important. These organizations could have provided the framework for establishing the strong social relationships that the younger white-collar group expressed an interest in building, a function that these organizations had performed in the past. In fact, the tonari gumi structures, even in decline, were instrumental in the development of the extensive landlady networks. The key element in their decline appears to be the apartment residents' apathy and lack of support. These organizations required high levels of cooperation in order to function. As the high levels of cooperation declined with the migration of the apartment residents into the neighborhood, the organizations decayed. The less effective they became, the less cooperation was forthcoming, and the rate of decay accelerated.

Support for this suggestion as to the causes of the decay of the Hanayama Neighborhood Association comes from a study of a neighborhood association in Kanazawa, a large city in Honshu. In this study, Falconeri suggests that the chonaikai, the neighborhood association, is a fragile gemeinschaft institution that rapid urbanization may inevitably destroy. As he describes the process,

...the neighborly milieu where public and private considerations have often meshed for the community good is now pervaded by a social ennui where self-interest and community disinterest may prevail. Under such conditions neighbors may conclude that such local organizations as the *chonaikai*...are no longer effective in maintaining social cohesion and neighborhood identity...(1976:34)

His findings are a fair description of the sequence in Hanayama. The migration of the disinterested entertainers undermined the effectiveness of the Neighborhood Association and the tonari gumi to the point where the younger white-collar apartment residents would have been able to use them for building social networks only with great difficulty. The combined disinterest of the entertainers and the younger white-collar apartment residents was sufficient to undermine their effectiveness for the entire neighborhood. Only a group such as the landladies who were determined to build up extensive social networks and were not constrained by other forces could utilize the tonari gumi once the decay was well started.

New Groups:

The two new groups in the neighborhood, the landladies and the entertainers, cannot be looked at in quite the same manner as those groups represented throughout the neighborhood's history, because they had not been in the neighborhood long enough to display patterns of adjustment. These two groups do, however, represent two very different adaptations to conditions in the most recent phase of the neighborhood.

Landladies:

The landladies, mostly older people, appeared to be taking the more traditional approach of constructing extensive neighborhood-based networks. Given the economics of running an apartment house, this was a viable choice. The landladies' businesses depended largely on personal reputation. Because they usually did not have large reserves of capital, prolonged vacancies could easily lead to economic disaster. Thus, it paid for the landladies to expend time and effort in the building up of their reputations through extensive social contacts. The density of the neighborhood did not affect their relationships with their own tenants or with the other older groups in the neighborhood, the older white-collar residents and the shopkeepers. They spent almost all of their time in the neighborhood and by 1975 were definitely established as long-term residents. Their economic stake in the neighborhood was greater than that of most of the older white-collar residents and roughly equal to that of the older group of shopkeepers. Although, as previously mentioned, renting did not automatically correlate with marginality, ownership, or part ownership, it was a clear indication of permanence. Permanence, in turn, was a key element in establishing network links, even if the permanence was perceived for the future rather than a past social fact because the permanence promotes higher levels of trust than would be otherwise possible.

Entertainers:

Contrasting strongly with almost all aspects of landladies' adaptation to the neighborhood was the adaptation of the entertainers. Although the entertainers as a social category have historical traditions of some depth (cf. Plath 1964), the group of entertainers living in Hanayama represented the bottom end of the entertainer social continuum. They were very young--averaging in their early twenties--had low incomes, occupations of relatively low prestige if some glamour, and low educational levels. As a descriptive sample of one apartment building in 1975, the occupations of the entertainers were bartender (2 males), waitress (1 female), bar hostess (13 females), coffee house waiter (1 male) and short-order cook (1 male). The average tenure lin the neighborhood for this group was a little less than 15 months; the median was 7 months.

The entertainers' adaptation to their environment was one of maintaining social distance from other people living in the name neighborhood. Almost all of the entertainers' relationships were outside the neighborhood, focused on the area where they were employed, the entertainment district of Susukino. The constraints operating on their behavior were many and varied. First, the entertainers worked nights, from about six in the evening to about two in the morning. Almost everyone else in the neighborhood worked during the day except some of the Japan Railways employees who worked variable shifts. Second, the entertainers had low prestige, which affected both their perceptions of other people in Hanayama and others' perceptions of them. Third, the entertainers as a group did not share many of the otherwise accepted values found in Hanayama, notably the value of extensive residential social networks. The entertainers perceived their current place of residence as transitional, a perception born out of their one-year average length of neighborhood residence. The entertainers saw themselves as being modern, not bound by traditional webs of social relationships. None of the entertainer households had more than one adult generation. None of the entertainers thought that traditional social bonding customs such as O-hirome was worthwhile. None of the entertainers thought that the Neighborhood Association or the tonari gumi were worth much, although a few did belong--invariably those who had lived in the neighborhood for several years or those whose landladies were han-cho, a tonari gumi head. These factors indicate constraints operating on the entertainers in their relationships with non-entertainers in the neighborhood, but it does not adequately explain the entertainers' lack of relationships with other Hanayama entertainers.

The lack of entertainer-entertainer relationships within the neighborhood appears to have been a function of how entertainer relationships were formed. Most of the entertainers found their jobs through social contacts formed in their area of origin outside Sapporo, sometimes apparently through direct recruitment by the entertainment establishments. The relationships that they formed in Sapporo appear to have been almost exclusively centered around their places of employment. Although most of the entertainers in the neighborhood knew a few other entertainers, usually at least one in the same building through whom they found their apartments, there were no mechanisms for nor interest in forming relationships with other entertainers working indifferent establishments. There was also some evidence, for example work choice during interview, indicating that the entertainers may have maintained the oyabun-kobun-type fictive kin relationships with work-related people similar to those described by Bennet and Ishino (1963). If this were true, then the paternalistic patron-client pattern of the oyabun-kobun bonds would constrain sharply the information of new network contracts. Finally, the transience of the entertainer tenure in the neighborhood would seem to affect entertainer-entertainer relationships as readily as it did entertainer-non-entertainer links.

It would be easy to dismiss the entertainers as a marginal population not sharing the same ultimate life goals of the rest of the people in Hanayama. Although the data do not clearly suggest this is not true, neither does it support the idea. Further, as discussed earlier, the assumption of different life goals or values appears to be an unnecessary step The behavior of the entertainers is adequately explained by the constraints that appear to exist for them. Their lack of formal education, age, and the transitory nature of their employment and residence all appear sufficient to explain their variant patterns.

Further, although many of the entertainers expressed rather disparaging comments about their natal towns and families, all of the entertainers interview maintained some sort of contact with their natal families. Most of them also maintained other contacts in their areas of origin such as childhood friends or distant relatives. The older entertainers were more likely to take such bonds seriously, to put more time, effort, and money into their maintenance than were the younger entertainers. However, all of the entertainers maintained at least an established minimum. The pattern seemed to be that when the entertainers first migrated to Sapporo they allowed the contacts in the natal areas to become rather tenuous, possible only exchanging New Year's cards. Then, after they grew a bit older, they began putting more into these rather minimal links. The few entertainers who were in their thirties had contacts with their natal areas that were roughly the same as those maintained by younger white-collar residents of the same age. There was however, no real attempt to maintain contact in Sapporo with other migrants form the same area of origin. Except for a few close friends, none of the Hanayama entertainers knew many other migrants from their natal areas, even though, in some cases, there were thousands of co-migrants in the city.

Conclusions:

The patterns of social relationships in Hanayama have shifted over the sixty year period in ways conforming to changes in the social and physical environment. Further, this shift in social behavior can be explained in social and physical terms. Each group adapted to the environment as the constraints acting on their behavior developed. One can, therefore, avoid the problems inherent in positing an ideological shift paralleling the political and economic changes that Japan has undergone during the last half century. This is not to say, with any assurance, that such an ideological shift has not occurred, just that such a shift does not appear to have occurred in Hanayama, and such a shift is not necessary for an explanation of the changes in behavior described earlier.

There are some implications concerning these two points that should be discussed. First, Sapporo is one of the most rapidly growing cities in a country noted for rapid urbanization, modernization, and industrialization. If the pattern of ideological shift is not obvious in a Sapporo neighborhood such as Hanayama, then it would seem less likely to appear elsewhere. However, a word of caution should go with this point. It is those social groups in the neighborhood for which I have the best data--older white-collar, younger white-collar, blue-collar, and shopkeeper--that show no evidence of an ideological shift of any great magnitude. To the contrary, the data suggests that these groups are holding constant ultimate life goals such as economic and personal security and satisfaction and values such as the worth and effectiveness of having extensive social networks based on employment, kinship, and residential proximity. What changed were their tactics for achieving these goals. However, these are the groups that would be the least likely to manifest an ideological shift. The group that would be the most likely to show such a shift, the entertainers, is the group for which there is the poorest data. On the basis of severely limited data, one can only say that it appears that the entertainers have maintained many of the same goals and values as the other groups in Hanayama. Their tactic, however, for achieving their goals are contrary to the tactics employed by members of other groups in Hanayama.

The second point has implications for convergence theory. Simply put, as exemplified by Kerr et al (1960), Moore and Feldman (1960) or Kahn (1971) convergence theory asserts that as societies modernize, industrialize, and urbanize, they become more and more like Western Europe and the United States in their cultural and social forms. My finding would suggest that while this may appear true on the social surface, the ideological, the way of thinking, can and probably does remain untouched. Individuals react to constraints surrounding them but these seem to be social and physical, as in the case of Hanayama. The processes of modernization, urbanization, and industrialization contain certain social and physical constraints that operate on everyone undergoing one or more of these processes. However, the fact that people are undergoing these processes says very little about the ideology they hold.

Convergence theory has suggested that we will somehow end up with a would wide cultural base. This material from a Sapporo neighborhood suggests that this may not be the case. The social and physical imperatives of "progress" in the forms of modernization, urbanization, and industrialization might be separable from cultural forms, not merged with them. In the case of Japan, the country often talked about by convergence advocates, the social and physical imperatives of industrialization appear to have left virtually untouched Japan's set of cultural patterns. If this is true, then convergence, in the sense of merging cultural patterns or, for that matter, anything much deeper than a common technological base, would seen extremely unlikely.

LIST OF REFERENCES

Abegglen, James
    1958   *Japanese Factory.* Glencoe: The Free Press
Ashihara, Yoshinobu (translated by Lynne E. Riggs)
    1989   *The Hidden Order: Tokyo through the Twentieth Century.* Tokyo:
           Kodansha
Barnes, J.A.
    1954   Class and Committee in a Norweigian Parish. *Human Relations*
           7:39-58
Barth, Frederik
    1965   *Models of Social Organization.* Royal Anthropological Institute
           Occasional Paper No. 23
    1967   Economic Spheres in Darfur IN *Themes in Economic*
           Anthropology. Raymond Firth (ed) London:Tavistock
Benedict, Ruth
    1946   *The Chrysanthemum and the Sword.* New York: World Publishing
Bennett, John and Iwao Ishino
    1963   *Paternalism in the Japanese Economy: Anthropological Studies of*
           <u>*Oyabun-Kobun*</u> *Patterns.* Minneapolis: University of Minnesota
           Press
Bestor, Theodore C.
    1989   *Neighborhood Tokyo.* Stanford: Stanford University Press
Bix, Herbert
    1986   *Peasant Protest in Japan, 1590-1884.* New Haven: Yale
           University Press
Bodley, John
    1987   *Victims of Progress.* 3rd Edition, Mt. View, California: Mayfield
           Publishers
Bott, Elizabeth
    1957   *Family and Social Network.* London: Tavistock
Cole, Robert
    1971   *Japanese Blue Collar.* Berkeley: University of California Press
Cornell, John B. and Robert J. Smith
    1956   *Two Japanese Villages.* Ann Arbor: Univeristy of Michigan Press
           Cybriwsky, Roman
    1991   *Tokyo: The Changing Profile of an Urban Giant.* Boston, MA:
           G.K.Hall & Co.
Dore, R.P.
    1958   *City Life in Japan.* Berkeley: University of California Press
    1973   *British Factory--Japanese Factory: The Origins of National*
           Diversity in Industrial Relations. Berkeley: University of
           California Press

Dower, John W.
    1975   Occupied Japan as History and Occupation History as Politics
           Journal of Asian Studies. Vol XXXIV, No. 2:484-504

Eames, Edwin and Judith Goode,
    1977   *Anthropology of the City: An Introduction to Urban Anthropology.*
           Englewood Cliffs, NJ: Prentice-Hall

Embree, John
    1939   *Suye Mura: A Japanese Village.* Chicago: University of Chicago
           Press

Epstein, A.L.
    1961   The Network and Urban Social Organization *Rhodes-Livingstone*
           Journal 29:29-62

Falconeri, G.R.
    1976   The Impact of Rapid Urban Change on Neighborhood Solidarity: A
           Case Study of a Japanese Neighborhood Association IN James W.
           White and Frank Munger (eds) *Social Change and Community*
           Politics in Urban Japan. Monography No. 4, Institute for
           Research in Social Science, Chapel Hill: University of North
           Carolina Press

Firth, Raymond
    1964   *Social Organization and Social Change. Essays on Social*
           Organization and Values. London School of Economics
           Monographs on Social Anthropology No. 28

Fox, Richard
    1977   *Urban Anthropology: Cities in Their Cultural Setting.* Englewood
           Cliffs, NJ: Prentice-Hall

Fujita, Kuniko and Richard Child Hill (eds)
    1993   *Japanese Cities in the World Economy.* Philadelphia: Temple
           University Press

Gans, Herbert
    1962   *The Urban Villagers: Group and Class in the Life of Italian-*
           Americans. New York: The Free Press

Gallin, Bernard and Rita S. Gallin
    1974   The Integration of Village Migrants in Taipei IN Mark Evlin and G.
           William Skinner (eds) *The Chinese City Between Two Worlds.*
           Stanford: Stanford University Press

Glickman, Norman J.
    1979   *The Growth and Management of the Japanese Urban System.*
           New York: Academic Press

Hannerz, Ulf
    1969   *Soulside: Inquiries into Ghetto Culture.* New York: Columbia
           University Press

Harris, Marvin
    1977   *Cannibals and Kings: The Origins of Cultures.* New York: Random House
    1979   *Cultural Materialism: The Struggle for a Science of Culture.* New York: Random House

Havens, Thomas
    1978   *Valley of Darkness: The Japanese People and World War* II. New York: W.W.Norton and Company

Helmer, John and Neil A. Eddington (eds)
    1973   *Urbanman.* New York: The Free Press

Hokkaidō Keisatsu Honbu
    1968   *Hokkaidō Keisatsushi* (The History of the Hokkaido Police). 2 Vols. Sapporo: *Hokkaidō Keisatsu Honbu* (Headquarters of the Hokkaido Police)

Hokkaidōchō
    1976   *Hokkaidō Tokeisho* (Hokkaido Statistical Book). Sapporo: *Hokkaidōchō* (Hokkaido Prefectural Office)

Hozomi, Shihgetoh
    1943   "The Tonari-Gumi of Japan" *Contemporary Japan.* 12(8):984-990

Hughes, Richard
    1987   *A Distant Shore*

International Geographers Union, Science Council of Japan, Regional Council in Japan
    1957   *Regional Geography of Japan, No. 1, Hokkaido Guidebook.* Tokyo: n.p.

James, Jennifer
    1972   Sweet Cream Ladies: An Introduction to Prostitute Taxonomy *Western Canada Journal of Anthropology* 3:102-118

Kahn, Herman
    1971   *The Emerging Japanese Superstate.* Englewood Cliffs, NJ: Prentice-Hall

Keifer, Christie W.
    1976   Leadership, Sociability, and Social Change in a White-Collar *Danchi* IN James W. White and Frank Munger (eds) *Social Change and Community Politics in Urban Japan.* Comparative Urban Studies, Monograph No. 4, Institute for Research in Social Science, Chapel Hill: University of North Carolina Press

Kerr, Clark et al
    1960   *Industrialism and Industrial Man.* Cambridge: Harvard University Press

Koyama, Takashi
    1970   A Rural-Urban Comparison of Kinship Relations in Japan. Hill and Konig (eds) *Families in the East and West.* The Hague: Mouton

224

Kuhn, Thomas
  1962   *The Structure of Scientific Revolution.*
Leeds, Anthony
  1968   The Anthropology of Cities: Some Methodological Issues IN
          E.M.Eddy (ed) *Urban Anthropology: Research Perspectives and
          Strategies.* Southern Anthropological Society Proceedings, No. 2
Lewis, I.M.(ed)
  1968   *History and Social Anthropology.* A.S.A. Monograph No. 7 New
          York: Tavistock
Little, Kenneth
  1965   *West African Urbanization: A Study of Voluntary Associations in
          Social Change.* New York: Cambridge University Press
Lomnitz, Larissa
  1977   *Networks and Marginality: Life in a Mexican Shantytown.* New
          York: Academic Press
Mangin, William P.
  1970   *Peasants in Cities: Readings in the Anthropology of Urbanization.*
          Boston: Houghton Mifflin
Mayer, P.
  1961   *Townsmen or Tribesmen: Conservatism and the Process of
          Urbanization in a South African City.* Capetown: Oxford
          University Press
  1962   Migrancy and the Study of Africans in Towns. *American
          Anthropologist* 64:572-592
Ministry of Foreign Affairs
  1970   *The Northern Territorial Issue.* Tokyo: n.p.
Mitchell, J. Clyde (ed)
  1969   *Social Networks in Urban Situations.* Manchester: University of
          Manchester Press
Montgomery, John D.
  1949   Administration of Occupied Japan: First Year *Human
          Organization.* 3:4-16
Mock, John
  1987   "Social Impact of Changing Domestic Architecture in a
          Neighborhood in Sapporo, Japan" *City & Society.* Vol 2, No. 1,
          June
  1993   "We Have Always Lived Under the Castle: Historical Symbols and
          the Maintenance of Cultural Meaning" in Gary McDonosh and
          Robert Rotenberg (eds) *The Cultural Meaning of Urban Space.*
          Bergin & Garvey
  1996   "Mother or *Mama*: The Political Economy of Bar Hostesses in
          Sapporo, Japan" in Imamura, Anne (ed) Re-imaging Japanese
          Women. Berkeley: University of California Press

Moore, W.E. and A. Feldman (eds)
    1960   *Labor Commitment and Social Change in Developing Areas.* New
           York: Social Science Research Council
Morse, Richard
    1971   Trends and Issues in Latin American Urban Research, 1965-1970
           Latin American Research Review 2:19-75
Muir, Richard
    1980   *The English Village.* New York: Thames and Hudson
Nadel, Stanley
    1942   *A Black Byzantium.* New York: Oxford University Press
Nakane, Chie
    1970   *Japanese Society.* Berkeley: University of California Press
Nimmo, William F.
    1988   *Behind a Curtain of Silence: Japanese in Soviet Custody, 1945-
           1956.* New York: Greenwood
Nojiiri, Yoriko
    1974   *Family and Social Networks in Modern Japan: A Study of an
           Urban Sample.* Ph.D. Dissertation (Sociology), Case Western
           Reserve University
Norbeck, Edward
    1954   *Takashima: A Japanese Fishing Community.* Salt Lake City:
           University of Utah Press
Peattie, Lisa
    1968   *The View from the Barrio.* Ann Arber: University of Michigan
           Press
Perin, Constance
    1977   *Everything in its Place: Social Order and Land Use in America.*
           Princeton: Princeton University Press
Pike, Kenneth
    1967   *Language in Relation to a Unified Theory of the Structure of
           Human Behavior.*
           2nd Edition The Hague: Mouton
Plath, David
    1964   *The After Hours: Modern Japan and the Search for Enjoyment.*
           Berkeley: University of California Press
Ramsey, Charles and Robert J. Smith
    1960   Japanese and American Perceptions of Occupations *The American
           Journal of Sociology* 5:475-479
Reischauer, Edwin O.
    1977   *The Japanese.* Cambridge: Harvard University Press
Roberts, Brian
    1973   *Organizing Strangers: Poor Families in Guatamala City.* Austin:
           University of Texas Press

Roberts, Glenda
 1994 *Staying on the Line: Blue-Collar Women in Contemporary Japan.*
   Honolulu: University of Hawaii Press
Sapporo City
 1975 *Sapporo Tokeisho* (Sapporo Statistical Book). Sapporo: The City
   of Sapporo
 1976 *Sapporo-shi Seigaiyō* (Sapporo Government Synopsis). Sapporo:
   The City of Sapporo
Scalapino, Robert A. and Junnosuke Masumi
 1962 *Parties and Politics in Contemporary Japan.* Berkeley: University
   of California Press
Shoji, Heikichi
 1967 *Hokkaido Yuri Shikō* (A Historical Treatise of the Hokkaido Red
   Light District). Sapporo: Kita Shobōkan
Skinner, Kenneth A.
 1979 Salaryman Comics in Japan: Images in Self-Perception. *Journal of*
   Popular Culture 1:141-151
Spradley, James
 1972 Adaptive Strategies of Urban Nomads: The Ethnoscience of Tramp
   Cultures IN T. Weaver and D. White (eds) *The Anthropology of*
   Urban Environments. The Society for Applied Anthropology
   Monographs
Strobel, Margret Ann
 1975 *Muslim Women in Mombasa, Kenya, 1890-1973* Ph.D.
   Dissertation (History), University of California at Los Angeles
Tauber, Irene
 1958 *The Population of Japan.* Princeton: Princeton University Press
Thompson, Richard A.
 1973 A Theory of Instrumental Social Networks *Journal of*
   Anthropological Research 4
Trewartha, Glenn T.
 1965 *Japan: A Geography.* Madison: University of Wisconsin Press
U.S.Strategic Bombing Survey, Overall Effects Division
 1946 *The Effects of Strategic Bombing on Japan's War Economy.*
   Washington, D.C.
Vogel, Ezra
 1967 *Japan's New Middle Class: The Salary Man and His Family in a*
   Tokyo Suburb. Berkeley: University of California Press
 1979 *Japan as Number One.* Cambridge: Harvard University Press
Ward, Robert E.
 1967 *Japan's Political System.* Englewood Cliffs, NJ: Prentice Hall

White, James W.
    1978   Internal Migration in Prewar Japan *Journal of Japanese Studies*
         1:81-123
Wilkinson, Thomas O.
    1964   *A Functional Classification of Japanese Cities: 1920-50.*
         Demography 1
    1965   The Urbanization of Japanese Labor, 1868-1955. Amherst:
         University of Massachusetts Press
Wilmott, D.E.
    1960   *The Chinese in Semarang: A Changing Minority Community in*
         Indonesia. Ithaca: Cornell University Press
Yazaki, Takeo
    1963   *The Japanese City: A Sociological Analysis.* Tokyo: The Japnese
         Publications Trading Company
Young, M. and P. Wilmott
    1957   *Family and Kinship in East London.* Baltimore: Pelican Books

INDEX

JAPANESE STUDIES